Mary, Michael, and Lucifer

Latin American Monographs, No. 69
Institute of Latin American Studies
The University of Texas at Austin

MARY, MICHAEL, AND LUCIFER
Folk Catholicism in Central Mexico

By John M. Ingham

 University of Texas Press, Austin

Library of Congress Cataloging-in-Publication Data

Ingham, John M., 1940–
  Mary, Michael, and Lucifer

(Latin American monographs/Institute of Latin
American Studies, the University of Texas at Austin; no. 69)
  Bibliography: p.
  Includes index.
  1. Catholic Church—Mexico—Tlayacapan—History—20th century.
  2. Tlayacapan (Mexico)—Religious life and customs. I. Title. II. Series: Latin
American monographs (University of Texas at Austin. Institute of Latin American
Studies); no. 69.
BX1431.T55I54   1986   306'.6'097249   85-22703
ISBN 0-292-75089-7
ISBN 0-292-75110-9 pbk.

First Paperback Printing, 1989

Requests for permission to reproduce material from
this work should be sent to:
  Permissions
  University of Texas Press
  P.O. Box 7819
  Austin, Texas 78713-7819

Contents

Tables

Maps

Figures

Preface

This book, a study of traditional culture in Tlayacapan, has emerged over a period of nineteen years and as a result of eight field trips amounting to a total of more than two years. In it I present a series of arguments unlike anything I could have anticipated when my research began in 1965. At that time, I was not well prepared to foresee the place of family life and Catholicism in village culture. I lacked firsthand experience with marriage and parenting, and having little knowledge of Catholicism, I was not equipped to see its more subtle manifestations. Misreading the villagers' anticlericalism, I concluded that they were less religious than they really were. My initial choice of research topic also delayed the present analysis, as, interested in the role of achievement motivation in rural entrepreneurship, I focused more on modernization than on traditional culture.

My research on agricultural innovation continued through a second field trip in the summer of 1968. The topic was not without scholarly interest, but in retrospect I can see that it delayed insight into the pattern and meaning of village life.

Fortunately, the cumulative experience of fieldwork eventually led to more concern with culture. In this I was helped by my key informants. During my first year in Tlayacapan I lived in the home of María Flores de Estrada and her two children, Mago and Oscar. María was forthcoming about what it was like to be a woman in Tlayacapan and knowledgeable about folk medicine. An excellent cook, she ran a restaurant in her home. Assisting her in the restaurant were two elderly ladies, Doña Petra and her sister, Doña Juana. Don Otilio, María's uncle, took his meals with us. Doñas Petra and Juana talked about the suffering during the Revolution, about the way things used to be and the way they ought to be; Don Otilio, a Zapatista in the Revolution, sometimes could be induced to tell his war stories. Occasionally, Don Otilio and Doña Petra engaged in feisty repartee, giving me some of my first impressions of gender conflict in Tlayacapan. María's children were treasuries of information about riddles, folktales, and children's games.

The first year I found myself doing a good deal of serious drinking with the men of the village. Drinking was a social fact, and my personal inclination to abstain was usually deemed irrelevant. Nonetheless, the price paid in hangovers was repaid in friendships and better understanding of the profane side of the male role. Early in that first year I was befriended by Angel Rojas, a villager also known as El Diablo. Angel was a raconteur and, as his nickname implies, something of a trickster and mischief maker. Having lost an eye to a bull's horn in *jaripeo* (festive bull riding), Angel wore sunglasses; he even looked the part of a marginal man. He no longer rode bulls but he remained an aficionado. We attended *jaripeos* in several neighboring towns and villages, usually coming home to Tlayacapan something less than sober. During short periods of fieldwork in the summers of 1970 and 1971 I stayed with Angel and his wife, Guadalupe, and focused on folk medicine and the village's system of neighborhood chapels, saints, and fiestas. By then I was leaving my TAT and Rorschach cards at home.

In 1971 I met Don Lucio, a shaman who professed to be able to control the weather and cure a variety of illnesses. He lived in a nearby hamlet of a neighboring *municipio*, but he had patients and disciples in Tlayacapan and represented a type of ritual specialist that had been present in Tlayacapan a generation earlier. Moreover, he used ritual figurines in his practices that are manufactured exclusively in Tlayacapan for the entire region. It became apparent that shamanism should be part of my account of the traditional culture of Tlayacapan.

A turning point came in 1973, when I returned to Tlayacapan for seven months to study social and cultural factors in fertility. The research included interviews with 50 men and 140 women (the latter were interviewed by female assistants), and ethnographic inquiry into male-female relations and customs and beliefs relating to sex, conception, contraception, pregnancy, birth, nursing, and child rearing. More than any other period in the field, this one drew my attention to the central place of the family in traditional culture. I was helped by Froilán and Apolonia ("Pola") Santamaría, with whom I stayed. Both were superb informants, Doña Pola exceptionally so. Much of what I have learned about the sanctity of the home and the concerns of women came from her.

The study of fertility led me to rethink the entire culture, including ritual kinship, the pantheon of supernatural beings, machismo or hypermasculinity in the male role, the predicament of women, and the problem of affliction. The outline of an argument took shape and, with it in mind, I gathered additional material in 1978, 1980, and 1984.

These later visits were exercises in salvage ethnography. In various ways the village was no longer the traditional community described in this book. I was astonished by how rapidly the years had come and gone and the changes they had wrought. Godparenthood, many of the fiestas, and Carnival and the fairs remained viable institutions, but traditional beliefs about illness, weather working, and supernatural figures were on the wane. And while these customs were passing, the village was modernizing as never before. Children had grown up and become parents, and old folks had grown truly old. With sorrow I heard them say it would be the last time we would see each other. For Doña Petra, the orphan of the Revolution, life had always been sad, but now, toothless and losing vision and hearing, it was even sadder. In 1982 Don Otilio had taken a bad fall and was confined to home, no longer able to sit in the plaza with his friends and aging comrades-in-arms. We gave each other a warm *abrazo* and, anticipating his death the following year, he said that we would "see each other on the other side."

Ineluctably, a whole world was slipping away. This book attempts to retrieve some of that world from the onslaught of time and the implacable machine of human progress. It describes traditional culture. Written in what anthropologists call the ethnographic present, it records a way of life that is disappearing. Some of it is little more than a memory.

This study rests on the work, contributions, and support of many persons and institutions. The importance of reproduction for religious symbolism was suggested by Sarah C. Blaffer's monograph on the black-man figure in highland Maya culture. It disclosed the manner in which images of evil beings reinforce domestic roles, particularly the role of women in household labor and biological and social reproduction. My study was also inspired by Stephen Gudeman's work, which established the importance of the theological notion of spiritual procreation for the understanding of godparenthood and stimulated a comprehensive rethinking of Tlayacapan in terms of Catholic dogma and doctrine.

I am indebted for assistance in carrying out my investigations to Mexico's Instituto Nacional de Antropología e Historia, which gave me permission to do research in Tlayacapan, to the Foreign Area Fellowship Program of the Social Science Research Council and the American Council of Learned Societies for funding my first field trip, and to the Center for Population Research (Grant 1 RO1 HD 07452-01) of the National Institute of Child Health and Human Development, which supported the research on cultural and social aspects of fertility in 1973. A National Endowment for the Humanities postdoctoral fellowship at the University of Chicago in 1971-1972 provided an opportunity for me to further my understanding of Tlayacapan's pre-Hispanic heritage.

Many people contributed to the fieldwork itself. Alberto Anzures and Jaime Rojas did yeoman service in taking a census of the village; Eva Segura and Olivia Carrión were adept in interviewing women for me; Mario Dávila, Scott Robinson, and Gobi Stromberg, all anthropologists, did substantial ethnographic work in the village in support of my research; and finally, and most important, I am indebted to the villagers themselves. This book is based on conversations with hundreds of people; although I cannot thank them by name, I must mention María Flores de Estrada and her family, Froilán Santamaría and his wife, Apolonia, and their children, and Angel Rojas and his wife, Guadalupe, and their children. Their hospitality gave me not one but several homes in Tlayacapan. Thanks, too, are in order for Don Lucio, the folk curer, for what he taught me about Saint Michael, weather working, and a good deal more. My informants were promised that I would write a book about their beliefs and customs. I have been a long time delivering on the promise, and for that they have my apologies.

Dan Faggerstrom, Deborah Anderson, and Mariana Madrigal helped with the analysis of statistical data and archival research. Discussions with Louis Casagrande, Alberto Rivera Gutiérrez, Kenneth Smith, and Mark Mosko, former graduate students and teaching assistants, stimulated a number of insights. I am thankful to Eileen Flory for drawing maps and figures.

I would also like to thank Cambridge University Press for permission to use portions of my "Human Sacrifice at Tenochtitlan," *Comparative Studies of Society and History* 26:379–400, in Chapters 3 and 6, and the Royal Anthropological Institute of Great Britain and Ireland for permission to use material from my "The Asymmetrical Implications of Godparenthood in Tlayacapan, Morelos," *Man* 5:281–289, in Chapter 5.

I am especially grateful to George M. Foster. He brought Tlayacapan to my attention and was a constant source of encouragement and advice. His thorough reading of an earlier draft of this book was especially helpful. The manuscript also benefited from readings by several anonymous reviewers as well as Stephen Gudeman and Don Handelman. Eugenia Smith, Sylvia W. Rosen, Mary M. Grove, Alberto Rivera Gutiérrez, and Julie Simpson provided valuable editorial assistance.

Some notes about the text are necessary. Money expressed in pesos is based on the 1965-1966 exchange rate of 12.50 pesos to the dollar. In most of the book I have used actual names, except where the incidents reported might prove embarrassing, in which case I have used pseudonyms or initials.

Mary, Michael, and Lucifer

1. Introduction

The physical signs of Roman Catholicism pervade the Mexican countryside. Colonial churches and neighborhood chapels, wayside shrines, and mountaintop crosses dot the landscape. Catholicism also permeates the traditional cultures of rural communities, although this ideational influence is less immediately obvious. It is often couched in enigmatic idiom and imagery, and it is further obscured by the vestiges of pagan customs and the anticlerical attitudes of many villagers. These heterodox tendencies have even led some observers to conclude that Catholicism in rural Mexico is little more than a thin veneer on indigenous practice.

In this study of Tlayacapan, a village of Spanish-speaking peasants in Morelos, I demonstrate the importance of Catholic themes and patterns in traditional culture. My argument is both historical and symbolic. Historical materials reveal the similarity between folk Catholicism in Tlayacapan and once-accepted lay religiosity in rural Europe and they indicate the rigor with which the missionary friars imposed Christian mores on the village in the early colonial period. A symbolic approach to the culture has similar implications, for it shows that beliefs and practices that seem heterodox and superstitious are often folk transformations and variations of received dogma and doctrine. Elements of pre-Hispanic religion persist—indeed, they do so to an extraordinary degree—but I shall argue that they express rather than contradict the Catholic worldview.

In addition to demonstrating the theological sensibility that lies within folk customs, I am suggesting that religion in Tlayacapan is a part of social life, even in its most practical moments. I describe religion as a cohesive and persistent ideological system, but I also relate it to the needs and experiences of social actors. Like many other scholars, I see culture, and especially religious culture, as a system of signification through which social order is experienced, communicated, and reproduced (see Williams 1981:11-13).

Folk Catholicism and the Corporate Community

Social affiliation and opposition are part of what is communicated through religious symbolism in Tlayacapan. As in other traditional societies, symbols and rituals express social solidarity and social distance. Symbolic classification reiterates social segmentation.

This familiar Durkheimian-structuralist principle, nevertheless, does not disclose or elucidate all the nuances of social meaning in folk religion. For one thing, it exaggerates the logical form of symbolic opposition and thus overlooks the way in which ambiguities and ironies in social life are expressed in religious discourse and symbolism. In Tlayacapan religious imagery is more dialectical than the model of simple binary opposition would suggest. Contrasting images have attributes of logical opposition but they also exhibit implicit similarities, implying secretly that they are versions of one another. Symbolic ambiguity—hidden conjunctions within disjunctions—may in turn resonate with conflicts, dilemmas, and contradictions in social life or with emotional ambivalence and contradictory motivation in social actors (see El Guindi and Selby 1976).

Hierarchy and Production

The Durkheimian-structuralist approach is also problematic as a theory of symbolic content. What is needed is more specificity about the human activity in social relations. Here, the Marxist perspective is at least suggestive, for in claiming that society is a system for organizing production, Marxists impute economic and political intentionality to social organization and social conflict. As in the Durkheimian framework, religion is related to social relations, but these are defined by Marxists as socioeconomic and political relations. As we shall see, production per se and social relations of production are prominent themes in religious imagery in Morelos.

One might argue further along Marxist lines that these symbolic representations are mystifications of political economy. This is not exactly my position. Religion in Morelos imbues political and economic realities with cosmic mystery and rephrases them in fantastic form, but it does not necessarily obfuscate them. It may disclose their features, and in ritual contexts it may even constitute them.

Nor am I entirely comfortable with the view that religion is primarily an expression of power and a means of instilling obedience in subordinate social strata (see Asad 1983). The discipline imposed by the missionary friars in the sixteenth century was severe, but it is clear that the Indians responded with enthusiasm and reworked Catholic teachings according to their own needs and understandings. Folk Catholicism in rural Mexico today is not part of a state apparatus, nor is it merely a tool of provincial elites. Although it formulates and sanctifies positive sociality, it provides an idiom for critical commentary on negative social relations. It thus reflects the interests of the poor as well as those of the wealthy. Ultimately, it is as much a peasant construction as the product of theological ratiocination by elite clergy.

Reproduction

Reproduction forms part of the content of folk Catholicism in Tlayacapan. Reproductive metaphors figure in ritual kinship, secular festivals, and demonology, among other things. Indeed, they permeate the culture. My approach to this imagery is twofold. Using historical and ethnohistorical sources, I trace its antecedents in orthodox Catholicism and pre-Hispanic religion. I also show that it is related to practical motives and ordinary experience.

Children are important in the adaptive strategies of peasant families in rural Mexico. They provide parents with inexpensive labor and, in later years, with economic support. Understandably, most peasants have large families. This much is well known. Less recognized and studied is the tendency for peasants to practice reproductive restraint. In Mexico this phenomenon is particularly noticeable in subsistence-oriented, Indian communities (Hicks 1974). Several studies suggest that in more isolated communities the economic benefits of large families are less salient, whereas in market-oriented communities cash cropping and wage labor increase the marginal economic utility of children and thereby encourage higher fertility (see Collier 1975; Loucky 1979; Warman 1976). Additional involvement in the market economy may work against this trend as the acceptance of modern living standards increases the actual and anticipated costs of raising children (Kelly 1979). In other words, demographic transition in rural Mexico may be a three-stage process: (a) subsistence agriculture with moderate fertility and customary restraints on reproduction; (b) economic modernization and rising birth rates; and (c) modern living standards with declining fertility. During the last forty to fifty years, Tlayacapan has passed from the first, through the second, to the third. Much of its family organization and culture, however, derives from the traditional mode of production and reproduction.

To some extent, my depiction of the family's patriarchal role structure resembles the observations of other students of the Mexican family. It is unconventional in illustrating a connection between the regulation of reproduction and certain features of male and female roles. According to my view of the family, the suppression of sexuality within marriage promotes the extramarital sexual behavior of some men and, correlatively, an intensification of the mother-child relationship. Marriages, we shall see, oscillate between brief moments of procreation and long periods of sexual abstinence during which mothers nurse their children and men redirect their sexual desires elsewhere.

Other anthropologists have noticed that the Holy Family models the ideal family in Mexican culture (Crumrine 1983; Nelson 1971). The observation applies in Tlayacapan. The family is identified with supernatural exemplars in ritual and idiom. My emphasis on the cycle of husband-wife relations and parent-child relations within the family nonetheless adds a novel perspective on the symbolic and psychological implications of the Mexican family. Inasmuch as the marital relationship has natural and spiritual phases, I am led to consider associations between marital roles and negative as well as positive supernatural figures. I also examine the way in which the parent-child relationship may lay an emotional basis for later perceptions of supernatural figures.

Social Solidarity

Ritual expressions of solidarity between families in Morelos are grounded in collective resources and economic cooperation. Arturo Warman (1976) mentions the connection between communal land and fiesta organization in eastern Morelos, and Guillermo de la Peña (1980:72) and Claudio Lomnitz-Adler (1982) have similarly shown that in upland Morelos barrio organization and fiestas were a means of protecting and affirming rights in communal lands (see also Greenberg 1981).

Communal tenure is not the only basis of fiesta organization. Philip K. Bock (1980) demonstrates the continuing importance of barrio organization and the symbolism of saints, animals, and flowers in Tepoztlán and concludes that neighborhood ties and traditional customs offer protection and relief from the risks and frustrations of modernization. Even when communal tenure is replaced in part or whole by private ownership of land, economic conditions may provide an impetus for neighborhood and community solidarity and participation in religious celebrations. Villagers are more apt to obtain employment, peons, loans, customers, and political favors if they have good relations with friends or patrons in other families. Throughout Morelos peasants have responded to modern market conditions with labor- and capital-intensive truck farming. The costs and risks of this cash cropping have in turn reinforced interfamily assistance and joint economic enterprises and, with them, expressions of ritual solidarity (see Warman 1976).

Fiestas for the saints are symbolic, ritual events, yet little has been written about how they fit into a general system of ritual celebration or, with few exceptions (see Foster 1979; Gudeman 1976a), about their religious meaning. Waldemar Smith (1977), for example, simply disregards the question of cultural rationale and argues that Indians have fiestas because they are denied opportunities to invest their wealth in other, more productive, ways. This is an oversimplification. The feasts of communities and neighborhoods have positive consequences and meanings for the people who live and participate in them. In this book I show that fiestas are a folk elaboration of the universal spiritual family. Godparenthood, I suggest, belongs to this same complex of spiritual kinship. It is at once a part of the apparatus of initiation into the spiritual family and a form of spiritual kinship itself. Like the fiesta, godparenthood effects a synthesis of religious meaning and social function.

Spiritual kinship opposes and transcends the natural family as a matter of principle, but the dialectic between the two is not merely ideological. It is played out in the ambivalent attitudes and actions of individuals. As George M. Foster (1963) points out for Tzintzuntzan, villagers prefer to live *sin compromisos* (without obligations), although they appreciate the advantages of social ties. They follow a mixed strategy of pursuing economic independence and maintaining mutually supportive relationships with others. Conflict between satisfying the immediate needs of one's self or family and the inclination to participate in social collectivities and interfamily relationships has implications for the structuring of social solidarity itself. Here, I suggest, sacramental bonds between households (that is, the feast and godparenthood) mediate and redefine separate interests without necessarily denying them. Ritual, for example, establishes communion between persons of unequal status, but it also legitimates their particular activities and possessions. This mediation is implied by the distribution of benefits, material and symbolic, expected and realized in sacred relationships.

The Problem of Evil

The manifold personifications of evil in belief and ritual become more intelligible in relation to the family and spiritual kinship. Evil beings invert the images of the saints, and agents of the Devil are diametrically opposed in their characteristics to godparents and mayordomos, the sponsors of spiritual kinship. Evil in fact may lurk almost anywhere beyond the family and the pale of spiritual family. As elsewhere in Latin America, it has a Sartrean quality; it represents the menace of the Other coming toward the Self (see Correa 1960; Selby 1974; Taussig 1977; Warren 1978). Attributions of evildoing are commonly directed at persons in other neighborhoods, villages, or social classes. Formerly, owners of the nearby sugarcane plantations and unsociable members of the local elite were often suspected of trafficking with the Devil. It is perhaps significant that these persons tended to have a marginal relation to the fiesta system (see also Greenberg 1981; Warman 1976; Wolf 1957). Attributions of evil are not limited to socially distant others, however. The inclination of families to place their own interests first makes the problem of evil widespread, for what may be good fortune for one family or group may spell misfortune for another.

Evil then is also intelligible in the manner in which it opposes the interests of individual families. In particular, it endangers production and reproduction, the two principal sources of peasant security; evil beings in fact are both acquisitive and hypersexual (see Blaffer 1972; Brandes 1979).

Demonic influence also has sexual connotations. I show, for example, that demonic affliction is a symbolic transformation of spiritual procreation, just as the latter is a variant of natural reproduction.

There are interesting complexities and subtleties in the opposition between good and evil. The fact that families must reproduce themselves places them in a morally ambiguous position. The husband and wife approximate the examples of Joseph and Mary in certain respects, but in reproducing they share in the sin of Adam and Eve. Insofar as the primordial couple is associated with the value of children and the pleasures of sexual intercourse, it constitutes a positive image, notwithstanding its relation with the serpent. Despite the positive connotations of spirituality, there is in ritual and belief an evident fascination with Adamic figures and what might be called forbidden fruit.

The struggle with evil also has ironic implications. Martyrdom is one method of combating evil. Christ's ordeal on the cross is thought to represent a victory over evil, and this theme is replicated in the martyrdom of saints, a common theme in Mexican folk Catholicism and a model for resignation and stoicism in the face of adversity in everyday life. Octavio Paz (1961) has commented insightfully on the presence of these traits in Mexican character and has related them to the image of the bleeding and humiliated Christ, which he sees as a transfiguration of the Mexican's own identity.

Nevertheless, martyrdom is not always effective. Given the realities of peasant existence, an active approach is often more advantageous, and this fact illuminates the references to Saint Michael the Archangel and other fighting saints in traditional culture as well as many of the curiously heterodox and paradoxical features of the male role. I show that the moral struggle demands that men moderate their expressions of spirituality with counterbalancing expressions of virility, or manly nature; such behavior may even lead them to mimic the forces of evil themselves.

In Tlayacapan representations of the struggle between good and evil have apocalyptic overtones. Why this should be so is uncertain, but there is reason to think that the villagers were exposed to the contents of the Book of Revelation (the Apocalypse) soon after conversion in the sixteenth century. Lafaye (1976) mentions that the missionary friars tended to interpret the Conquest and their work among the Indians as a realization of apocalyptic expectation; they believed they were experiencing the final days, the climactic struggle between good and evil. Presumably, they conveyed this impression to the Indians.

In any event, traditional culture in Tlayacapan alludes to several of the major actors in Revelation, including Satan, Michael the Archangel, the woman and child, and the harlot. In Revelation, Satan appears as a red dragon that tries to devour the woman's newborn. The woman stands on a moon. The dragon is forced out of heaven by Michael. Cast down to earth, he turns into the beasts of the land and sea and continues to threaten the woman and child. The harlot, the female opposite of the woman, drinks the blood of martyred saints. Implicit in the culture of Tlayacapan, moreover, is the same historical vision one finds in Revelation: Christ's mission, also the aim of the church, is to incorporate nature into the spiritual family; Satan works against this trend, seeking recruits for his own family.

The Corporate Community in Morelos: A Dialectical Perspective

The ideas presented here about the social and economic foundations of lay religiosity in Tlayacapan build on the earlier controversy over Tepoztlán, a village that lies just to the west of Tlayacapan. In his book on Tepoztlán, Robert Redfield (1930) implied that traditional culture and communal and neighborhood organization compose a harmonious whole. Taking a different view of the same community, Oscar Lewis (1951) noted the pervasiveness of conflict and mistrust, which he attributed to economic scarcity and social inequality.

Reflecting on these seemingly contradictory accounts, Redfield later proposed that social life in the village is a "combination of opposites" (1955:135-136). Economic need and enmity, he was willing to admit, are part of peasant experience, but so are positive sociality and a shared way of life. In *The Primitive World and Its Transformations* he indicted that the dialectical character of the peasant community arises from the influence of civilization, social inequality, and the market economy, on the one hand, and the persistence of the traditional moral solidarity of the folk community, on the other (1953:39-40). In this book I try to deepen and broaden this dialectical perspective, first, by showing that strife between families is an inevitable by-product of the domestic mode of production and the traditional organization of reproduction, and, second, by showing that conflict and solidarity are complementary themes in religious ritual and symbolism.

Syncretism

The plausibility of emphasizing the Catholicity of traditional culture turns in part on what we make of syncretism. Religious syncretism in Tlayacapan has led de la Peña (1980:289) to minimize the place of Catholicism in village life. He depicts folk religion as a potpourri: some beliefs derive from Christian tradition, others are probably pre-Hispanic, and still others are of uncertain origin. In any event, he doubts that contemporary folk religion preserves any of the coherence of antecedent traditions. Instead, he maintains, the meaning of ritual varies with social context. He mentions that many villagers, especially men, do not attend mass, confess, or take communion with regularity, and he cites the opinions of clergy that the villagers are in effect theologically ignorant and immoral. In addition, he implies that recent expressions of anticlericalism testify to the heterodoxy of folk religion in Tlayacapan.

The supposition that religious syncretism is symptomatic of a superficial Catholicism is contradicted, however, by an ethnographic oddity found nearly everywhere in the Mexican countryside: the greatest dedication to the saints and other Catholic customs occurs in traditional communities, those that most preserve pre-Hispanic religious beliefs and practices. Commenting on this phenomenon in Yucatan, Redfield (1941:101) reasoned that the missionary work among the Indians ceased without the friars having completely eradicated indigenous customs. Left without benefit of clergy, the Indians simply perpetuated both Christian and native customs, unaware of their supposed incompatibility.

Redfield's formulation may explain conditions in remote regions of Mexico, but in the central highlands, where sixteenth-century friars went to great pains to inculcate a proper religiosity, and where clergy have been present ever since, the formulation offers an unlikely solution to the problem of syncretism. The failure becomes all the more apparent when we learn that local religion in sixteenth-century Spain had heterodox elements, often with the approval of clergy.

My view follows Foster's (1960) documentation of Iberian influence in Latin America. It also finds support in Robert Ricard's work on the evangelizing methods of the mendicant orders in New Spain. He says that many customs that seem heterodox are at least partly European in origin and notes that some beliefs and practices represent the unguided work of folk imagination on perfectly orthodox conceptions. And he warns against making too much of pagan survival:

The theory of the "mixed religion" commits the error of sticking exclusively to the form of these celebrations, in which survival of paganism is naturally detected. . . . What does it matter, then, that the Indian of today, to honor the Virgin of Guadalupe, makes the same gesture that his ancestors made in honor of Tonantzin, if he really means to honor the Virgin and not Tonantzin? In my opinion it is as frivolous to consider these feasts of substitution as pre-Conquest survivals as it would be childish to consider the use of Latin in the Church a survival of Roman paganism. (1966:280)

The persistence of indigenous culture may be less a measure of its strength than an effect of Catholicism itself. For one thing, the church had a history of making concessions to local cultures as a matter of missionary expediency even before the friars arrived in Mexico. Missionaries adapted indigenous songs and dances to Christian ritual with the aim of speeding conversion. When local customs were not encouraged and even canonized, they were often tolerated. As missionaries accepted and accommodated local custom, the orthodox ritual and the received supernatural pantheon of the church were affected. The company of saints replaced and assimilated tribal and clan gods, acquiring in the process their associations with meteorological phenomena, agricultural fertility, and healing. Similarly, Adamic and demonic images assimilated pagan gods noteworthy for their sexuality and destructiveness. Indeed, the gamut of mythical figures in the Catholic pantheon models the historical process of converting native peoples to the faith. The Holy Family and the saints represent persons who are already within the fold, whereas the figures of the fallen Adam and Eve symbolize the pagans who are yet to be incorporated into the church. The struggle between the Devil and God for the fealty of souls has a precise historical counterpart in the missionary work of discouraging old cults and instilling new faith. Moreover, the ontological distinctions between good and evil and spirit and nature in the Catholic worldview support the persistence of pagan images, at least implicitly. The strong positive valuation of the spiritual in orthodox liturgy conjures up, by way of the dialectical implications of the term, contrasting conceptions of nature and evil, which the laity then represents in ritual drama. Within the (universal) Catholic worldview, the gods and rituals of heathen peoples are associated with nature and evil by definition.

In sixteenth-century Mexico, the parallels between Catholic supernatural figures and indigenous gods were especially remarkable, and the resulting syncretism was unusually coherent. The Catholic worldview was able to assimilate not only some of the content of indigenous religion but also its underlying structure. One noteworthy feature of this synthesis was the identification of the supernatural patrons of the indigenous elite with the forces of evil, and the supernatural advocates of commoners with Adamic and holy figures in the Christian pantheon. Thus religious syncretism in the sixteenth century implied moral criticism of secular wealth and power and expressed the aspirations of the common people. The efforts of the early friars to defend the Indians against economic and social abuse by secular Spaniards probably further enhanced Catholicism's appeal to Indian peasants. Later, of course, the friars were replaced by the secular clergy, who were more apt to sympathize with provincial Spanish elites than with the Indian community. Yet by then the Indians had fashioned their own Catholicism—a blend of pre-Hispanic religion, European Catholicism, and symbolic representations of colonial society—which gave them not only a blueprint for survival but a critique of domination also.

2. Setting, People, and Village

Tlayacapan lies in the northern uplands of Morelos, a small state just to the south of the Federal District and the State of Mexico (see map 1). The Municipio of Tlayacapan (that is, the main village and the surrounding hamlets) is bordered by the *municipios* of Tepoztlán to the west, Tlalnepantla to the north, Totolapan to the northeast, Atlatlahuacan to the east, and Yautepec to the south. At an elevation of sixteen hundred meters, the main village is said to be in *tierra templada*, country that for most of the year is neither too hot nor too cold. To the south lie the sugarcane districts and towns of the *tierra caliente*, or hot country. Towns like Tlalnepantla farther up the mountains are said to lie in *tierra fría*.

Tlayacapan is the administrative center of the *municipio* of the same name. In addition to the main village, the *municipio* includes the hamlets of San Agustín, San Andrés, San José, and, on the edge of the *tierra caliente*, a small settlement amid the ruins of the old hacienda of Pantitlán. The main village is also a market center for the hamlets. Hamlet residents can be seen in the main village during the weekly market and in large stores shopping for dry goods and other necessities. The inhabitants of hamlets, and especially those of San José, are somewhat more conservative culturally than those of the main village. In the 1960s all but a few people in Tlayacapan spoke only Spanish, whereas in the hamlet of San José many were still bilingual in Spanish and Nahuatl, or Mexicano, as it is called locally. People in the hamlets may be somewhat more inclined to conserve traditional curing and weather-working ritual, but their smaller populations support less elaborate ceremonial complexes. For the people in the hamlets, the main village is a market and, to a lesser extent, a ritual center. They are drawn to the market in Tlayacapan, particularly in anticipation of All Saints' and All Souls' Days, and some of them come into town for Carnival, fairs, and major fiestas.

Its physical setting gives Tlayacapan a storybook quality. To the northwest, west, and south of the village is an arc of prominent hills and bluffs: Tonantzin (Our Mother), Zuapapalotzin (Hill of Butterflies),

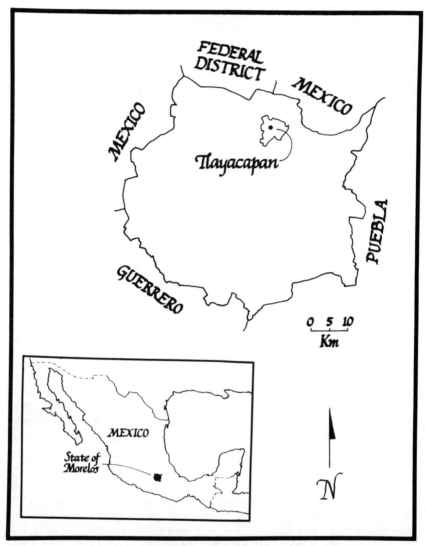

Map 1. Location of Tlayacapan

Tlatoani (The One Who Speaks), and Huitzlaltzin (The Spines). The most notable hill to the south was known as Tlayacapa in the sixteenth century (de Curiel 1905:8) but today, remarkably, the villagers know it only by the name Sombrerito, after its hatlike summit. Several kilometers to the north, pine-and oak-covered high country separates the area from the Valley of Mexico; and to the northeast rise the snow-capped giants of Popocatépetl and Iztaccihuatl. Immediately surrounding the village and hamlets are patchworks of fields that are intersected here and there by small ravines or barrancas. Writing in the sixteenth century, Fray Diego Durán compared the region to Eden:

This is certainly one of the most beautiful and delightful lands in the world, and if it were not for the great heat it would be another earthly paradise. There are beautiful springs, wide rivers full of fish, the freshest of woods, and fruits of many kinds, some native to the land and others to Spain, which supply all the neighboring cities. And it is full of a thousand fragrant flowers. (Durán 1967:2:23)

Although often pleasant, the mood of the countryside varies with the seasons. The rainy period, beginning in mid-June and lasting through October, gives the landscape a brilliant mantle of greenery but also brings great, thundering electrical storms, especially in July and August. During October and November the weather moderates and becomes springlike. In late November the days turn cool and the nights even cooler. December and January are winter months, cool and dry. February and March are often windy—"Febrero loco y marzo otro poco." Preparations for planting begin in April and continue into the hot, dry days of May and early June. Seed goes into the ground with the first good rains, sometimes in May but usually by early June; crops are harvested in October and November, according to the pattern in the dry farming region immediately surrounding the village. The community also has irrigated lands in the *tierra caliente*, which are cultivated continuously, usually yielding two crops a year.

Cultural and social characteristics distinguish Tlayacapan and other upland communities from the *tierra caliente* communities to the south. The latter exhibit more acculturation to Spanish language and culture but also more anomie and social disorganization. Villages there tend to be riven by strife and factionalism. Alcohol consumption is high, and aggressive, even murderous, displays of machismo are commonplace. Indeed, the homicide rate in the hot country of Morelos is one of the highest in the world.[1] One Tlayacapense described the area as follows: "There in the *tierra caliente* a man only thinks about getting a horse, saddle, and pistol. There they are more aggressive, they like to fight. They plant sugarcane and rice and don't save their money and fix up their homes like Tlayacapenses. Many live in shacks." Smiling at the irony, his wife added, "They spend money on fine horses, saddles, big guns, fine clothes, and an expensive hat, then ride up to their little shacks and have to stoop to go through the little doors!"

The communities in the uplands, by contrast, are more socially cohesive and bound by a stronger idiom of moral solidarity. Inhabitants are village-born natives, for the most part, whereas the populations of the lowland communities include many immigrants from other villages and states. The ties of kinship and neighborhood and, with them, religious fiestas and their supporting sodalities are more developed in the uplands. What is more, the percentage of couples married by church ceremony is higher than in the *tierra caliente.*[2]

Nahuatl language has disappeared in most of the *municipios* of Morelos, and even in the more conservative settlements it is often spoken only by an aging minority. Nonetheless, the distribution of Nahuatl has some relevance to my theme. It persists in communities that, generally speaking, had a marginal relation to the haciendas of the colonial period and nineteenth century. Most of these conservative communities are in the northern part of the state, although two of them—Puente de Ixtla and Temixco—border the sugarcane districts on the south and west.

The most likely explanation for this pattern is that traditional communal land tenure, as elsewhere in Mexico, reinforced Indian ethnicity.[3] Throughout the sugarcane districts, the haciendas had a long history of expropriating the communal lands of nearby Indian communities. Communal fiestas for patron saints were one expression of solidarity in the face of such external threats. Communal landholding has probably strengthened the fiestas within the barrios as well. Communal tenure was a characteristic of the pre-Hispanic clan and the colonial barrio that replaced it.

The expansion of the haciendas at the expense of the Indian community was not the only factor in the decline of communal landholding and Indian ethnicity in Morelos, however. There are *municipios* on the periphery of the sugarcane districts that switched to Spanish from Nahuatl as early as the end of the eighteenth century. Nonetheless, we can still detect the pattern Redfield observed in Yucatan: in general, those communities that are linguistically and ethnically Indian are the most Catholic.

Although the people of Tlayacapan are Spanish speaking, they are often regarded as *indios* by people in the hot country and by urban Mexicans. Tlayacapenses occasionally refer to themselves as "*indios,*" although they usually prefer to avoid this label by describing themselves as campesinos (country people). The word *indio* is derogatory; it implies backwardness, lack of sophistication, and poverty. This is not to say, however, that the villagers are ashamed of their Indian heritage. Most villagers typically speak as though their ancestors were in Tlayacapan before the Conquest. In effect, they think of themselves as indigenous people or natives of the soil. Spaniards are seen as having had an exogenous influence: either they corrupted the innocent natures of the indigenous people by introducing vices, or they had a spiritualizing and civilizing effect. When putting distance between themselves and their Indian past and emphasizing the changes wrought by Catholicism and European culture, the villages are apt to say, "Now we are civilized."

The Village

Tlayacapan is a nucleated settlement (map 2). It is laid out according to a

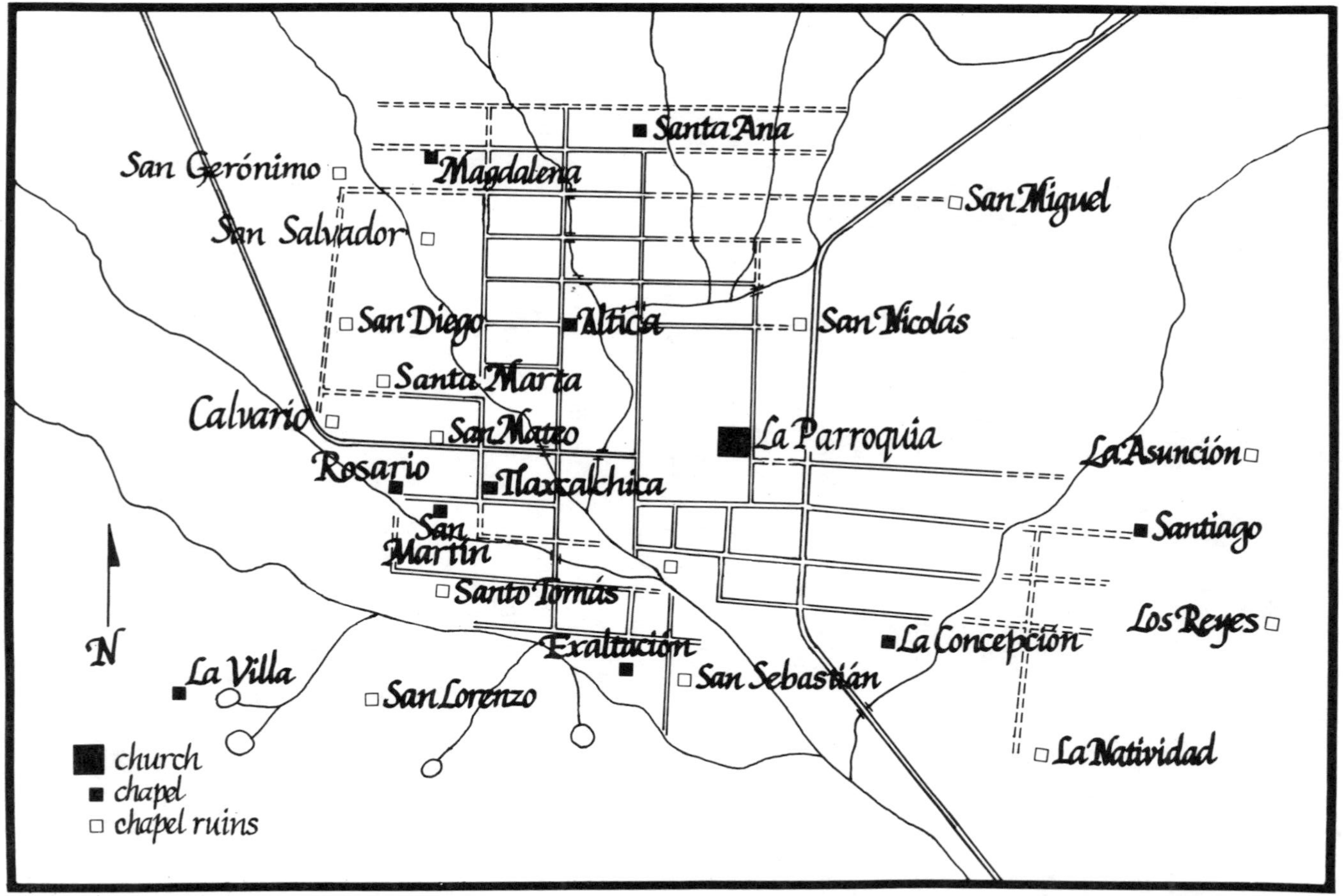

Map 2. Tlayacapan

San Gerónimo
San Miguel
San Salvador
Santa Ana
La Asunción
Santiago
Los Reyes
La Natividad
Magdalena
San Nicolás
La Concepción
San Diego
Altica
La Parroquía
La Concepción
Santa María
San Marcos
San Sebastián
Santo Tomás
Rosario
Tlaxcalapan
San Martín
Calvario
Exaltación
San Lorenzo
La Villa

N

■ church
■ chapel
□ chapel ruins

neat grid of streets running north and south and east and west, with most of its adobe houses butting up against one another in tidy rows. Seen from a nearby hilltop, the houses appear to cluster for protection about the large church at the center of the community. Indeed, the church holds the image of San Juan Bautista, the village's patron saint.

Facing the central plaza from the east, the church and its attached convent (now used as a rectory) sit at the back of a large atrium, a walled, grassy, open space containing a shady stand of eucalyptus trees. The atrium is where the villagers reenact the Passion of Christ during Holy Week and where little boys practice soccer after school. A long, narrow marketplace traverses the plaza's eastern boundary, and until recently a row of small shops defined its western border. In the marketplace women sell fruits and vegetables and butchers tend small stands where they display beef and pork. The northern end of the plaza area is bordered by the town hall. A colonial two-story building, with porticoes on its ground floor and a clock tower above, it is the second most impressive structure in the village. Just in front of the town hall is a *zócalo* (square) with benches, in many ways a focus of social activity. It is where town meetings are held and the destination of masked dancers during Carnival. It is also a favorite gathering place for men who simply want to pass time. Several of the largest houses in the village front the plaza along its southern boundary, and many of the rest, along with the busiest stores, are found within a block or two of the plaza on the main streets leading into it. Particularly noteworthy is an abandoned building with a colonnade to the west of the plaza, the "candle factory." Houses on the opposing sides of a street a block to the south of the southeast corner of the plaza once had an unusual linking arch. The large open area in the middle of the plaza is used as a corral for bull riding during Carnival and some fiestas.

The main north-south street passes between the marketplace and the church wall and terminates to the north at the chapel of Santa Ana, and to the south at the chapel of Exaltación. The main east-west street traverses the southern side of the plaza and ends at the chapel of Rosario in the west and the chapel of Santiago in the east. In addition to these chapels, many others are scattered throughout the village. Most house the images of one or more saints and are associated with particular barrios.

In 1965 ten chapels were in good repair, and another nine were in various stages of dilapidation. The remains of six more — San Sebastián, Santo Tomás, Calvario, Santa Marta, San Salvador, and one of uncertain name — were barely discernible, and most villagers had no knowledge of them. Portions of some have been incorporated into walls of homes, but nothing remains of others but pieces of foundation.

The aging Don Refugio mentioned that once there were twenty-seven "churches" in Tlayacapan, a number that he said included the main church. In the traditional scheme, most of these chapels were the namesakes and ritual foci of particular barrios or neighborhoods. Don Modesto, also advanced in years, said that there were twenty-eight neighborhoods, each with a Nahuatl name; and Don Baldomero had heard that there used to be twenty-eight chapels.

Land records suggest that there may have been a chapel for San Isidro a kilometer or so to the northeast of the village and another named Las Animas to the southeast of the village, and there are ruins of a chapel called San Pedro a couple of kilometers to the northwest. A sixteenth-century report for Tlayacapan indicates that San Pedro was an independent hamlet; it lists several other small hamlets to the north of the village, but no San Isidro. The latter was probably part of San Agustín (García Pimentel 1904:119–120). If San Pedro, San Isidro, and Las Animas were external to the chapel system of Tlayacapan, then there is tangible evidence for twenty-five chapels.

As a rule, both saint and chapel are cared for by the families of the surrounding neighborhood and especially by mayordomos or mayordomas, the men and women who organize the saint's fiesta. The figures of the saints are carved in wood and painted. Many are life-sized and some, diminutive. Several chapels (Altica, Tlaxcalchica, and Exaltación) contain stone crosses, either as primary objects of veneration or in addition to a saint. The images are thought to be miraculous and are treated with respect and veneration. The villagers understand that the figures represent persons who once lived but they also believe that the figures themselves are able to convey supernatural benediction, some more miraculously than others. Among the chapel saints, the greatest miracle workers are the Señor de la Exaltación, an image of the crucified Christ, and the Virgen del Tránsito, an image of Mary as she rises to heaven (this image is in the chapel of San Martín for safekeeping but pertains to La Villa, an isolated chapel without a neighborhood of its own). The reputations of both images extend beyond the village. The Virgen is particularly esteemed by the people of Tepoztlán, many of whom attend her fiesta.

All neighborhoods belong to one or another of four major barrios, the boundaries of which can be roughly imagined as two diagonal lines running southeast-northwest and southwest-northeast and intersecting at the plaza. The major barrio in the south is known as Exaltación, after the main chapel in that quarter, and the one in the west is called Rosario, after its main chapel. The northern barrio, Santa Ana, is customarily called América, after its Carnival dance group. The major barrio in the east is called either Santiago or Tezcalpa, after the name of a hamlet several kilometers farther east.

Today there are thirteen functioning barrios. Among them, only Exaltación, Santiago, Santa Ana, Altica, Magdalena, Tlaxcalchica, and Rosario still have intact chapels and annual fiestas. The barrios of San

Miguel, San Nicolás, San Mateo, and San Diego are thought to exist but their chapels are in ruins. Tlaxcolpa, one well-defined barrio, is really a sub-barrio and never had a chapel. A small number of families living on or near the plaza say they belong to "El Centro." This group does not encompass all wealthy families, however. Currently, wealthy families can be found in various parts of the village. The number of households and people in each barrio in 1966 is shown in table 1.

It does not now appear that the saints of the four main chapels are held to be the patrons of the major barrios, nor is there any indication that such was the practice in the past. Yet the major barrios were associated with saints in another way. Older informants relate that the village used to be divided into two factions, each of which gave its support to a favorite saint. One championed San Juan Bautista, the patron saint of the entire community, and the other, San Nicolás. Two images of each saint occupied conspicuous positions on the walls around the altar of the main church. San Juan was supported by mayordomos in Santa Ana, and San Nicolás, by mayordomos in Santiago (which encompassed the small barrio of San Nicolás). Some informants indicated that Exaltación sided with Santiago and Rosario with Santa Ana in the rivalry, but others implied that the loyalties of the latter two barrios were divided. In the early 1960s several other saints were present in the main church, some of whom are still honored with fiestas and masses.

Table 1
Barrios, Households, and Population, Tlayacapan, 1966

Barrio	No. of Households	Population
El Centro	13	90
Exaltación		
Exaltación	31	171
Tlaxcolpa	34	198
Santiago		
Santiago	148	772
San Miguel	1	6
Santa Ana		
Santa Ana	69	381
Altica	98	576
Magdalena	10	67
San Nicolás	4	25
Rosario		
Rosario	34	214
San Mateo	31	241
Tlaxcalchica	24	153
San Diego	6	35
Total	503	2,929

Most are now supported by the entire village, but some may have been connected with factionalism in the past.

In addition to being loyal to certain saints, major barrios maintain particular crosses. Santiago, which does not have a hill immediately behind it, has two crosses within the barrio. Exaltación tends a cross on La Ventanilla and another on Sombrerito. Rosario maintains crosses on hills to the southwest of the village as well as a cross in Tlaxcalchica. Santa Ana has a cross on the hill of Mixtepec to the north and a cross in the chapel of Altica. All the crosses are celebrated on the third of May, the Day of the Santa Cruz, with festivities similar to the fiestas for the saints.

The major barrios also have ceremonial importance in connection with Carnival. The masked dancers of Carnival belong to one of three *comparsas*, or dance groups. The group called América pertains to Santa Ana; Azteca encompasses the major barrios of Rosario and Exaltación; and Unión represents Santiago. The wealthy families of El Centro make up a fourth dance group, La Central.

The major barrios are also distinguished by secular differences. Santiago is by far the most culturally conservative of the four barrios and the most Indian. Nahuatl patronyms (really, toponyms) persist there more than in other barrios. It is also unusual in that it contains families that dedicate themselves, either full or part time, to making domestic pottery, censers, and candle holders (Rojas Rabiela 1973). Santa Ana may be the next most conservative neighborhood. It includes families that make small clay figurines that shamans throughout the region use in curing and as offerings to rain spirits (ibid.). On the whole, Exaltación and Rosario, which some regard as a single barrio, seem more acculturated.

There is rivalry among barrios, particularly in the staging of impressive annual celebrations of patron saints. Standards require ample fireworks, good music, and, most important, a generous banquet lest there be any doubt about a barrio's commitment to its patron. During Carnival, the major barrios compete with each other in fielding large numbers of masked, costumed dancers and arranging memorable formal dances for young people. In the past, young men often taunted and insulted each other across the boundaries of the major barrios, and a young man who dared to court a young woman in another major barrio ran the risk of being beaten. Even today there is good-natured teasing among people of different barrios. Residents of Santiago are sometimes called *brujos* (witches) and they, in turn, call others *naguales* (were-animals).

The antagonism among the four large barrios is reflected in a strong tendency toward large-barrio endogamy. The barrios per se included within the wards tend toward exogamy; roughly 70 percent of marriages are contracted between persons of different barrios. This figure, however, probably represents a random mate selection, not a prescriptive marriage rule; about 70 percent of eligible partners are found outside the barrio. On the other hand, large-barrio or ward endogamy clearly exceeds what might be expected from a random model; the percentage of endogamy ranges from about 40 to 75, whereas households by ward make up between about 10 and 36 percent of total households (see Ingham 1971:620).

Many homes and house compounds in Tlayacapan shelter joint or extended families: 32 percent of the households are patrilineally extended or consist of agnatic joint families; 5 percent are matrilineally extended; and another 3 percent are multifamily arrangements of different types. Sixty percent contain nuclear families, childless couples, or single persons.

Socioeconomic Differences

Tlayacapan is a highly stratified community. Although the wealthiest villagers no longer compose a well-delineated elite, the differences between the rich and poor are still considerable. When I took a census of the community in 1966, many villagers remarked on their poverty with humor and sarcasm. Replying to a question about how much land her husband held, one woman said, "He doesn't even have dirt under his fingernails—he cut them off." Another woman, whose husband was an illegitimate child and had inherited nothing, answered the same question by saying, "Nothing. All they gave him was his life." Still another woman, asked if her husband could read, replied, "No, but he knows how to drink." When asked whether her husband planted tomatoes, a woman said, "He plants children, that's all!"

The average house had two rooms, electricity, a radio, two or three beds, and a floor of unglazed tile. Averages obscure variations, however. At the poor end of the spectrum, families lived in one-room houses with dirt floors and unplastered walls; they used kerosene lamps and slept on *petates* (fiber mats) that were rolled up during the day. At the more affluent end, the houses had several rooms, many beds, ceramic tile floors, television sets, and modern furniture in the front room.

A ranking of village households according to their material possessions gives a rough indication of the magnitude of socioeconomic differences in the community. I gave a household one point for each of the following: ownership of a home; each room after the first (that is, three points for four rooms); electricity; gas stove; sewing machine; radio; television; and each store-bought bed. Table 2 displays the results of this scaling procedure. The category 0-4 corresponds roughly to what the villagers would call "poor" or "humble" living conditions. Although villagers know that elsewhere in the world there are persons who are truly wealthy, the categories 9-12 and 13+ correspond to the "wealthy" in a local sense.

Diets also reveal differences in living standards. In most families people start the day with tortillas, beans, sometimes an egg, a little chile sauce, and

Table 2
Households and Socioeconomic Status, Tlayacapan, 1966

| | No. of Points | | | | |
	0-4	5-8	9-12	13+	N
% of households	38.0	42.3	16.5	3.2	503

coffee heavily sugared. The main meal, taken in the afternoon, ideally includes noodles or rice, a meat soup, and beans with tortillas. At the evening meal, white bread, pastries, and coffee, often used to flavor a glass of milk, are served. The poorest families, however, enjoy meat much less often; beans, chiles, and tortillas, perhaps with a little coffee, may be their fare meal after meal and day after day. Several family budgets, which I recorded in detail, showed that wealthy families often spent three times as much on food per person as did poor families. When judging a family's social position, in fact, villagers are apt to consider how well the family eats. A village joke on this subject places San Isidro and San Rafael in a cornfield where San Isidro is weeding the corn and San Rafael is planting weeds. Tired of weeding, San Isidro wants to know why San Rafael is planting weeds. San Rafael replies, "The poor have to eat something."

Land tenure also demonstrates economic inequality. There are three kinds of land in Tlayacapan: private, ejido, and communal. Most of the arable acreage near the village is privately owned. The fields west of the village are preferred because they are less rocky and hold more moisture than the less-productive lands lying to the east, which are owned in large part by the residents of the barrio of Santiago. Communal land includes hills, forested areas, and some arable land lying to the east of the village. Much of the arable land has been divided into small plots, which particular families hold in usufruct. Because the uplands are not irrigated, there is only dry farming on private and communal land. The ejido lands, which were taken from the hacienda of Oacalco after the Revolution, lie to the south of the village in the *tierra caliente*. They also have been divided into small plots and assigned to individuals. If the land is in production it can be inherited; unlike private land, it cannot be legally sold or mortgaged, although, in practice, one or another deal may be made surreptitiously.

Like other indicators of wealth, the amount of land held varies from one extreme to another; in the 1960s about 15 percent of the households had no land, whereas some of the wealthiest households had more than 20 hectares each. About 49 percent of the households had one or more ejido plots; approximately 45 percent had private land; and about 10 percent had communal plots. Some families had two or even three types of land. The average ejido plot was slightly more than a hectare in size; that of private land, about 3.5 hectare; and the typical communal plot was less than a hectare.[4]

Roughly 86 percent of the heads of household consider themselves farmers. Even if they do not have land they earn their living by working in the fields. Among the forty-one families that make their living primarily as potters, a number also farm. Fewer villagers are store owners, teachers, barbers, carpenters, bread makers, butchers, tinsmiths, or blacksmiths; there are also a cobbler and a rocket maker. A few men earn extra money by playing in the village band. The families that rank high on the measure of socioeconomic status described previously tend to have more land, although the correlation is not perfect. Land ownership is not an index of the incomes of nonfarming families. Later, when I examine the relation between status and ritual sponsorship, I rely more on the measure of socioeconomic status than on land tenure data.

Wealth differences are related to barrio divisions. In terms of the socioeconomic scale, Rosario is the wealthiest barrio, followed in order by Santa Ana, Exaltación, and Santiago (Ingham 1969:76). Land is unevenly distributed according to this same pattern; there are more landless families in Exaltación and Santiago. Fewer families in the latter barrio have communal and ejido plots, and the average size of such plots is smaller than in the other barrios (ibid.:360).

These differences between the barrios are related to the distribution of political power in the community. The three loci of political power in the village consist of the *ayuntamiento* (municipal government), the commissioner of ejido lands, and the commissioner of communal lands. The *ayuntamiento* includes the president, the treasurer, and the judge.[5] With few exceptions, since the 1920s these offices have been filled by men from the major barrios of Rosario and Santa Ana.

The Round of Life

The more dramatic ritual events of the year (barrio and village fiestas, Carnival, and fairs) are interspersed with periods of work, commerce, and leisure, including the less dramatic ritual of the Sabbath. Life in Tlayacapan, for men and women, is mostly work, the effort of provisioning and caring for one's family. For men, the task is more seasonal, particularly if they are dry farmers, although for those who have irrigated land in the ejido, farming can be almost as continual as the work of women, which is unremitting. Even dry farmers will try to work year round by hiring themselves out as peons to their compadres and friends who have irrigated land or by working in some other capacity, say, as potters, bricklayers, or bread makers. During the spring, summer, and autumn months, when much work must be done in the fields, men and boys can be seen getting early starts as they drive their mules or lumbering oxen before them. Women's work begins even earlier. Before the introduction of mechanized mills, women had to arise before dawn to grind the maize on their *metates* for the tortillas. After breakfast, the women shop in the marketplace, clean house, and mend or wash clothes. When such chores are done, they must begin preparing the afternoon meal, caring all the while for their children.

Most farmers and field hands return from the fields during the late afternoon or early evening. By dusk most women have finished their chores. Evening, then, provides a brief respite from the daily labors. Many villagers like to sit on their doorsteps, perhaps to chat with neighbors about babies, weather, or the prices the crops are fetching in the market, while the children play traditional games in the street. Some men relax by drinking in the cantinas. Later in the evening, when most people have bolted their doors against the night, young men may serenade their sweethearts, and still later, the quiet might be broken by the caterwauls and plaintive songs of men who are drinking and carousing in the streets.

Saturday mornings bring the *tianguis*, or weekly market. Much larger than the markets during the week, the Saturday market, with all its color, noise, and commotion, resembles a fair. Vendors arrive from surrounding communities and cities to peddle produce, clothing, sewing supplies, kitchen utensils, and tools. Artisans from other villages sell their handiwork, and potters from the barrio of Santiago show up to vend their pots, tortilla griddles, and the giant kettles used for preparing fiesta meals. Among the sellers are persons who hawk a miraculous potion that is purported to relieve everything from kidney pains to headaches, and residents of Tlalnepantla who sell pulque—the maguey beer. Shoppers from surrounding hamlets help to crowd the plaza.

While some men gather at the booths to drink pulque, others do more serious drinking in the cantinas near the plaza (really, general stores that serve as cantinas). Wary of the strangers and drunkards, mothers try to keep a close watch on their daughters. Some may be suspicious of the young men of the village as well, although serious suitors may still manage to address a few courting words to young women.

When women are out of the house they must be careful to protect their honor and the reputations of their families. In the marketplace, they also must guard against economic abuse. Both buyers and sellers are apprehensive about being cheated. Sellers maintain the appearance of civility by giving regular customers a little extra, but self-preservation is clearly the dominant attitude. The competition among vendors often leads to quarrels, and all participants have a conspicuous interest in current prices. None want to be made the fool by buying dear or selling cheap.

Sunday, ideally, is a day of rest from the struggle of making a living and the anxieties of buying and selling. Properly spent, Sunday is a day for family and fellowship. Preparations begin on Saturday afternoon, when women sweep the streets in front of their houses and men get haircuts. On Sunday, some villagers, wearing their better clothes, attend mass. Relatives may come to visit from the city, and almost always a household or two are holding a fiesta to celebrate a baptism, confirmation, or first communion. In the afternoon many men gather at the soccer field in the school yard, if the local team has a home game, and some men, as on Saturday, play cards or billiards or drink beer with their friends.

3. History

Before the Conquest, Tlayacapan belonged to the Xochimilca, a Nahuatl-speaking tribe that settled in the southern end of the Valley of Mexico and then spread into the uplands of north-central Morelos (Durán 1967:2:22). Although little is known directly about pre-Hispanic Tlayacapan except for what is contained in the brief sixteenth-century "Relación de Totolapa y su partido" (de Curiel 1905), we can assume that the village shared the basic features of Nahuatl social organization and religion found throughout the central highlands.

Patrilocal residence was the norm; a bride generally left her natal household and joined her husband in his father's household. The *Relación* says,

In their marriages they kept this order: the father and relatives of the groom sent the bride many presents, which were dresses, food, male servants and maids who served her; the day of the wedding the father and relatives of the groom went to her house for her and they brought her to his house on their shoulders, where they tied or joined the manta of the groom and the "huipil" of the bride in sign that they were married; the feast for the bride was very great, with dances, food, and banquet, for a space of seven days, during which they became drunk as they do to the present day. (Ibid.:8-9)

The father was the "root" and "stock" of the family, the provider, and principal authority figure. The mother was expected to be chaste, obedient, and self-sacrificing; to bear children; and to cook, weave, and clean house. Her most laborious chore was grinding the lime-soaked maize into dough on the *metate*, a task that epitomized the woman's role then, even as it has until recent times (Sahagún 1956:1:355; 3:98).

Proper children were obedient and hard working. When they entered adolescence they were expected to suppress erotic urges. Boys were counseled to abstain from sexual relations before marriage; for daughters, abstinence was obligatory. The proper daughter spurned men and avoided women of questionable morals. Adulterers were stoned and dragged through the streets, then dumped outside the city as food for wild animals (Durán

1967:1:36). The ancient Nahua believed that illicit sexual relationships and desires could cause sickness and even death. An infant could become sick if an adulterer simply came near the pregnant mother or newborn (Alarcón 1953:110-112).

The *Calpulli*

A series of households belonged to a clanlike group called a *calpulli*. Each of the various *calpultin* (pl.) in a community had its own *calpultéotl*, or titulary deity, an image of which was kept in a special oratory and celebrated with movable and fixed festivals.

Passages in Zorita (1963:105, 184) imply that the *calpulli* chiefs and their children were nobles, and census data for sixteenth-century Morelos indicate the *calpultin* contained one or more noble lineages as well as commoners (Carrasco 1976a, 1976b). One plausible view is that it was a conical clan or ramage, a corporate group whose members were related to one another through actual or fictive kinship and ranked in status according to their imagined genealogical closeness to the god or founding ancestor (Wolf 1959:136). The nobles would have composed the senior lines or agnatic core of the *calpulli*, commoners the junior or cadet lines. The gods were conflated with persons who had lived, and nobles asserted their close affiliation with the gods in dress and demeanor. According to Zorita (1963:105-106), the *calpulli* "is a barrio of known people or an ancient lineage which holds its lands and boundaries from a time of great antiquity. These lands belong to the said kindred, barrio, or lineage, and they call such lands calpulli, meaning the lands of that barrio or lineage." House sites and fields belonged to the entire *calpulli* in common, although particular plots for homes and farming were distributed to individual families by the nobles or elders according to their needs and usufruct rules. Commoners could maintain possession of plots and even pass them on to their children if they kept their fields in production, continued to reside in the *calpulli*, and paid tribute to the *calpulli* chief to compensate him for expenses incurred in preparations for *calpulli* festivals (Zorita 1963:106-107, 110, 181, 184). The festivals were also funded by collective labor on temple lands (Durán 1967:2:83).

In keeping with the four-part division of the cosmos, many communities in the central highlands were partitioned into four large wards comprising various *calpultin* each; this was the case in Tenochtitlan, the dominant Aztec city. The number of *calpultin* per se varied from one community to another, although everywhere it tended to conform to cosmological numerology. There is evidence, for example, that twenty, twenty-five, or twenty-six may have represented the ideal number of *calpultin*. In describing the great festival of Tlacaxipehualiztli, Fray Durán wrote, "If twenty barrios existed, twenty men went about impersonating this universal god." These impersonators were sacrificed and their skins were removed. Later, the skins were worn by beggars who went from house to house. "These mendicants were twenty or twenty-five, depending on the number of barrios" (ibid.:1:96, 100-101).

Gods

Passages in some of the pre-Hispanic codices seem to allude to a concept of twenty-five or twenty-six founding ancestors. In the Codex Borgianus, for example, there appears a series of twenty-five couples numbered two through twenty-six. Eduard Seler (1963:2:149) showed that the series contains twelve couples associated with the night and twelve with the day. The twenty-fifth couple, bearing the number twenty-six, apparently represented the primordial male and female, who were known, among others, by the names Ometecuhtli and Omecihuatl. Seler discerned that this couple, occupying the thirteenth or highest heaven, complemented the two groups of twelve couples, in effect, adding a couple to each. The strange enumeration from two to twenty-six, in other words, is explained by the supposition that one—presumably ancestral—couple was counted twice, and indeed it may be added that Ometecuhtli means "twice a man" and that Omecihuatl means "twice a woman" (Sahagún 1956:3:188). There is reason to assume that male-female pairs in Aztec iconography represent ancestors; in Durán (1967:vol. 1, plates), each of the seven caves of Chicomoztoc, the place of origin of the seven tribes, contains a male-female pair.

Of religion, the sixteenth-century *relación* about Tlayacapan says only that the people of the region "worshiped the Devil, which took many forms and figures. They sacrificed to him, offering him 'copal' and cutting their ears, or passing the point of a maguey spine through the skin of one of their legs below the knee, and they offered him the blood that came out of their ears" (de Curiel 1905:8). The "Devil" in this passage doubtless refers to the gods of the many *calpultin* in the villages of the region. In conformity with the multilayered segmentations of society, each locality had a multiplicity of such patron deities. Nonetheless, there were many resemblances between gods of different communities, and it seems likely that all the gods in ancient Mexico were ultimately variants of a primordial pantheon, possibly the twenty-five or twenty-six divine pairs represented in the religious codices.

The gods were aligned with one or another of the four regions of the cosmos and varied in their importance and characteristics. According to Aztec myth, Ometecuhtli and Omecihuatl gave birth to four sons, each of whom became the principal god of a region: Tezcatlipoca, of the North; Quetzalcoatl, of the West; Huitzilopochtli, of the South; and Xipe Totec, of the East (Garibay K. 1965:23-24).

Quetzalcoatl, the Plumed Serpent, was the god of wind and ally of the rain gods. He carried water for the rain gods and swept the paths clear in preparation for their arrival. As a mythical personage in the ancient city of Tula, he was the inventor and patron of crafts. Along with the goddess Cihuacoatl-Tonantzin, he helped to create the race of commoners. Cihuacoatl and Quetzalcoatl were both associated with the deer (see chap. 6). In myth women transformed themselves into deer, and the killing of deer had sexual connotations (Codex Chimalpopoca 1945:123-124). Contemporary myths suggest that Quetzalcoatl was ambiguously a patron of deer hunters and deerlike, and hence a victim of hunters (see Benítez 1980).

Tezcatlipoca was the patron of warriors. As principal god of the North he was associated with Huehueteotl or Xiutecuhtli, the god of fire; Mictlantecuhtli, the god of death who ruled over Mictlan, the mythical land of the dead; and Mixcoatl, god of the hunt. Tezcatlipoca at one point transformed himself into Mixcoatl to invent fire (Garibay K. 1956:33). Along with the help of Huitzilopochtli and Tlacuepan, Tezcatlipoca defeated and humiliated Quetzalcoatl in Tula and caused him to flee the city. Using various strategems, he tricked Quetzalcoatl into drunkenness and incest.

Xipe Totec, the god of the flayed skin, represented maize, rain, and rejuvenation. Xipe was a patron of metalworkers. His hymn also links him with Quetzalcoatl:

> Thou, Night-Drinker
> Why dost thou mask thyself?
> Put on thy disguise, thy golden cape!
> My God, thy jade water descended;
> Precious Cypress!
> Feathered turquoise/fire serpent!
> Maybe I shall die,
> I the tender maize plant;
> My heart is jade,
> But I shall see gold there.
> I shall rejoice if I ripen early.
> The war-chief is born!
> My God, let there be an abundance of maize plants,
> In a few places at least.
> I shall rejoice if it ripen early,
> The war-chief is born![1]

The East was also the region of Tlaloc, the principal rain god, and Chalchiuhuitlicue, the goddess of water, who also took the guise of Chicomecoatl, goddess of sustenance, and Xilonen, the goddess of tender maize. Another major god of the East was Tlahuizcalpantecuhtli, morning star and soul of the self-immolated Quetzalcoatl.

Huitzilopochtli was the tribal patron of the Aztecs at Tenochtitlan. A diurnal counterpart of Tezcatlipoca and manifestation of the sun, he was a fearsome warrior, a killer of peoples and destroyer of towns who carried a fire-breathing dragon or serpent.

There was a pattern in this arrangement of the gods. The gods of the East and West had strong associations with rain and fertility, whereas those of the North and South were linked more with fire (fig. 1). These properties of the four directions were apparent also in the depiction of the four *tlaloque* or rain gods in the Codex Borgianus: the *tlaloque* of the North and South appear with drought, lightning (fire), and pests that eat the maize; the *tlaloque* of the East and West appear with abundant rain and healthy maize (see fig. 2). These associations were in turn correlated with social symbolism: the gods of the North and South were patrons of warriors or

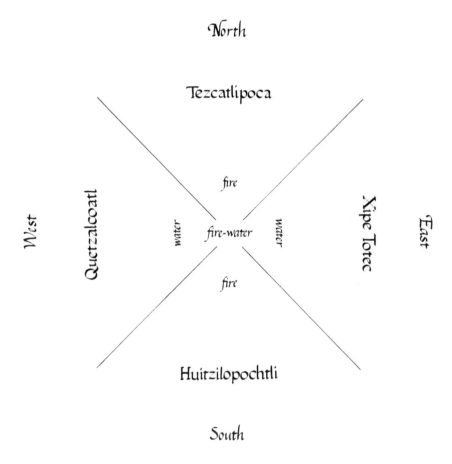

Fig. 1. Gods, Elements and Directions

West   North

South   East

Fig. 2. The *Tlaloque* (after Codex Borgianus, Seler 1963:plate 27)

nobles, whereas those of the East and West were patrons of commoners, or farmers and artisans. *Atl-tlachinolli*, or water and fire, was a symbol for warfare, the activity that produced and reproduced domination. War was fire consuming water.

The connections between gods and elements, it should be noted, were not without ambiguity. All the gods were nobles and, hence, warriors. Moreover, since the *calpultin* contained nobles and commoners, their gods were patrons of nobles and warriors. In some measure, then, the mystical properties of fire and water suffused all directions, although their proportions varied: the West was more associated with water, the East with fire. The opposition between water and fire, in other words, was repeated among the water gods themselves.

Clans, Gods, and Time

The celebrations of the gods were scheduled with two calendars: one was a solar calendar of 365 days; the other was the Tonalpohualli, a calendar of 260 days. Sometimes called the divinatory calendar because it was used for prognostication, the latter consisted of two cycles, one of thirteen numerals and the other of twenty signs. The count proceeded from 1 Crocodile to 2 Wind, 3 House, 4 Lizard, and so on, beginning again with 1 Crocodile after 260 days. Each of the four quarters of the world was linked with five of the twenty signs.

In the Tonalamatl (Book of Days), which is included in some of the religious codices, the Tonalpohualli is laid out in twenty groups of thirteen days. Each group is accompanied by drawings of one or two deities and what may be the accoutrements of appropriate rituals or festivals. In a comparative study of the extant versions, Seler (1963:2:174) found that a total of twenty-five deities are pictured in the Tonalamatl, of whom one is Ometecuhtli, sometimes shown with Omecihuatl. Celebrations for *calpulli* deities were scheduled with the Tonalpohualli, apparently because it was a birthday calendar (Durán 1967:1:233-237; Sahagún 1956:1:133-137, 236, 238, 239, 241). Nobles were named after their birthdays on the Tonalpohualli, and nobles and gods were closely affiliated. From these data, it would appear that the Tonalamatl was, in part, a means of keeping track of the birthday festivals of the gods. Durán (1967:1:235) observed that after the Conquest, headmen of the barrios sometimes tried to hold the fiestas for their barrio saints on their own birthdays.

The solar calendar, which consisted of eighteen periods of twenty days plus five empty days, was used to schedule the most impressive festivals of the annual round. These festivals, centered on the major gods of the pantheon, appear to have been organized and sponsored by a limited number of high-ranking *calpultin* (Ingham 1971). Several of these solar festivals dramatized the hierarchical relations between gods of fire and water, and of these, two solar festivals, Quecholli and Tlacaxipehualiztli, will prove especially pertinent to later discussions of syncretism.

The highlight of Quecholli was a ceremonial hunt of deer and other animals by men disguised as Mixcoatl. After the hunt, the game was roasted over a great bonfire (Durán 1967:1:75-76). As part of the festival, arrows were made, offered to Huitzilopochtli, and redistributed. Captives were carried to the top of the pyramid for sacrifice "as if they were deer" (Sahagún 1956:1:127, 201-202). Since Mixcoatl was a transformation of Tezcatlipoca and the deer was associated with Quetzalcoatl, the ritual slaying of the deer was structurally parallel to the defeat of Quetzalcoatl by Tezcatlipoca.

A relationship of domination also obtained between the sun and maize, or between Huitzilopochtli and Xipe Totec. The festival of Tlacaxipehualiztli honored both gods (ibid.:142-143). In preparation for the festival, a captive was dressed to represent Xipe, and in each *calpulli* a captive was dressed in the likeness of its *calpultéotl*. The hearts of these captives were ripped out at dawn before the temple of Huitzilopochtli and offered to the sun. Then commoners came forward and made offerings of ears of dried maize. Later in the day the flesh of the victims was cooked with maize and consumed by relatives of the captors and other nobles. Before the bodies were butchered, the skins were removed and nobles were dressed in them along with the costumes worn by the victims. These nobles were tied to a series of captives by ropes that symbolized the unity of the god with his captives. Since the god-impersonators were identified with Xipe by virtue of wearing human skins, all the captives were in effect Xipe warriors. These warriors, armed only with wooden swords and balls, were obliged to defend themselves against warriors dressed as eagles and jaguars, or warriors of the sun. As each Xipe warrior was dispatched, his heart was torn out and offered to the sun (Durán 1967:1:96-99). Xipe's hymn suggests that the human skins were an allusion to regeneration and, perhaps, to the mantle of the maize plant, which turns gold with maturity. This inference is supported by the festival of Ochpaniztli, wherein impersonators of Toci (mother of the gods) and the *cinteteo* (the maize gods of the four directions) wore human skins (Sahagún 1956:1:195).

Quetzalcoatl and Xipe were similar figures in that both were associated with water and fertility. Huitzilopochtli—Tonatiuh and Tezcatlipoca-Mixcoatl resembled one another in that both were associated with fire and war. The relationship between Tezcatlipoca-Mixcoatl and Quetzalcoatl-deer, then, was analogous to that between Huitzilopochtli-Tonatiuh and Xipe Totec, the maize god. In each instance, gods associated with fire dominated and assimilated those associated with water and fertility (see fig. 3; see Ingham 1984).

The Conquest and the Colonial Period

The first meeting between Tlayacapan and the Spaniards is described in Bernal Díaz del Castillo's classic account of the Conquest. After *la noche triste*, when the Spaniards fled Tenochtitlan, and before the final defeat of the Mexica, Cortés undertook a campaign to the south to secure alliances with the people of Chalco, traditional enemies of both Tenochtitlan and Tlayacapan. The Spaniards found that the villagers of Tlayacapan had fortified the hills around the community. Laying siege, the Spaniards eventually forced a surrender, but only after suffering heavy casualties from the stones and boulders that were thrown at them and rolled down the hills

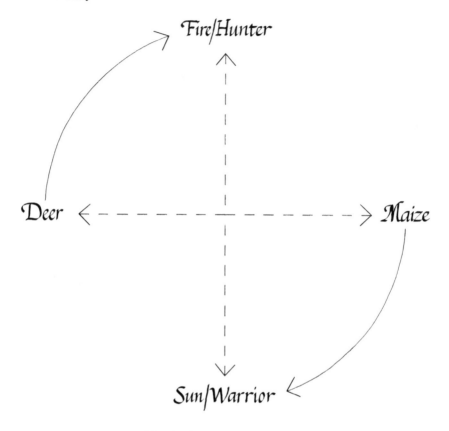

Fig. 3. Fire, Deer, and Maize

upon them. From a military point of view, the chronicler concedes the victory to the Tlayacapenses but notes that they gave fealty to Cortés when he promised not to harm them. Cortés then went on to Oaxtepec, Yautepec, and Tepoztlán, where he met little opposition (Díaz del Castillo 1956:372).

Local legend upholds the chronicler's story that the Mexicans rolled rocks down on the Spaniards and mentions that the hillsides were strewn with Spanish bodies. The ruins of the fortifications described in Díaz del Castillo's account are still visible; they must have been as impenetrable as he reported. The local version, however, says nothing about suing for peace; it is said that Cortés retreated by way of Santa Catarina to Oaxtepec. Later, when the new Mexica ruler, Cuauhtemoc, sent out to his allies a request for aid, local authorities conscripted warriors for the struggle with the Spaniards and gathered them for a census at a place near Nepopualco called Stone of the Counter. Tlayacapan, it was claimed, sent many men into the final battle but few if any returned. There was then no question of further resistance.

In 1534 Augustinian friars established a monastery in the nearby town of Totolapan and a periodic visitation (*visita*) in Tlayacapan. An early source says that they were received in the area with great enthusiasm and devotion (Grijalva 1624:13). A chapel was constructed in Tlayacapan and, as in many other communities, a large open-air atrium with oratories at its four corners was used for baptisms and masses. Tlayacapan was raised to monastery rank in 1554, and additional religious construction followed, including a large, imposing church, attached monastery, and many neighborhood chapels (de Curiel 1905:11). The hundreds of tons of earthen and stone platform under the atrium, church, and monastery suggest that they were built on the toppled remains of a great pyramid (McAndrew 1965:244). As in other communities in which they worked, the Augustinians restructured and congregated Tlayacapan according to an explicit Hispanic design: a marketplace, or *tianguis*, and central plaza were laid out next to the church and bordered by a municipal building and school; streets and lanes were organized into a grid pattern.

The Augustinians were probably more severe than other orders in suppressing indigenous religion. Idols and shrines were destroyed and obvious instances of paganism were actively discouraged. Schools for young people were held in the patios of the church, in which the children were taught to assist in the mass, to read and write, and to sing and play musical instruments. In these classes boys and girls were carefully divided. Before they were allowed to marry they were rigorously examined in matters of doctrine. Indians gathered in their barrios in the evenings and mornings to sing the four prayers and hymns. On days of fiestas, they congregated at the barrio cross and then moved in procession to the church, singing hymns and reciting prayers. On Sundays and feast days, the people gathered in the atrium or cemetery of the church under the shade trees, the men to one side and the women to the other. The officials of the town and the barrios called roll, and those who were absent without excuse were punished, sometimes harshly. The Indians repeated portions of the catechism two or three times, after which the sermon was preached and the mass was held. The whole community attended vespers on Fridays, and a cofradía supported masses for the spirits of the dead in Purgatory on Mondays and another, devoted to the Virgin, sang a mass for the living on Saturdays (Grijalva 1624:72-73; Ricard 1966:107-108).

The Augustinians as a whole were notable for their confidence in the spiritual capacities of the Indians. They introduced communion and even extreme unction, something the Franciscans were unwilling to do (Ricard 1966:108). The Augustinians gave all the Indians instruction in the Eucharist, informing them that Christ was present in the smallest particle of the sacred wafer and warning that they must be in a state of grace and were not to eat or drink after the preceding midnight. On each Sunday of Lent, they were given more detailed teaching and examined on the catechism, after which those who passed were selected for communion on the following Saturday. On Friday, the communicants listened to special instruction and on Saturday they further prepared themselves by dressing as if for a wedding and by remaining silent. As the act of grace was about to be consummated, they recited in chorus in Nahuatl Saint Thomas Aquinas's *Omnipotens sempiterne Deus* as well as his prayer of the act of grace (ibid.:125).

The friars introduced the sacraments and orthodox liturgy into the religious lives of the Indians, of course, but they and lay Spaniards also transmitted elements of local religion, which was flourishing in sixteenth-century Spain. The cults of saints in local chapels and shrines had been part of this lay religiosity since the eleventh century, when ecclesiastical acceptance of saintly images freed devotion from exclusive attention to the relics of martyr, hermit, and bishop saints in cathedrals, parish churches, and monasteries (Christian 1981).

Some saints were advocates of entire communities, whereas others were the special patrons of particular barrios or neighborhoods and guilds. At each of the two levels, the brotherhoods cared for the saints and sponsored their fiestas. Brotherhoods that centered on the saints of barrio and guild chapels occupied themselves with day-to-day devotions, funerals, and charity for the poor, whereas those devoted to saints of the parish church were more concerned with joint processions and other shared vows. The saints in the neighborhood chapels were usually specialists of local origin in contrast to the townwide devotions, which were more apt to center on Mary or the Apostolic saints. Smaller villages had an average of two chapels, whereas towns of five hundred to a thousand households tended to have five or six. The fame of images and the importance of their chapels varied greatly and underwent changes in time. The chapels of especially miraculous saints became shrines and drew pilgrims from other towns. About one town in six had a shrine (ibid.).

The saints were thought to offer protection against hail, drought, and epidemics. These disasters were assumed to be the work of the Devil but they could also represent punishment by the saints for insincere and insufficient religiosity. Fires, floods, earthquakes, lightning, and pestilence on saints' days were taken as signs that saints needed or wanted more attention. Vows made by individuals, barrios, guilds, and villages might consist of building and maintaining a chapel or sponsoring feasts, processions, or bullfights.

Many saints were reputed to have special powers and provinces. Saint Sebastian offered protection against pestilence and disease, as did Mary and Anne to a lesser extent (ibid.:42, 43). Insects attacking vines were the province of Saint Gregory of Nazianzus, Saint Gregory the Pope, and Saint Pataleon (ibid.:43). Mary was preferred in matters of biological fertility, and Mary and the Cross of May were sought to end drought (ibid.:46, 47). The Cross of May was also thought to offer protection against hail and vine worms (ibid.:116). "In late medieval theology, the cross was a sign of great power to turn back the devil, and hail and locusts were as much of 'the enemy' as Albigensians, Turks, and Moors" (ibid.:184). The common association of Mary and the Cross with rain was not coincidental, since most of the Marian visions reported included the cross. The doctors of the church—Saint Augustin, Saint Thomas Aquinas, and Saint Ambrose—were also thought to have the power to conjure locusts (ibid.:44). Saint Barbara had the power to send lightning but could also offer protection against it (ibid.:35).

Protection for the crops was a major preoccupation of folk religion. Lay practitioners traveled through the countryside selling their services of warding off disease, hailstorms, and insects by magical means. Known as *ensalmadores* (charm curers), necromancers, or conjurers of clouds, they competed with the parish priests, who offered exorcisms for these same problems. Some of the wizards, apparently, were themselves clerics. Among other things, they put insects on trial and excommunicated them. The weather workers were hired by communities to conjure away the hail-bearing clouds or to make the hail dissolve into rain. In some places the wizards and the clergy held contests to determine who could deal more effectively with the clouds (ibid.:29-30).

There were also other heterodox elements in local religion. Clerics complained of dancing, feasting, and drinking, plays and farces, and ribald and lewd songs during the vigils before feasts (ibid.:164). Some dances and plays portrayed the struggles between the Moors and Christians, with Santiago leading the latter. Feasts, Carnival, and fairs could also be the occasion for masquerades and dances featuring Old Men and Old Women, Devils, Demons, Hobbyhorses, and Big Heads, and as elsewhere in sixteenth-century Europe there could be performances of the commedia dell' arte in which Harlequin and other scandalous figures were represented. Many festivals included bullfights and in some places ritual bear hunts similar to the ritual deer hunts in other countries (Caro Baroja 1965; Kurath 1949).

Part of the religious heritage of Catholicism was an ongoing struggle between the particular and the universal, the laity and the clergy, about proper practice. Priests were often loyal to the folk customs of their native villages, but when working in alien parishes or the outlying districts they usually tried to impose the received standards of the universal religion. And these efforts to control local religion increased in the sixteenth century under the influence of Erasmianism and the Counter-Reformation. The saints were said to be mere idols and doubt was expressed about their capacity to perform miracles. Throughout the latter half of the sixteenth century special efforts were made to discourage bullfighting, albeit with limited success (Christian 1981:158-180).

Barrio Organization

In Tlayacapan images of the *calpulli* gods were destroyed along with their shrines, and the community was reorganized, but the general pattern of social and ritual organization persisted. The old gods were replaced by Christian saints, and the *calpultin* endured intact (see Carrasco 1976b). Spanish civil authorities redefined the *calpulli* as a barrio and treated it as an administrative unit, but this practice did not appreciably alter its traditional organization nor its relation to the rest of the community; the pre-Hispanic *calpulli* had also been an administrative unit. The community was still divided into four large *campanes*, or wards, each containing smaller barrios.

Although saint and fiesta replaced god and festival, the barrio remained a cohesive unit grounded in common religious devotion. The Christian calendar did not duplicate the indigenous calendars, but the general character of the distinction between festivals of the Tonalpohualli and those of the solar calendar endured in the difference between ordinary barrio fiestas, on the one hand, and the village-level fiestas, Carnival, and fairs, on the other. As we shall see later, the pre-Hispanic ritual deer hunts and mock combats gave way to Passion plays, masquerades, mock and actual bullfights, and European versions of the hunt of the primordial animal.

The friars probably had misgivings about these unorthodox aspects of Catholic practice in the Indian community, especially when the customs had indigenous origins. There is, for example, the implied criticism of festive drunkenness in the "Relación de Totolapa y su partido." The clerics no doubt criticized pagan customs of European origin as well, and such criticism—and corresponding anticlericalism—probably increased once the friars were replaced by the secular clergy. In 1756 the community planned to celebrate a bullfight on a Sunday, and the priest opposed the plan. When the villagers insisted on making the bulls part of their fiesta, the priest excommunicated the entire community, and the villagers rioted. They forced the priest to flee the community, burned his house, and held their fiesta without him.[2]

Throughout the central highlands Spanish officials identified *calpulli* chiefs and elders (that is, the nobles) as mayordomos, who in this capacity continued to be responsible for organizing religious celebrations. Following the pre-Hispanic pattern, the men of a barrio, under the direction of their mayordomos, worked communal plots that had been specifically designated for the support of the chapel. They also supported their religious feasts with tribute paid to the barrio elders or mayordomos and, in return, received the usufruct to a house site and agricultural land. The record of a 1769 dispute over property rights in the barrio of San Nicolás gives a valuable glimpse of barrio organization in the colonial period. The litigants were a mestizo woman and the Indian alcalde.

The woman (Josepha María Vida) was the widow of an Indian of the pueblo (Andrés

Santa María); she and her husband lived in a house of the barrio of San Nicolás, to which he paid regular tribute. The woman appeared before the Spanish authorities because, after the death of her husband, the alcalde had tried to use his authority to give the house to another Indian. She alleged that the house had been, originally, the private property of her husband's father (Diego Gregorio), and that her husband inherited that property and finally it was willed to her. Furthermore, she said that one of her sons, who was living with her, continued to pay tribute to the barrio. Therefore, Josepha was using a double argument to affirm her rights over the house; on the one side, she was alleging it to be private property; on the other, if the housed did belong to the barrio, she had a right to use it because her son was paying tribute.

The alcalde (Joseph Aleuterio Nopaltitla) answered that the house never had been anybody's private property and that Josepha María had no legal document to demonstrate that it might be hers. He noted that the woman was a mestiza—that is, she had no right to belong to an Indian barrio—but that he had not threatened her with eviction as long as she lived with her husband, who was an Indian and member of the barrio. The alcalde also gave a different version of how the house was put in the hands of the father-in-law of the woman, the Indian Diego Gregorio. According to this version, Diego Gregorio was originally from the barrio of Santa Ana, married an Indian woman of the barrio of San Nicolás, and went to live with his father-in-law. What he later inherited was not the private property of the house, but membership in the barrio, with its norms and obligations. Finally, the alcalde said that during the fight he had not acted on his own initiative but at the request of the Indian officials of the barrio, who wanted to reassign the house now that none of the sons of Josepha María were disposed to fulfill their obligations as members of the barrio.

The alcalde took to the magistrate three witnesses who corroborated his testimony. It is advisable to note that in his statement he did not question the normative principles on which the argument of the woman was based, but only stated that the facts presented by Josepha María were distorted, that is to say, that the house was not private property but property of the barrio, and that her children were not paying tribute. The witnesses were Indian officials of the same barrio of San Nicolás: the mayordomo, the *caballero-pixque* (the horse tender of the church stable), and the water carrier (the one in charge of carrying water to the priests). All confirmed what the alcalde had said; they added that *it was the custom that those who belonged to a barrio cooperated in its fiestas, and also that they performed small tasks in the republic, and that owing to this cooperation they were granted a house and a plot of land* [emphasis added]. The witnesses were very annoyed with the sons of Josepha María, because they had refused to pay tribute to the barrio and to do the work of same; moreover, they had tried to obtain a house in other barrios, and now, being children of the mestiza, they had the pretension to possess a house privately, like the *gente de razón* [educated people, Creoles].

After the statement of the witnesses, the court declared that Josepha María and her children could remain in the house with the condition that they comply with their obligations toward the barrio. (AGN, *Ramo de Tierras*, 1769, exp. 4, f. 10; quoted in de la Peña 1980:70-71)

As in the *calpulli* system before the Conquest, patrilocal residence was the norm, but it was possible to attach oneself to another barrio through uxorilocal residence, providing that one met the obligations of membership in the new barrio. Also as in the pre-Hispanic system, it was usually commoners, not the elite of the barrio, who changed barrio affiliation.

Exceptions to the usual residence pattern must have occurred throughout the colonial period, but they were probably particularly frequent in the early seventeenth century, the low point in a century-long period of population decline resulting from European diseases. As the decimation continued in the latter half of the sixteenth century and into the next, outlying neighborhoods were evidently vacated and their chapels were abandoned. Survivors must have moved into neighborhoods closer to the plaza, diminishing the strength of agnation within them.

This development, however, did not mark a sharp break with the past. Even before the Conquest, the *calpulli* was often a heterogeneous mixture of agnatic core and collateral elements, including immigrant nonagnates. It was a kinship group by fiction as much as genealogical fact. Following the reconstitution of the *calpultin* in the seventeenth century, their agnatic character must have reasserted itself as a result of patrilocal residence. There is even a hint in early nineteenth-century census data of agnatic lineages within the barrios (see below), although kinship was unquestionably less salient in defining barrio membership than it had once been. More germane to the question of continuity is the way the semifictive kinship in *calpulli* organization before the Conquest gave way to a Christian idiom of spiritual kinship afterward (see chapter 5).

Social Hierarchy

Intermarriage between Spanish men—the social elite of the community as a whole—and Indian women created a class of mestizos who, ordinarily, were not members of the Indian barrios. The *Relación* of 1743 indicates that there were 61 Spanish families, 75 mestizo families, and 1,222 Indian families in the entire *municipio* (Rojas Rabiela 1980:60). The mestizos were known as *gente de razón* (people of reason).

The Independence Period

In the nineteenth century the dominant families of Tlayacapan were known as "the rich," "those of the plaza," and "those of the government." They in turn referred to Indians as "the humble ones." The rich owned the stores, most of the cattle, and the butcher shops. Their homes were more imposing and elegant than those of the poor; some had two stories, porticoes, and interior patios with reflecting pools and flower gardens. When overseeing the work in the fields, the wealthy men wore slacks, shirts, and boots; in town, they wore dark suits. The upper-class women wore fashionable shoes and dresses.

Poor villagers lived in smaller adobe houses with tile roofs, although the poorest roofed their houses with thatch. Men wore the typical white pajamas of the Mexican peasant (at least by the end of the nineteenth century), with leather huaraches for footwear. Women wore a black *nagua* (wrap-around skirt) with a white band near the waist and secured with a red sash, with a white embroidered blouse and heavy black *huipil*. Most women went barefoot. As the mestizo population grew, however, traditional female attire gave way to simple cotton dresses and European-style shawls. By the time of the Revolution of 1910, only a few women dressed in the traditional manner.

Many mestizos were artisans or skilled laborers. Unpublished census summaries found among old documents in the town hall's clock tower show the division of labor in the nineteenth century. In one undated census, 62 percent of the men had Spanish surnames and 38 percent had only Christian names to which "José" was prefixed. Lacking surnames, these villagers were listed under the Nahuatl names for the streets on which they lived (to this day, villagers recall that it was the custom for the "Indian" villagers to use street names as surnames). Eighty-nine percent of the population lacking last names were laborers, and 65 percent of the men with Spanish surnames were shopkeepers or craftsmen of some type. An unpublished census dated 1843 indicates that there were 13 agriculturalists and 324 *jornaleros*, or common workers, along with makers of candy, candles, rockets, shoes, and hats as well as tailors, silversmiths and blacksmiths, barbers, and musicians.

Descendants of the pre-Revolution elite say that the rich sympathized with the poor. They gave them employment and sometimes acted as godparents to their children. One could argue, however, that the sympathy was self-serving. Some rich people lent money at high rates of interest, and many bought crops *al tiempo*, before the harvest was in, for only one-third or one-half as much as it would fetch later in the marketplace. If a poor villager looked desperate, the rich buyer might try to drive an even harder bargain. Don Otilio said, "When they seemed broken, well, they broke them some more." It is clear from current recollections that the rich were strict disciplinarians: alcoholic and indolent villagers were reported to the authorities in Yautepec, who in turn had them drafted into the army. Luis Arabia, a store owner, used to mix beans and rice together; when there was no other work to be done, his clerks were kept busy sorting the beans and rice into separate piles. Luis was equally demanding of himself; it is said that he spent the whole of Sunday mass on his knees, his arms outstretched.

An article about Tlayacapan published in 1885 by Cecilio A. Robelo describes Tlayacapan much as it appeared eighty years later. Basing his remarks on a brief visit as well as on one of those elusive unpublished "manuscripts" that are the frustration of ethnohistorians, he says that there were nineteen existing chapels but adds that there had once been twenty-five, each with its own barrio. He mentions the great *pochote* or ceiba tree that still stands in front of the town hall, the spaciousness of the plaza, the straight and well-ordered streets, and the flat-roofed houses, some with porticoes and elegant patios (1885:109).

The village in those days, he says, had a sad and gloomy appearance: streets were deserted, great houses were lying abandoned, and the walls of houses and chapels were in disrepair. He attributes the decline to independence (or the insurrection, as the Indians called it), the expulsion of the Spaniards, and the Revolution of Ayutla, but also mentions the arrival of the railroad in the lowlands of Morelos—Cuautla in 1881 and Yautepec in 1883—which served to confirm the increasingly marginal economic position of the community (ibid.:110).

The conditions Robelo mentions only account for the decline of the Spanish elite and the mestizo commercial sector. The subsistence-oriented Indians in the barrios were less affected by the declining commercial fortunes of the village. Actually, the population of the village from 1850 to the Revolution of 1910 remained roughly the same, at about twenty-five hundred persons. Periodic outbreaks of cholera, measles, and smallpox curtailed population growth, and demographic increase was probably limited as well by sexual restraint and long nursing periods as well as by resistance to immigration. Interestingly, in the hot country, where villages were more open, growth was noticeably greater than in the uplands.[3]

In 1885 fields around the village lacked irrigation and people took their water from the *jagueyes* (hillside reservoirs). To increase or supplement their incomes some villagers fertilized their fields and others worked as artisans, either in silverworking, saddlery, wax candle making, pottery, rocket making, or hat making. The list of nonagricultural occupations is somewhat more attenuated than what appears in the 1843 census, suggesting that the economic decline had indeed affected the division of labor. The mention of silverworking in 1885 is interesting, since it appeared earlier, in the census of 1843. Robelo discusses the abandoned mines in the area in some detail, implying that a silver- and goldworking industry had played a part in the earlier economic prosperity.

According to Robelo, Carnival in Tlayacapan in the late nineteenth century was vigorous, despite the economic downtrend. He says that as many as 2,000 persons wore masks, including women, who took special care with their costumes. The figure seems a bit exaggerated, since the entire population of the village was only 2,454. Presumably the women he refers to were the wealthy, who put on costumes and discreet masks for an elite ball. Despite this general enthusiasm for the festivities, however, the priest in 1885 tried to dissuade the villagers from staging their Carnival, and as the festival approached, his advice changed to imprecation and cursing. The "misguided sheep," however, "followed the devouring wolf," and the priest resigned himself to watching the people "swarm like ants" from the top of the church (Robelo 1885:111-112).

From the early colonial period, haciendas dominated the lowlands to the south of the village. Several of these estates were in operation by 1540, and haciendas steadily proliferated and extended their domains thereafter, particularly during the early colonial period, when the Indian communities were in decline (Barrett 1970). The sugarcane industry was depressed in the late seventeenth and early eighteenth centuries, as low prices, poor management, the decline of the slave population, and prohibition of rum manufacture curtailed operations and forced bankruptcies. But the industry revived by the middle of the eighteenth century, thus renewing the competition with the corporate communities. Meanwhile, the increasing numbers of Indians and especially non-Indians raised fruits, vegetables, and indigo and competed with the haciendas for land, water, and markets. Since some non-Indians rented Indian lands, they had a unity of interest with the Indians vis-à-vis the haciendas. Throughout Morelos, corporate communities continued to assert their Indianness in legal forums even though many of their residents were mestizos. The haciendas for their part had the same aims as would their descendants, who tried to appropriate Indian lands under the Reform Laws in the next century: they would eliminate the outmoded institution of the corporate community and extend their version of capitalist relations of production instead. The haciendas produced maize and other crops as well as cane and it seems unlikely that they were dependent on the uplands for food. They were also largely self-sufficient in labor. Conversely, work on the haciendas was less significant as a source of income in the late colonial period than it had been earlier and would again become in the nineteenth century (Martin 1982).

The demand for labor on the haciendas increased in the latter half of the nineteenth century, particularly after the construction of a narrow-gauge railroad and the introduction of heavy milling machinery allowed increased production for commercial markets. At the end of the nineteenth century more than forty haciendas dotted the fertile and irrigated bottomlands of Morelos. Old men recall that before 1910 most men worked on the haciendas. Some walked daily to the hacienda of San Carlos or Oacalco (Pantitlán had been abandoned some years earlier). They arose at four in the morning to be at work by six, because late workers were not paid. Others worked on more-distant haciendas from Monday through Saturday and returned to the village only for a day of rest on Sunday. On Wednesdays the workers were paid the *socorro*, an advance on their salaries, and the remainder was paid on Saturdays. Men received thirty-five to forty centavos each, barely enough to meet the subsistence needs of a family. The foreman, mounted on horseback, used a whip to keep the men in line. The hacendados themselves were absentee landlords, although they, their families, and guests could be seen on occasional visits wearing fine riding clothes and mounted on expensive horses.

A now-familiar view of the relation between the haciendas has them appropriating lands throughout the colonial period and then, with special ferocity, following the passage of laws of disentailment in 1856 and the arrival of the railroad and the gas centrifuge in the early 1880s (see Womack 1969). There is a measure of truth in this picture, but most of the Indian lands were already appropriated by the end of the seventeenth century. In general, the new industrial potential for sugarcane production in the 1880s was realized through an expansion of irrigation works and a reappropriation of rental lands already belonging to the haciendas (Crespo and Frey 1982). The exceptions to this pattern typically occurred at the margins of the *tierra caliente*, and one of these involved the relationship between Tlayacapan and the hacienda at Oacalco.

Tensions over Tlayacapan's *tierra caliente* communal lands (Cacahuatlan) had already reached a high pitch by the middle of the nineteenth century. Oacalco tried to claim the field, but in May of 1849 an armed group of four hundred to five hundred Tlayacapenses announced their intention of retrieving the land, which was mentioned in their colonial land titles (títulos primordiales). The civil authorities, to avoid bloodshed and doubtless because their own interests were at stake, took charge of the protest and led the men to Cacahuatlan, where they were joined by others from Tepoztlán, Oaxtepec, and Santa Catarina. The protest was popular and was soon imitated by other communities in the region,[4] but in 1856 Oacalco gained control of some three hundred hectares in Cacahuatlan.[5]

Acculturation, increasing division of labor, and wage labor on the haciendas may also have been responses to the appropriation of communal lands within the village itself. The process of converting communal tenure was probably a gradual one with beginnings in the monetization of the economy in the late eighteenth century. The Reform Laws, which separated church and state, and so legalized the appropriation of barrio and church lands, merely marked a stage in a long process. Independence itself signaled the rise of liberal, antichurch forces that were oriented to appropriating land through political means. The labeling of men as *"jornaleros"* in the 1843 census may imply that most villagers either were already working in part or entirely for the rich Spaniards in the village or on the haciendas, or had carved a place for themselves in some form of skilled labor. The census may futher imply that some tracts were privately owned by 1843 or were at least being rented by elite families and that many poor men worked as wage laborers. The census of 1900, which aggregates data for the present *municipios* of Tlayacapan and Atlatlahuacan, gives the same impression. There were 67 agriculturalists, 2 cattlemen, 54 shopkeepers, 1,105 field hands, and various artisans of different types.[6] Nonetheless, it seems likely that many field hands continued to hold communal plots. Although the Reform Laws were promulgated in 1859, throughout Morelos private entitlement to communal lands was either reconfirmed or granted for the first time in 1909.[7]

De la Peña (1980:85) may be correct in claiming that the Reform Laws undermined the economic basis of barrio solidarity. By 1909 barrio officials probably had little say in the distribution and administration of communal lands. The process of secularization, however, was gradual rather than precipitous. Certainly de la Peña's suggestion that the Reform Laws initiated the abandonment of chapels is improbable. Given that Robelo found chapels in ruins in 1885, it seems more likely, as suggested earlier, that they began to deteriorate in the seventeenth century.

The Revolution of 1910

An agrarian problem had been building in Morelos since the resurgence of the indigenous population in the middle of the seventeenth century and the recovery of the sugar industry in the middle of the eighteenth century. The crisis culminated, of course, in the Revolution of 1910. In Tlayacapan violence first occurred on Good Friday in 1911, when a Zapatista force came through the village pursued by federal troops. In those days, most villagers considered themselves supporters of the insurrectionist Madero. A year later it seemed that Madero had failed the Revolution, and Zapata raised the call against him. Zapatistas next fought against Victoriano Huerta, the general who replaced Madero. After a brief triumph, the Zaptistas again had to take up arms, this time against Carranza. Members of wealthy families usually say that the Zapatistas were harder on the village, but the humble people say that the government forces caused more suffering. The seizures of animals, property, and food, and incidents of rape and murder are still remembered.

The hills around Tlayacapan offered natural hiding places that were frequently used by Zapatista troops. A lookout always was posted on the top of Sombrerito; when armed forces approached, the lookout sounded the alarm and the villagers fled to the hills. Some village men were revolutionaries, but many avoided the fighting and others fought only intermittently. The villagers suffered, nonetheless, particularly the poor. The rich sat out the hostilities in distant urban areas and some never returned.

Doña Delfina Salazar, the daughter of the most powerful man in Tlayacapan on the eve of the Revolution, recalled that Zapata and his generals had their headquarters in her home for twenty days in 1915. Although she was only a girl at the time, she remembered that Emiliano was a kind man and this his brother was a drunkard and woman chaser. Doña Delfina's recollection is interesting, for it suggests that the most powerful man in Tlayacapan, a cattleman as well as store owner, shared political interests with Zapata, who also came from a cattle-raising family. Salazar, that is to say, was interested in protecting the communal pasturelands and thus the principle of communal lands in general. Zapata certainly supported local cattle owners; several letters he wrote to the president of Tlayacapan during the Revolution urge harsh treatment for cattle thieves.[8] In 1915 the villagers recovered the lands of Cacahuatlan.[9]

Other Zapatista generals stayed in Tlayacapan, and some did not treat the local elite as kindly. General Domínguez killed Guadalupe Copas—the president of Tlayacapan—simply because he failed to feed the general's horses as ordered. Domínguez even killed his own brother when the latter was disabled. Another Zapatista general memorable for his ruthlessness was Diego Ruiz, nicknamed El Diablo, a man who dressed in black and carried two pistols and a carbine.

The worst period was that of the *linea del fuego*, a line of Carrancista soldiers who came over the mountains from the north in 1916. Villagers say they had permission to take whatever they wanted. Hard fighting devastated the vicinity: Tlayacapan was sacked and partly burned, and later a typhoid epidemic struck the village. The dead were not properly buried; they were simply rolled up in mats and left in the graveyard. Little planting was possible that year because of the disorder, so by the following year people were going hungry. To ward off starvation they ate guayabas, fried bananas, tortillas made from avocados, and even cornstalks. Children, orphaned and clothed in rags, wandered in search of food through streets overgrown with weeds.

After the Revolution

The Revolution was followed by land reform and other changes that eventually brought Tlayacapan into the modern world. In 1929 the government officially granted the village Cacahuatlan and other land formerly belonging to the hacienda of Oacalco in the form of an ejido. A smaller grant of land was made in 1939. These lands were highly fertile and, for the most part, irrigated.

The Revolution did not dramatically alter the class structure of local society, however. Some of the wealthy villagers who had taken refuge in cities and provincial towns did not return. The five or so families that had circulated the offices of the village government among themselves before the Revolution were no longer in control after the Revolution, but presidents of the village in the 1920s and 1930s were often related to them by kinship or marriage or were the children of less important pre-Revolution upper-class families. A 1929 report indicates that land distribution was highly uneven. Of eighty-six small property owners, seven had between seventy-five and sixteen hectares, whereas most had less than ten, and twenty-one had less than one hectare each. An unspecified number of villagers had cornfields on small communal plots.[10]

During the 1940s, villagers began to acquire mules and lightweight steel plows, which allowed them to farm more efficiently and to bring more land under cultivation. They cultivated rice and peanuts as cash crops on the ejido lands and the traditional staples of maize, beans, and squash in the fields around the village. The sugar industry was revived in the early 1940s and much of the ejido was planted in cane. The construction of an unpaved road in 1946 encouraged cash cropping by facilitating movement to urban markets. In the late 1950s, so-called green-revolution technology was brought to the area, and villagers began to grow tomatoes as a cash crop. Risky and capital intensive but often lucrative, the modern method of cultivating tomatoes transformed Tlayacapan in a matter of years into an unusually wealthy rural community. Many of the men who were leaders in the innovation were former braceros, temporary migrant laborers in the United States. As braceros they learned about the advantages of modern agricultural technology and, more important, acquired the needed capital to invest in seeds, fertilizers, insecticides, and other equipment for the new type of tomato cultivation.

The revival of the agricultural economy was accompanied by demographic recovery. The population of the *municipio* grew gradually from about 1,500 at the end of the Revolution to 2,421 in 1940. By 1980 it was 7,950. Both mortality reduction and fertility contributed to the pace of increase. Following the introduction of sulfa drugs in the 1940s and then antibiotics in the 1950s, the death rate fell, from 29 per 1,000 in 1940 to a low of 9 per 1,000 in 1970. The traditional birth rate is uncertain, but may have fluctuated between 35 and 40 per 1,000. By 1940 it was 43 per 1,000 and by the mid-1960s it was close to 49 per 1,000. Thereafter, it declined, to about 38 per 1,000 in 1980.[11]

Although sugarcane cultivation generated cash income, and thus supported this growing population, it re-created patterns of dependency typical of the period before the Revolution. The relations of production in sugarcane cultivation amount to a share-cropping arrangement. The cane planter is advanced money, given fertilizer, and is provided irrigation water by the refinery, which charges interest on the value of these things. The refinery hires its own workers to harvest the cane and charges the service against the cane planter's account. Sugarcane takes twelve to eighteen months to mature, but after the first cutting it can be cut several more times at about one-year intervals before replanting is necessary.

Planters earn little from the first crop and nothing during the first twelve to eighteen months, so that they must finance themselves for this period by some other means. Many borrow money from the refinery at interest, making cane planting even less profitable than it might appear. The refinery, however, does not make loans easily. One joke has a man asking the refinery for money for *el hambre* (hunger), but the refinery official thinks he is saying, *para alambre*, "for wire," and grants the money readily. Some planters obtain money for peons and then do the work themselves. Another strategem is to resell fertilizer that the refinery has charged to the planter's account. The refinery, aware of these practices, does not discourage them, since indebtedness binds the planter to the refinery. This dependency is further encouraged in other ways: a government health center in Yautepec is available to cane planters, but not to other ejido holders or to nonejidatarios; and many cane planters claim that the refinery cheats them by not weighting the cane accurately.

An examination of the itemized costs of one planter showed the average gross income per tarea, or one-tenth of a hectare, to be 400 pesos a year. For the first crop his debt with interest to the refinery was 336 pesos, leaving 64 pesos. During the next two years his annual debt was 143 pesos per tarea. So in a period of slightly over three years, his net earnings were 578 pesos per tarea, or less than 963 pesos per year for five tareas. Earnings from a maize field vary somewhat, depending on how much bean is intermixed with the maize and on use of fertilizer, but most maize farmers estimate that they can earn 1,250 pesos or more on five tareas (see de la Peña 1980:217).

Many more times these amounts have been earned in tomato cultivation, but there are disadvantages: the plant is easily damaged by bad weather, insects, and fungi; prices fluctuate wildly; the plants require more work than maize or sugarcane; and their cultivation is more complex. In addition, tomatoes demand a sizable investment of money. Abrán Alarcón, twenty-two years of age, planted nine tareas of tomatoes in 1965 and kept a careful diary of the venture. He worked his tomato garden for sixty-five days with several peons. His investment, including the cost of labor, fertilizers, wire, stakes, insecticides, and other equipment was 6,822 pesos, not including 2,000 pesos spent on insecticide sprayers. He grossed 65,000 pesos on that particular crop, but he and other peasants have lost their crops to hail and, moreover, prices are not always so high. On some occasions prices have been so low as to make harvesting a patch of tomatoes not worth the effort. Tlayacapan competes with other tomato-growing areas in Mexico and is subject to price fluctuations related to weather in tomato-growing areas in the United States.

Tlayacapenses have tried to reduce the risk in tomato planting. They have found that prices are sometimes better in Oaxaca than in Mexico City, and unripe tomatoes sold to buyers from Texas can bring good prices. Tomatoes grown in the winter produce a smaller crop, but they mature when there is high demand. Most peasants protect themselves by planting maize in addition to tomatoes.

Most tomato planters plant on credit. They may borrow from a local moneylender or at interest from a produce wholesaler on condition that the planter sell the crop to that wholesaler. Since planters are not able to check prices daily, they are vulnerable to exploitation. Not surprisingly, those who can do so operate with their own capital. They either sell to a trucker when the crop is still in the field, reducing risk but also foregoing possible higher profits, or they try to sell small amounts of tomatoes in local markets (Ingham 1969:61-73).

The costs and liabilities of involvement in the market economy have reinforced intrafamilial and interfamilial patterns of solidarity in the village. Sons and fathers and brothers cooperate even more than they did in the past to ensure a supply of labor and to mitigate its high cost. The costs of production are also reduced through interfamily cooperation. Friends or compadres may become partners, or *socios*, in a planting project in which they pool family labor, draft animals and tractors, and other resources. Friendships and compadrazgo can also ensure a supply of labor or access to tractors or draft animals. A man can ask his compadre for help or the privilege of temporarily employing his compadre's peons or request the rental of his tractor or team of oxen with some assurance of an affirmative reply even when labor and equipment are in scarce supply (see Warman 1976).

It may be that religious fiestas persisted in the modern period because, along with compadrazgo, they were a means of reinforcing and sacralizing cooperative social relations. At the same time, economic modernization was encouraging acquisitiveness (an ethic that runs counter to that implied by ritual sponsorship) and was enlarging the number of people at the upper end of the socioeconomic continuum who, by virtue of their pecuniary values, were inclined to exempt themselves from active participation in folk ritual. Modernization, by exaggerating the economic disparities between rich and poor, also tended to increase the sense of alienation from traditional culture among the latter. Villagers at the extremes of the socioeconomic continuum, then, tended to find a community of interest with the clergy, who beginning in the 1960s renewed their traditional hostility to folk Catholicism with unusual fervor.

The first priest to figure in this drama was Father P., who arrived in 1955. A kindly and sincere man, he soon showed seemingly genuine concern for the villagers. Much about their way of life troubled him, however. As he saw matters, marriage was a bond more of convenience than of love, and poor men often squandered on immoderate drinking the money they should have used to support their families. Furthermore, there were many pagan elements in the folk religion.

To instill correct Catholicism, he organized devotional groups for the care of the church, encouraged participants to attend mass, and tried to instruct them in the proper understanding of the religion and its practices. He also made participation in the groups more appealing by offering free medicines (although not a doctor, he operated a lucrative medical practice along with performing his priestly duties). He accused the mayordomos of promoting drinking, eating, and bull riding rather than sincere devotion. To discourage such activities, he sometimes refused to say masses for the saints, and he even managed to persuade a few mayordomos that the *mayordomías* should be abandoned. He also did not want to say prayers for the dead in the cemetery during All Souls'. Explaining his reasoning to Doña Pechi, his housekeeper, he said, "The dead do not return." Doña Pechi was never one to acquiesce. "Well," she said, "they may not come, but if you do not say prayers [for the dead] and masses [for the saints], how will you maintain yourself? The saints are our customs!"

Father P. even kept a large dog in the convent to prevent the mayordomos from climbing the roof of the church to ring the bells during fiestas. His most controversial act, however, was to begin the removal of the church's side altars to the saints; the altars to the Vírgenes Purísima and Guadalupe were demolished along with the pulpits, much to the outrage of the villagers. Amid the mounting turmoil, Father P. was accused of breaking his vow of celibacy, and to avoid further controversy the bishop transferred him in 1968 to another parish.

Father P.'s initiatives against the folk Catholicism of Tlayacapan were not taken independently. They were conceived of and supported by the bishop of the diocese, Sergio Méndez Arceo, a leader in the so-called reform movement in the Mexican church and an advocate for a more progressive role for the church generally. He wanted to return Catholicism to the fundamentals of the faith, to substitute inner belief for outer form. He stressed the Bible over pious books and catechisms, and the rite of the mass over the cults of the saints. In his view the laities of the rural communities of the diocese had construed the saints not simply as intercessors but as deities with the power to grant salvation. To the bishop, the fiestas were a mixture of pagan and Christian practice, as much occasions for drinking, dancing, and revelry as for sincere devotion. Suppression of the cults of the saints, then, was a part of the reform program (de la Peña 1980:292–295).

With these aims in mind, he rehabilitated the cathedral in Cuernavaca, replacing its baroque clutter with clean, simple lines. Side altars and plaster were removed from the walls to reveal delicate sixteenth-century murals. The main altar also was removed and replaced with a more modern altar in gold and flat black. New stained-glass windows and baptismal font further enhanced the church's pristine simplicity. The general effect was indeed stunning. The bishop's "Pan-American Mass," held every Sunday and featuring mariachi bands and South American folk music, gained popularity among tourists and rich Mexicans.

In Tlayacapan Father P. was replaced by Father M., who finished the job of eliminating the side altars. The bishop and Father M. explained to the villagers that there was only one God and that the saints were merely statues of wood and plaster, nothing else. While removing the side altars, Father M. was accused of digging for gold that was thought to be buried underneath them. When a large hole was found under the altar of San Juan Bautista, the village's patron saint, a rumor spread that Father M. had offered to help Doña Nate find buried treasure in her house and that he had an electronic metal detector.

Father M. did little to endear himself to the villagers. Indeed, on occasion he refused to say masses for the saints and not infrequently was openly disrespectful of village customs. One day when Doña Pechi and her friends entered the church carrying crowns of cypress, censers, a bottle of liquor, and a plate of sand for the mass held one year after a funeral, Father M. suspiciously eyed the smoke from the censers and mockingly asked the women what it meant. Embarrassed, they hung their heads and said nothing. Adding to their humiliation, he accused them of being either "deaf or dumb." Later, as they were standing in the churchyard, Doña Pechi tried to console the crestfallen women, telling them, "We are neither deaf nor dumb, and if we had not been in the church we would have insulted his mother." Father M., Doña Pechi says, was just a Carrancista (that is, a soldier who looted the village during the Revolution).

In the latter part of 1969, the bishop sent still another priest to Tlayacapan, Father C. He was the Jesuit son of an aristrocatic Creole family living in Jalisco. A gentleman of many facets, he was a priest, an architect, and sculptor. Tall, portly, and light complexioned, he spoke smoothly with a lisp. He was a darling of the ruling class and a close friend of the bishop. Father C. had applied his architectural skills to the restoration of the Cuernavaca cathedral upon his return from Europe, where he had spent ten years. When he expressed an interest in living in the countryside and working on his sculpture, Bishop Méndez Arceo directed him to Tlayacapan, one of the most charming and unspoiled communities in the diocese. The understanding, apparently, was that Father C. would work on his art but also lend his support to the moral and socioeconomic development of Tlayacapan. The bishop asked Father M. to treat Father C. well and to introduce him to the community. After walking the town and talking with village officials, Father C. learned that the community lacked running water, a secondary school, and a medical clinic. The community would surely benefit from a school and a clinic, but water was especially urgent. It was also essential to Father C.'s comfort and plans.

Father C. began to recruit friends to help him with his civic projects. Among them were several anthropologists (they would study the social and economic needs and characteristics of the community), a Spanish lawyer and his wife, a doctor, a young mathematics professor, and another priest, Father Chavo, who had taught in a village school in northern Guerrero. By May 1970, six months after the arrival of Father C., his recruits had settled in the village. They called themselves "the *calpulli*," an indication of their romanticism but, in retrospect, also an ironic choice of word: ensuing events showed that Father C. and his sophisticated friends seriously underestimated the strength of traditional customs, the social solidarity of the community and its barrios, and the villagers' willingness to resist external meddling in their affairs.

Father C. was introduced to the community at a town meeting. He outlined his plans for progress and spoke of the secondary school that he would have in operation by the following fall. Although it would take longer to provide running water, he thought he could solve that problem, too. Before he arrived there had been talk in the state government of pumping water from Oaxtepec up into the highlands, but it seemed that the cost would prevent the project from ever getting beyond the planning stage. Father C. proposed a well instead. On behalf of the villagers he obtained a loan of nearly a half million pesos to finance the project and made arrangements with a drilling company. Equipment was brought to the village and a productive aquifer was struck at 232 meters in the summer of 1971.

Father C.'s group took a socioeconomic census of the village to create a data base for assessing households for the cost of the water system according to their ability to pay. The state and federal governments cooperated by providing the pump and distribution pipes, and villagers contributed manual labor to dig ditches. A committee was formed to administer the finances. In theory, all the villagers were members and a standing committee on material improvements was supposed to take a leading role. In practice, however, it soon became apparent that Father C. was in control, especially of the finances. Nonetheless, the village had water and for the moment, at least, Father C. was an immensely popular figure.

Meanwhile, he bought a lot on the site of the old chapel of Santo Tomás and built on its foundations, using adobe and tile to fashion an elegant country home with many rooms, almost monastic, with its interior courtyard. With a road under construction, Tlayacapan would soon be only an hour's drive from Mexico City to the north. Given its colonial flavor, magnificent surroundings, and new supply of fresh water, Tlayacapan was bound to become a weekend retreat and even a bedroom community for the urban rich who sought escape from the air pollution and congestion of the city. Father C.'s house became the showcase of what he, the architect, could offer. On weekends his wealthy relatives and friends arrived in their expensive limousines to enjoy his country hospitality. He plied them with drinks and peddled his sculpture and his architectural skills. Soon, other residences like his were under construction. Not anticipating the rapid appreciation in land values that would soon occur, the villagers sold land for these projects at a pittance. Father C. once told me, "Well, I have to live, too"—that is to say, in a style commensurate with his social station. To be sure, he rationalized that he was giving the villagers work and a source of income. And a small group of adobe workers, carpenters, electricians, and other skilled workers became beholden to him. In turn, he lavished favors and bestowed respect on his supporters. He lent money and his car and introduced his ambitious young foremen as "architects" and "engineers."

In time, however, Father Chavo and several other members of the "*calpulli*," not to mention many villagers, began to have misgivings about the propriety of Father C.'s role in administrative matters. When he ignored these concerns they broke off their association with him and began withdrawing their support. Some of these dissidents began publishing a pamphlet critical of Father C. Father Chavo at first remained silent, but when the dissidents left the community, he took over the pamphlet and continued the criticism. He became more critical of the bishop as he learned more about the folk Catholicism. He argued with the bishop in favor of staging the Concilio, the dramatization of the Passion of Christ, which the bishop had prohibited throughout the diocese. He also befriended the mayordomos of the Santa Cruz in Altica and the Virgen de Dolores in Santa Ana, undergoing what might be called a conversion experience. Reflecting on the period some years later, he said that he had found more evangelism and more humanism in the fiestas of what he called the "cultura Xochimilca-Tlayacapense" than in the so-called progressive ceremonies of Bishop Méndez Arceo, with their mariachi bands and liturgical trappings. Eventually, Father Chavo published a letter in which he accused the bishop of being a friend of the rich and an enemy of the people and their customs.

In the spring of 1973, when Jacinto Banderas, one of Father C.'s supporters, became president of the village for the second time, the priest's position seemed secure, although in reality it had begun to deteriorate. He had announced that some households had not paid their assessments and, consequently, that the water committee could not pay off the loan. He proposed that water be sold to neighboring communities, especially to a subdivision of weekend homes being developed nearby. When this was done and he later claimed that the water project was still in the red, suspicion and outright opposition mounted rapidly. He did not help his case when he tried to answer questions about the water-works finances by mimeographing his explanation as a cartoon strip and defending it in a village assembly. The tactic only enhanced his growing reputation for arrogance.

By the end of 1974 a group of villagers, led by Alberto Flores, the schoolteacher, became increasingly active in taking their complaints against Father C. to the state and even federal governments. And their complaints did not go unattended. There was something inherently distressing to the sensibilities of Mexican politicians about a Jesuit priest's extralegal political control in a Mexican community.

An audit of the water committee's records was carried out by the state government in November 1974. Although it showed everything to be in order, some villagers were not satisfied. According to their informal calculations, based on what they had been able to reconstruct of the committee's income and expenses, considerable funds had yet to be accounted for. A town meeting in February 1975 ended in pushing and shoving and the threat of bloodshed. The bishop came to the village to defend Father C., and priests throughout the diocese denounced his enemies as a handful of troublemakers. Both sides in the dispute mobilized as much political influence as they could at the state and federal government levels.

On 18 September 1975 Alberto Flores and his supporters seized the town hall in a coup d'état and ejected Jacinto Banderas from the office of president. They then made representations to the governor of the state and demanded an extraordinary election to create a popular government in the community. A referendum was held on 12 October 1975 and most villagers voted against Banderas and Father C. Later, arrangements were made for a second audit, but Father C. left the village before it could take place. Many people now say that his leaving proves he was guilty of embezzlement; if there had been nothing to hide, they say, he would have stayed and defended himself (see de la Peña 1980:300–307).

Father M. had been run out of the village somewhat earlier. Apart from the resentment he had created by destroying the side altars and denigrating traditional customs, he had supported Father C. Moreover, a rumor had spread that he, Father C., and the bishop planned to turn the convent into a hotel. They had already permitted an architect and his family to take up residence in its rooms. As far as the villagers were concerned, the convent belonged not to the church or the federal government but to the village, and no decisions were going to be made about its use without their consent.

Father J. replaced Father M. His attacks on the saints were even more disparaging. He told a group of mayordomos, for example, that their image of the Christ of the Resurrection, which was clothed in red, reminded him of a "red grasshopper," an allusion to a comic television personality. When some men asked him to allow the posadas in the church at Christmas time, he called them "dark Indians" to their faces. The indomitable Doña Pechi gave him a piece of her mind, though. She told him he was a "fool." "We may be Indians," she said, "but this is our place. It belongs to us. You are just a passerby, like a soldier." When Father J. tried to sell some timber that had been given to the church by a film company, the wood was seized as a truck was about to carry it out of the village and Father J. was promptly run out of the village. He had lasted only two years.

Although the recent conflict between the villagers and clergy was unusual in certain regards and peculiarly related to recent developments within the church, it was a chapter among many in a long history of differing interpretations of Catholicism by clergy and villagers. The clergy has for centuries been less than sympathetic to folk customs, and villagers' sentiments about the clergy have been correspondingly ambivalent. The bishop's attacks on the saints recall in particular the efforts to suppress local Catholicism in sixteenth-century Spain, which were motivated, much like the rethinking that came out of Vatican II, by a desire to stem the spread of Protestantism. The attempt to suppress local religiosity in Morelos met with little more success than similar efforts in the sixteenth-century, however.

The limited success of the Counter-Reformation in suppressing local religion, then as now, must be understood in terms of the meaning and value of the latter to the local people and, in Morelos at least, of the corporate character of the upland villages. The bishop and his priests misunderstood and underestimated both.

So, too, I think, have Roberto Varela and Guillermo de la Peña, anthropologists and acquaintances of Father C. Varela (1984b:203-207) claims that the events of the 1970s show that the smaller villages of Morelos had limited capacity to resist outside interference, although he acknowledges that they generally experience little outside intervention. If anything, the events show that the clerics were soundly rejected once their attitudes and activities proved incongruent with the values and interests of the villagers.

De la Peña in a similar vein maintains that village authorities lack the power for an undertaking on the scale of the well project and that in such cases an outside patron, like Father C., is necessary. It is true that for such projects the village usually cannot raise the necessary funding on its own, but it does not follow that the patronage must take the form of private entrepreneurship and adventurism, as was the case with Father C. In the last forty years alone village authorities have had a part in various public works, including two renovations of the village plaza, a grammar school, a sewer system, cobbling and recobbling of village streets, a library, and renovation of the municipal palace. Most of these projects depended on state and federal aid, but the impetus for many of them nonetheless originated in the local *ayuntamiento*, which lobbied for them at higher levels of government.

The motives in the struggle were not as simply materialistic as Varela and de la Peña imply. Both mention the role of the schoolteachers in the opposition to Father C., but they wrongly suggest that they were motivated primarily by envy and desire for power. Varela even sees the fight as one over control of a material resource (that is, water). The schoolteachers were rudely treated by the teachers in Father C.'s new secondary school and they were understandably resentful, but in struggling against Father C. the schoolteachers were not merely seeking revenge for lost power. It oversimplifies their motives to suggest that this was the only reason for their activism or that they wanted control of the water system themselves. In recent history, schoolteachers have served in the town government because their education enables them to communicate with educated outsiders and because they are respected as keepers and interpreters of civic values. The schoolteachers were offended by Father C. and his associates because what they were doing was a throwback to pre-Revolution *cacicazgo* and a violation of revolutionary and democratic values they were teaching in school. Similarly, de la Peña oversimplifies when he insinuates that the associates of Father C. who turned against him were motivated by resentment of his power and their low pay. Their criticisms of Father C. derived as much from their idealism and principles as from political or economic interests.

Ironically, Varela and de la Peña give too little attention to the way in which practical interests shaped the struggle. Father C. would have had hardly any support in the end if he had not created a constituency through economic incentives. As noted earlier, these included the employment generated by his building activities. He also had support among the parents of children in the secondary school and, presumably, among those who stood to benefit from sale of land for weekend homes (not all villagers had suitable land to sell). Father C. also enlarged his following by lending money.

Barrio rivalries and related economic and political interests also entered into the struggle. The América dance group was almost unanimously opposed to Father C., whereas most of the villagers in Unión supported him, and many in Azteca did so, too. It is significant that Father C. lived in Azteca and Father Chavo worked in América, but another reason for the interbarrio differences may be the history of Santiago's exclusion from major political positions within the community. Alliance with Father C. may have represented a means of acquiring power the people of Santiago had been denied.

Overview

By the turn of the century most of the villagers of Tlayacapan were speaking Spanish and wearing mestizo clothes, and today they understate or deny their Indianness in most contexts, and yet, as we shall see, there is much Indian heritage in their culture. Evidently, ethnic identity and cultural heritage are not perfectly correlated.

Folk Catholicism has not been impervious to social and economic change. Some beliefs and customs have changed or disappeared, and yet in the main folk Catholicism has proved remarkably durable. This observation, however, only tends to confirm the interconnection between socioeconomic relations and conditions and folk religion, for there has been a great deal of continuity in the former as well as the latter. Society was highly stratified before the Conquest and remained so after the Conquest. The *calpulli* system persisted as a barrio system and retained its foundations in communal land until the early twentieth century. Communal land, especially as ejido land, is still important and may continue to encourage ritual organization. Moreover, economic cooperation has given neighborhoods as much importance as they lost through the secularization of communal land. Despite the Revolution, the hacienda at Oacalco persists and remains a source of irritation to the villagers. One could argue that modernization and cash cropping is a new trend, with unprecedented implications, but it is not. As in other parts of Middle America, wage labor, cash cropping, and craft production have supplemented subsistence farming since early colonial and even pre-Hispanic times. What has changed is the scale of production for the market, and with it dependence on modern agricultural technology and desire for manufactured goods.

The disappearance of Indian identity may also lie in history, namely, the character of the local elite during the late colonial and early national periods. If the evidence is to be believed, acculturation to mestizo identity was well under way by the early nineteenth century in Tlayacapan. The local elite was not simply or primarily a landholding elite. Among the most important families were a number who were dedicated to shopkeeping and cattle raising, enterprises that did not entail competition for Indian lands. Even members of the elite who were agriculturalists may have been land renters rather than land owners. Many of the elite families, then, would have had an interest in protecting village lands. The interests of the poor villagers were not identical with those of the elite, of course, and could even conflict with them, but evidently they were not so opposed as to promote the perpetuation of strong ethnic distinctions between the two strata. Meanwhile, the presence of various trades in the community allowed an economic entrée to mestizo status. The mestizos might still have had usufruct to barrio lands but they were not exclusively dependent on them, and their commercial activities, we may suppose, led them to identify with the Creoles even though their stake in the community and its material resources supported continued dedication to the saints.

4. The Family

There is an extensive literature on the social and psychological organization of the Mexican family (Bermúdez 1955; Elu de Leñero 1969; Fromm and Maccoby 1970; Kahl 1967; Leñero Otero 1968; Lewis 1951; McGinn 1966; Nelson 1971; Romanucci-Ross 1973). The male is typically described as authoritarian toward and jealous of his wife and given to aggressiveness, heavy drinking, and the pursuit of sexual adventure outside the home. In contrast, the wife is portrayed as obedient, continent, and self-denying. Marital relationships are said to be puritanical, and some authors indicate that men may deliberately avoid arousing their wives sexually, fearing that arousal may encourage promiscuity. Some of the more sensitive investigators have been careful to note, however, that observed patterns may vary from these stereotypical characterizations. Some men are less given to machismo than others, and some wives are less subservient than other women and even openly defiant of male dominance (see Lewis 1951; Fromm and Maccoby 1970).

Machismo and its associated family values are often given historical or psychological explanations. Machismo, it may be argued, has roots in the feudal and warlike orientations of the Aztec and sixteenth-century Spanish cultures, and the conquistadors' practice of taking Indian wives. Psycho-analytically oriented interpretations have explained machismo as a defense or protest against dependency needs, mother-fixation, or confused sex-role identity (Aramoni 1965; Díaz Guerrero 1961; Fromm and Maccoby 1970; Paz 1961; Ramírez 1961; Ramírez and Parres 1957).[1]

Whatever the merit of the historical and psychological explanations, there are other reasons for male behavior. In peasant society the family is the basic unit of production and reproduction. In both its internal organization and relation to the outside world, the family can be understood as a system for achieving and reproducing security. Husbands and wives and parents and children are bonded by positive affect, of course, but also by mutual rights and obligations centering on work, obedience, and fidelity. Husbands support their families by laboring in the fields and, in return, they expect their wives to give them children and to work in the home. An effective household is impossible without a wife and the farmer without sons is at a great disadvantage. These considerations lead men to assert their authority and sexual prerogatives over their wives.

At the same time, other facets of the machismo syndrome may be related to the curbing of reproduction. The burden of additional children may cause economic stress and interfere with the proper care of existing children. The control of reproduction through sexual restraint is correlated with men's extramarital pursuits outside the home, a phenomenon that raises the problem of defending the honor of one's own woman against other males. In this chapter, I show how male and female roles are motivated by the necessities of production and reproduction. In later chapters, I shall focus more sharply on the religious meanings of male and female behavior and experience.

The House, Street, and Field

The family is domiciled in the *casa*. The word can be translated as "house," but its range of meaning is somewhat broader than the English word; it also implies "household" and "home." The house sits in a moral landscape that includes the chapels and church, the streets, fields, barrancas, and hills and mountains. The moral connotations of house, street, and fields are particularly germane to an understanding of the meanings of the family and its constituent roles.

The houses of most villagers now stand flush with the streets. The majority are one story but with high, red-tile roofs; they have thick adobe walls and even small buttresses. Large constructions, some are almost like small fortresses. Their imposing appearance is further enhanced by heavy wooden doors that are flanked on either side by one or two small windows sometimes covered with iron grating. The houses of the poor are less sturdily built and tend to be located back from the street on sites surrounded by walls of volcanic rock. During the colonial period many houses were probably so located and many, no doubt, had thatch roofs. People say the older style of situating houses back from the street made them look as though they had atriums or courtyards like those of the church and chapels.

The front room of the house is a formal space used for entertaining guests and holding ritual banquets, but often it doubles as a bedroom. Interior walls may be in disrepair and in need of whitewash or paint, but they are attractively decorated with calendars and other family memorabilia. The calendars, current and out of date, typically depict biblical scenes, Aztec mythology, or idealizations of family life in the Mexican countryside. Also decorating the walls may be political posters, family pictures, educational degrees (if any family members have earned them), paper and plastic flowers, and photographs of soccer teams cut from magazines and newspapers. The furniture includes sleeping mats or raised beds, small wooden chairs, wardrobes, and a table to hold the family shrine. The last is constructed of a large picture of the Virgen de Guadalupe, Jesus, or the Last Supper, surrounded by smaller pictures of the saints. Often there are votive candles and flowers on the table.

At the rear of the house, facing the patio, are a corridor and kitchen. The kitchen table is where the family eats its meals and friends and relatives gather informally. The walls are decorated with pottery and utensils hung in neat arrangements. Food and leftovers are stored in baskets hanging from roof beams, where they are out of reach of the chickens, cats, and dogs that have the run of this part of the house. The *metate*, the stone slab used in grinding maize and other foods, is kept near the hearth. The tortillas are cooked on a *comal*, an iron or clay griddle placed over the hearth.

Many villagers decorate the corridor or back wall of their houses with sedums, ferns, and other potted plants. Indeed, the rear of the house and the adjacent patio may teem with flora and fauna. In addition to chickens and pets that wander in and out, there may be caged birds and bowls of tropical fish in the corridor and garden plants in the patio. Fruit trees, such as hog plum, orange, lemon, lime, and guayaba, are popular, as are bougainvilleas, tulips, geraniums, poinsettias, roses, fuschias, and other flowering bushes and shrubs. Most women cultivate herbs for cooking and home remedies. Behind the patio some families fence off corrals for beasts of burden and pigs; and a kitchen garden and small orchard, which is called the *huerta* (the garden), may fill the back of the house site. There is something Eden-like in this profusion of life at the rear of the house (see Gudeman 1976a:58).

Despite these allusions to nature, the house has sacred qualities that align it with the realm of spirit. The adobe layer gives the new house a wooden cross and the priest blesses it. A house contains an altar—much like the church and chapels—reinforcing the explicit analogies that are drawn between house and chapels or church. In keeping with the sacredness of the house, others do not enter without permission, and even invited guests may display deference by being slow to enter. Accordingly, it is a mark of friendship and trust to invite others into the house. When villagers want to emphasize their hospitality to outsiders, they say, "Aquí tiene su casa" (Here you have a home). The house, we might say, subsumes a contrast between spirit and nature, which recurs in the relation between house and the profane world outside the house, although nature within the home generally has an innocent or sanctified aspect, whereas nature beyond the home may be sanctified but often has a fallen character.

In both a symbolic and an interactional sense, the home is a woman's domain, whoever the actual owner may be. Traditional values strongly associate the wife and mother with the home. The woman carries out most of her tasks there, and the household objects and their arrangement all bear the imprint of her esthetic tastes and activities. Within the home it is principally the woman who supervises the behavior of children and decides what needs to be done. Her power in the home is reflected as well in the control she has over the family purse. Mothers and wives usually insist that husbands turn over their earnings to them. In addition, many women contribute to the purse and increase their control of the family budget with economic pursuits of their own. These may include making pottery or ritual figurines, raising chickens and pigs, cultivating fruit trees and herbs, or curing. In fact, the confinement of virtuous women to the home replicates a powerful religious image, that of the Virgen de Guadalupe enshrined within her sanctuary (a picture of the Virgen is often the centerpiece of the family altar).

The moral valuation of motherhood and women's actual control of mundane affairs within the home tend to put men in a somewhat passive posture, despite the patriarchal values that they sometimes voice. Understandably, they often prefer to be away from this enclave of female affairs. They come home to eat and sleep, and sometimes they stay indoors to avoid threatening encounters in the street. If they are not eating or sleeping, however, they usually remove themselves from the women by sitting on the front porch, fiddling with equipment, tending to animals at the back of the house, or engaging in some other suitably masculine activity, such as threshing maize or making repairs.

The many houses of the village are connected to each other as well as to chapels and church, central plaza and marketplace, and fields at the edge of the village by streets and lanes. Portions of streets may be under the permanent protection of streetside crosses and shrines. They are places where civil greetings are exchanged between passersby and, at times, even seem to take on a sacred quality. As mentioned earlier, on Saturdays women sweep the streets in front of their homes in preparation for Sunday; when religious processions for the saints are about to pass, they sprinkle the streets with water and strew them with flower petals. Yet, on the whole and especially at night and during Carnival and fairs, the streets assume a more negative moral connotation: they are profane interstices between sacred places, the settings for vice and media for evil spirits.

These connotations of the street are expressed in the various measures that villagers take to protect the home from external dangers. When night falls or suspicious-looking strangers are about, householders close and brace doors and shutters. In addition, they use various amulets to protect the home. On September 26 or 27, villagers go into the countryside to pick the yellow flower *pericón* (*Tagetes lucida*), which they bundle and tie together to make small crosses, sometimes with a rose in the center.[2] On the morning of September 28 these crosses are hung above exterior doorways and windows and in the fields for protection against the Devil, who is said to run loose on September 29, the day of San Miguel Arcángel. The crosses soon dry out but they remain in place until the following September. Wooden crosses and crosses made from the palm branches that are blessed in the church on Palm Sunday may be hung over the inside of exterior doors and windows. Villagers also may burn the blessed palm along with rosemary and incense or throw pieces of the blessed palm into the patio during a storm to drive away the spirits of hail and wind. The rosemary and incense are blessed on Holy Saturday. Mustard seeds sometimes are scattered on roofs as protection against witches, and rue and basil may be kept in the patio or house as further protection against witchcraft. Garlic and onions protect shops. Displaying purple onions and burning a bull's horn are thought to discourage ghosts.

Women and children are deemed to be weaker than men and so more vulnerable to abuse and evil forces. They are expected to remain at home or to venture out only in the company of trusted companions or under parental supervision. Washing clothes, shopping, selling in the marketplace, and religious observances may taken them out of the home, but these activities should be performed as expeditiously as possible. Children who play in the street too much are thought to learn bad habits and to be more susceptible to the evil eye sickness and other diseases. Daughters require special vigilance; they may be sent out on errands, but they are warned not to tarry and scolded if they do. Even married women must be cautious: those who are seen "going up and down the street" are thought to lack self-respect. The street is simply not a place for a proper woman. Prostitutes are called, among other things, "women of the street." Doña Pola put the contrast between the house and street vividly when she said, "The woman of the house is sacred. The woman of the street has a *pingo* [devil]."[3]

Men are much freer to spend time in the street. If her husband is not at home, a wife may say that "he went to the street," a phrase that covers various activities outside the home. When in the street men may chat with friends on street corners or in the plaza; play dominoes, cards, or pool; or drink beer or rum in the cantinas. Many men seek extramarital sexual gratification "in the street." They travel to larger towns and cities to visit prostitutes from time to time and a few keep mistresses in the village itself. Wealthier men, of course, can better afford to maintain mistresses or to buy the favors of prostitutes, and it is generally expected that they will do so.

Men also engage in various pseudosexual behaviors outside the home. Male sociality, for example, is often and conspicuously exhibited in intimate body contact and sexual teasing: occasionally men grab each others' buttocks, and when drunk, they commonly wrap each other in physical embraces.[4] When they drink, men may toast "ellas y las botellas, aunque mal paguen" (women and bottles, although they don't pay). Advertisements for the most popular beer consumed in the village liken it to a "blonde with class" and "a blonde everyone loves." Men play mildly aggressive verbal games multilayered with innuendos about pretended desire to penetrate each other sexually. Serious aggression between males, which typically occurs in the street, is phrased as sexual penetration and domination.

When men are not in the street, they are usually in their fields. Being in the field is such a part of masculine behavior that men visit them even when there is little work to do. The fields, in some respects, are a home away from home. They enjoy the protection of crosses of *pericón*, as homes do, and some peasants keep small huts on their fields where they may stay during harvest season to protect their crops.

Whereas men's activity in the street often entails expenditures of wealth, activity in the fields is productive, parallel in this respect to the productive and reproductive activity of women in the home. Various usages in particular show the metaphorical imbrication between the generation of plants and human beings. The word *semen*, meaning the male reproductive fluid, is etymologically related to—and resonates phonetically with— *semilla* (seed) as well as several related words. "Seedings" are called *semenceras* or *sembraduras*; a "seed field" or "planted field" is a *siembra* or *sementera*; and a "seedling" is a *planta de semillero*. A field, like a woman, is either "fertile" or "sterile." Plants are "born," they are given "fertilizers," they are affected by "plagues" and given "medicines," and they "die." When maize is harvested, exploding rockets are set off in the fields and later the occasion is further celebrated by eating *mole* in the home. Since the serving of *mole* is associated with moments in the life cycle of individuals and saints, the implication would seem to be that the maize plant is saintly or personlike. As we shall see later, there is supporting evidence for this inference.

Husband and Wife

Women, of course, would prefer men to spend their time at work or at home. Women manage to limit the amount of time and money men spend in the street by maintaining tight control over the purse, and some wives even enter cantinas to extricate their husbands from drinking bouts. Men who withhold money from their wives are said to be *cuentachiles* (chile counters), a metaphorical expression that implies that men are stingy with sexual favors as well as money.

Neither husband nor wife expects romantic love to be the most important part of marriage for long, even though romantic attachment is valued. When people were asked to describe the ideal characteristics of a spouse, almost every woman said a man should be hard working, but few said a man should be affectionate and fewer still expressed the expectation that men would be faithful.

Most women take it for granted that men will seek sexual relations with other women; in many instances they grudgingly accept such peccadilloes if husbands provide them and their children with adequate support. Failing economic support, however, they may express their resentments openly, and some wives scold and complain, despite the beatings they may receive as a result. A few self-respecting wives even take punches at the husbands; one wife waited until her husband fell asleep and then hit him with a piece of lumber. As a last resort, a woman may enlist the help of a witch against her rival or poison her husband's food: a pinch of *toloache* (jimson weed) added to coffee is supposed to make a husband "stupid," and larger amounts render him insane or even kill him. Such poisonings are probably rare, but one imagines that the mere threat keeps some husbands in line.

The qualities men desire most in a wife are respect, industry, domesticity, and, above all, sexual fidelity. Few men say that they desire intelligence, affection, or physical beauty in a wife, because these are qualities that make women attractive as mistresses. Most men want their wives to be matronly and apron-clad, not attractive and sexy.

Men believe that a wife has a duty to respect her husband and that a disrespectful wife should be punished, physically if necessary. Even when men are reprimanded by the village president, many continue to insist that they have a right to beat their wives. One man has beaten his wife regularly throughout the many years of their marriage; he thinks it is her duty to provide him with a decent meal and his duty to teach her a lesson when she fails. He throws bowls of soup at her when the taste does not please him, and on one occasion he beat her severely with a length of bamboo simply because she did not bring his lunch to the field precisely at the agreed-on time. Another villager, who continually found fault with his wife's cooking, beat her almost daily. On his return home one day, Doña Petra overheard his wife remark, "Do you beat me now and we eat later, or do we eat now and you beat me when we finish?"

Behind the masculine standards for a wife's performance of her household duties is a desire to control women's labor but also, perhaps, a suspicion that the neglect of her work stems from the distractions of extramarital activities. When a man comes home to find the floor unswept, an infant's diaper unchanged, or his meal not ready, his wife may receive a pummeling. Some village men are so sensitive to hints of infidelity that they assume the worst when they hear someone whistling outside the house or small pebbles falling on the roof, or when they see a strange man standing on a nearby street corner.

Both men and women say that overly gentle or tolerant husbands may be expressing indifference toward their wives. One elderly man, noting that wife beating was more common once than it is today, voiced this idea when he said, "Women do not feel right if they are not beaten. They must be trained, like a good horse."

Some women feel as duty bound to submit to beatings as men feel in providing them. To suffer at the hands of their husbands and yet remain loyal to them is even a mark of wifely virtue. The elderly Dolores recalled that when her late husband beat her and then threw her clothes out the door she simply went outside, gathered them up, and returned through the back door. "A woman who is beaten and quits," she observed, "is not a real woman." On one occasion, when her husband severely injured her by clubbing her with a handstone, the neighbors became frightened and summoned the local constable, who jailed the husband. But Dolores refused to file a complaint against him and even tried to conceal her wounds. When her husband was released, he thanked her for not betraying him. "I am not," she said, "like those women who complain and then come back to lick their husbands' feet."

Wife beating and emotional estrangement of husband and wife do not occur in all marriages, and when they do, they are more typical of established marriages than of younger ones. Beginning with the romance of courtship and the first year or two of married life, the relationship gradually becomes utilitarian and child-centered as affectionate interaction between spouses gives way to the work of supporting and rearing a family.

Even in the past, courtship involved strong romantic feelings in both young men and women, despite the many restrictions that kept face-to-face meetings to a minimum. Sweethearts communicated principally through the exchange of letters. Older women wistfully recall that the letters were written in elegant script on colored stationery that was decorated with figures of hearts, flowers, and clasped hands. At night young men customarily serenaded their lady friends with guitars and song. In the words of Doña Pola, "The boys were outside all night losing sleep while the girls were snuggled up in bed inside."

Nowadays, parents present fewer obstacles to courtship, and mothers, who may be more permissive than fathers, may even allow suitors into the house to visit with the daughters. At night, sweethearts talk and cuddle in doorways. Some young men position themselves on nearby street corners, whistling to their sweethearts to arrange less conspicuous meetings. Young women may leave the house on errands that are little more than pretexts for spending time with their suitors, and mothers not infrequently act as allies in these gambits. Most fathers are aware of these departures from customary discretion, but they usually say nothing, thereby maintaining the appearance of supporting traditional values although tacitly condoning the newer and more liberal morality. Sweethearts may indulge in heavy petting once they become engaged, but a young woman's virginity is still carefully guarded until she marries or elopes. Virginity remains a desirable attribute in a potential wife, and a man who marries a previously married woman is deemed to be unfortunate, even a fool. Men do not want a woman who has been "handled" or "drilled out."

Young men are permitted to conduct themselves according to a different set of rules. They are expected to seek outlets for their sexual needs, and in early adolescence they begin to visit prostitutes. Some, following the example of some married men, engage in bestiality. Occasional activities of this sort do not compromise their worth as potential husbands, providing they are discreet, but when a youth has earned the reputation of being a drunkard or woman chaser or has had a love affair with a widow, he may find it difficult to arrange a marriage for himself; parents of eligible unmarried women often fear that a man's former partner may vent her jealousy in witchcraft.

Despite the sexual restrictions and double standards for young men and women, courtship and engagement are described by many villagers as the happiest time in their lives. "Courtship," Doña María observed, "is more beautiful than marriage. Husbands and wives quarrel and come to blows but sweethearts almost never fight. After they marry, people become less affectionate with each other." Although women are more likely than men to express such nostalgia, there is reason to suppose that men place a similar value on romance; at least, they display romantic attitudes toward prostitutes and mistresses, often interacting with them in a way that suggests as much interest in tender companionship as in sex per se. It is not uncommon for men to visit the "merry ladies" with no intention of having intercourse; instead, they merely sit with the women, engaging in friendly conversation and banter for hours at a time.

After marriage or elopement most couples take up residence with the groom's parents, whereas fewer move in with the bride's parents or set up independent households. Only a few couples set up independent households immediately after their wedding. On the average, young spouses spend five to six years in an extended family before establishing their own household. The duration of this arrangement follows no fixed rule, although, eventually, tight living quarters and the desire for independence encourage the breakup of the domestic group. Usually, several people sleep in a single room; the efforts to provide newlyweds with a modicum of privacy may be limited to placing their bed at one end of the room and their parents' and siblings' beds at the other end.

Young people face still other obstacles to physical intimacy. A young man's mother typically is jealous of her son's amorous attentions to young women and may actively try to discourage him from marrying. Later, after the marriage, she may vie with her daughter-in-law for her son's affections. Quarrels over finances and work assignments occur frequently, and depositions in the records of the village court show that meddlesome mothers-in-law not uncommonly play a significant role in marital separations.

Even when an engagement culminates in marriage, which lifts the near-total ban on sexual activity, couples are still not free of restraints. During the early years of marriage, at least, parental pressure and interference as well as the simple inconveniences of extended family life conspire to thwart sexual relations. Many young couples would no doubt set up indepenent households sooner if it were not for lack of economic resources and dependence on parents. Meanwhile, variations in cooking arrangements, budget management, and work assignments reflect these emotional tensions and the trend toward the dissociation of the larger unit. Even in their own households, however, other cultural restrictions continue to discourage the development of freedom and intimacy in sexual relations.

Sex, Conception, and Birth

Sexual intercourse between spouses is infrequent or absent during pregnancy and nursing. Many couples cease having intercourse immediately on discovering that the woman is pregnant, and others abstain after the first trimester. People believe that coitus can provoke miscarriage early in a term and harm the fetus later.

The pregnant woman is said to be "hot." This hotness, or the special nature of her condition, is thought to protect her against the stings of scorpions and to give her saliva the power to kill them. It also can cause an emotional illness in her husband, which may require that he sleep apart from her.

The physical separation of spouses continues during the nursing period. Pregnancy is said to make a mother's milk watery and salty and hence unsuitable for an infant, and women say that nursing a child throughout its infancy ensures its health. So husbands and wives abstain from sexual relations with each other for a year or more after childbirth to avoid the risk of pregnancy during the critical period of nursing. Older people say that in the past husbands would "care" for wives in this manner for as many as four years.[5] Many younger couples no longer observe the restriction, although there is general agreement that husbands and wives should not have sex during the *cuarentena* (quarantine), a customary forty-day period of postpartum seclusion. Villagers believe that sexual intercourse during the *cuarentena* can cause worms to grow in the vagina.

Sex is a source of shame. Many women view sexual intercourse as a disagreeable obligation in which they submit to male abuse; indeed, several married women told my female interviewers that it had never given them pleasure. Some women prefer to avoid sex by feigning illness or simply by telling their husbands outright to find someone else.

Women's lack of pleasure in sex derives, in part, from the tendency for some drunken men to demand sex with their wives, even though the latter may not be interested. Many drunken husbands return home too intoxicated for anything but sleep, but others arrive in a mood for lovemaking. They are, however, often aggressive and insensitive, and so, unattractive to their wives. Rebuffs, in turn, may leave them feeling rejected and lead to quarrels and wife beating, particularly if they arouse suspicions of infidelity.

Most villagers say that men have stronger natures than women, a notion that supports the double standard of sexual conduct. Although women are expected to be sexually passive and indifferent to the pleasures of sex, men recognize that women can and sometimes do enjoy it. Their anxiety about female impulses getting out of control may be expressed in jokes about women who enjoy sex.[6] At the same time, there is a belief that immoderate sexual activity is detrimental to a man's health. Frequent ejaculations are thought to desiccate the spinal column and to cause tuberculosis, and men who father large families are believed to be more likely to suffer from the disease. Men also attribute impotence, temporary debility, and lower back pain to excessive sexual intercourse.

Tlayacapenses use the word *naturaleza* to refer to the generative substance. In men at least, the latter is said to form in the brain, apparently from blood, and pass down the spinal column to the genitalia. A woman's *naturaleza* is believed to be present in the blood of her uterus. Conception is thought to involve a mixing or confrontation of the natures of a man and woman. If the *naturalezas* of both husband and wife are strong, they are likely to have many offspring, but if either or both have weak *naturaleza*, they may have few or no children. Interestingly, a woman's *naturaleza* makes a special contribution to the formation of sons, a man's to the formation of daughters. Women with strong *naturaleza* are more apt to give birth to sons, who are expected to take after their mothers in stature and appearance.[7] In any event, conception occurs only through the will of God. Without spirit or "the breath of life," there can be no conception. When a woman ceases to menstruate and it later becomes clear that she is pregnant, her blood is said to have "the breath of life." "Woman produces," one man remarked, "as dictated on high."

Spiritually ordained though it may be, pregnancy is considered akin to disease. The pregnant woman feels "fat" and "deformed" and she stays indoors even more than usual. People rarely describe a woman as being simply "pregnant"; they say that she is "embarrassed," "in an interesting state," "in a bad state," or "sick." A woman "gets well" by delivering a child or "cures herself" by aborting or being sterilized. When asked if a pregnant woman was truly sick, Doña Pola was taken aback, but only for a moment. Collecting her wits, she quickly replied, "But of course it is bad; after all, a person can die!"

In keeping with the cultural emphasis on the delicacy of her condition, a pregnant woman tries to protect herself from stressful experiences and evil spirits. A fright, a blow, or the lifting of a heavy object may cause miscarriage. Failure to satisfy the mother's food cravings may cause the baby to be born with birthmarks. Exposure to eclipses can cause neonates to be born with harelips.

At parturition a woman is attended by a midwife. Traditionally, women about to deliver assumed a sitting position and held onto a rope strung from the rafters of the house; today most women take a prone position for delivery. Immediately after birth, the midwife ties a roll of cloth, called a "doll," to the mother's abdomen to prevent the womb from falling. A fallen womb is known to be a cause of sterility. The inability to have children also may be attributed to "frigidity" in the womb. Cold enters the womb and gives it a leathery quality, preventing conception; it can happen, for example, when a woman eats "cold" foods (for example, watermelon, oranges) during her menstrual period. As part of the mother's care, steps must be taken to "close" her waist (that is, tighten the pelvis) lest cold enter. The pelvis is tightened by baths in the *temazcal* (sweat bath) and in *agua de cocimiento* (an infusion of rosemary, *pericón*, and other warming herbs).

Villagers believe that if dogs eat the placenta and umbilical cord, harm will come to the mother and infant, so some people bury those by-products of birth under the hearth. It is also thought that the neonate is a tempting prize for witches, evil spirits, and the Devil, who is always on the lookout for new souls. To protect the infant, some people keep a cat in the same room or put an upside-down sombrero under the infant's crib. Formerly, people may have made offerings to spirits (*los aires*) that inhabit the ground under the mother's bed so that they would not molest the infant. This practice is still observed in a nearby hamlet.

Reproduction, Production, and Security

There are compelling reasons for wanting children in Tlayacapan: having children indicates maturity and adulthood; a man demonstrates manhood by fathering children; and a woman confirms her womanhood by bearing them. Adults are regarded as "young people" until they have married and produced children.

People say that life without children is a life of "sadness." Young children provide joy, and older children help and support. Fathers value the labor of sons in the fields, and mothers, the work of daughters in the home. Both boys and girls make valuable economic contributions to the family from early childhood on, and sons do as much work as grown men by the time they are thirteen or fourteen. By that age, daughters can handle the strenuous work of the *metate*. Parents hope and expect that their children will care for them when they are old and feeble.

Despite the incentives for having large families, parents have reasons for delaying pregnancies or even limiting the total number of offspring. Although postpartum sexual abstinence is thought to favor the nursing infant, one informant explained that it is also a form of birth control. Village women are aware that nursing can inhibit menstruation and conception, so we may infer that sexual abstinence and nursing together are complementary forms of birth control. In general, women are sensitive to the physical and emotional burdens imposed by pregnancy and child rearing. Many speak of the pain, physical wear and tear, and risks to life that attend bearing children.

Some informants mention economic stress as a disadvantage of large families. This awareness of the economic issue is not confined to poor families, however. Since better-off families spend more on food, clothing, and education, they also perceive the expense of additional children. Interviews in 1973 with fifty couples and another ninety women showed that most villagers did not want what they considered to be large families. When the fifty couples (men and women were interviewed separately) were asked to define "large" and "small" family, the women defined "large" families as a mean of 9.2 children, and the men as 6.3. The spouses agreed more closely in their definitions of "small" family: the mean numbers were 2.7 (women) and 2.4 (men) children. Sixty-two percent of the women and 74 percent of the men preferred small families. In addition, few women who already had 2 or more children wanted an additional child; for all women the mean number of desired additional children was slightly less than 1.

These data imply that the typical couple has wanted what might be called a moderately large family, one neither too small nor too large. In traditional culture, the achievement of this aim was more a consequence of sexual mores and customary role behavior than of conscious planning. Extended nursing periods and postpartum sexual abstinence ensured long birth intervals and moderately sized families.

Various scholars have argued that machismo contributes significantly to high fertility in Latin America (Corwin 1963; Kahl 1967; Stycos 1955). In Tlayacapan a childless man is said to be "empty," like a piece of fruit with no pit. Others may ridicule him, saying, "Lend her to me, I'll get her pregnant." Drunkenness, which is a part of the machismo syndrome in Tlayacapan, may also promote reproduction to the degree that it lowers sexual inhibitions and emboldens husbands to make sexual demands on their wives, despite customary restrictions on sexual behavior. Nonetheless, the relation between machismo and fertility may not be so simple. Sexual and pseudosexual behavior in the street may complement sexual restraint within marriage. To the extent that street machismo is a redirection of sexual impulses away from wives, it really supports marital continence.

The desire to limit family size is suggested by attempted and actual abortions. To avoid unwanted pregnancies, many women use abortifacients, sometimes at the urging of husbands who worry about their ability to support more children. A variety of teas made from anise, rue, cumin, oregano, and other herbs are thought to stimulate menstrual flow. Some women insist that these herbs are effective, although others say they have had little success with them. One midwife said, "They can take oregano until it is coming out of their ears, but it won't help." When young women come to her asking for something to prevent pregnancy, she is unlikely to offer much encouragement. "My dear child," she told one informant, "if I knew, do you think that I would have had so many myself?" A few women seek the help of abortionists outside the village, although it is known that their more drastic methods can have tragic results.

The villagers are aware that the church considers abortion a sin, yet the practical reasons for terminating pregnancy may more than balance the religious strictures against it. The dilemma is handled by redefining the function of abortifacients. Instead of thinking of them as a means of ending pregnancy, women regard them as medicines for keeping their periods regular. Abortion in the second trimester, which requires more violent means and which clearly destroys a fetus, occurs but is generally regarded as wrong.[8]

The preference for moderately but not excessively large families is the product of contradictory forces, some favoring and others discouraging reproduction. Historically, the balance has fluctuated along with shifting economic conditions. As Tlayacapan has been drawn into the modern national and world economy, the economic value of children has increased along with desires for manufactured goods. The truck farming of tomatoes beginning in the late 1950s and continuing to the present has in particular created a strong demand for labor.

The demand has been satisfied in part by making better use of family members. Young boys are put to work planting seed and spreading fertilizer. When the need for labor is acute, even women work in the fields. Labor requirements have also been met by an increase in the average size of the family, which has resulted in part from a decrease in mortality, particularly among infants and children, but also from an increase in fertility during the late 1950s and 1960s. This trend is evident in birth rates reported in chapter 3. It is further suggested by the 1960, 1970, and 1980 censuses, which give the mean number of children ever born live (table 3). Data on birth intervals gathered through interviews with women in 1973 also imply an increase in fertility during the 1950s and 1960s (see table 4). Reported intervals between the first and second child were greater in-older informants, a finding that conforms with the villagers' own impressions that postpartum sexual abstinence is now being ignored, particularly by young couples. The interval of 2.5 years reported by women 29 years of age and under probably represents little or no sexual restraint. Intervals of roughly 27 months can be expected from a combination of lactation amenorrhea, the effects of periodic infertility in the menstrual cycle, and the 9 months of pregnancy.[9]

The rise in the fertility of married women was offset somewhat by a change in the average age at marriage. Between 1940 and 1970 the mean age at marriage for women gradually rose from 16.5 to 20 years. Yet, once the younger women married, they had children in quicker succession, and fewer

Table 3
Mean Number of Children Ever Born Live, per Woman, Tlayacapan,
1960, 1970, 1980

	1960	1970	1980
No. of women	1,227	1,668	2,579
Mean no. of children	2.7	3.4	3.0

Source: Estados Unidos Mexicanos (1963:261; 1971:134-135; 1983:93).

Table 4
Age Cohorts and Birth Intervals, Tlayacapan, 1973

Age	Mean	S.D.	N
40+	3.8	2.5	15
30-39	3.1	1.6	17
15-29	2.5	1.5	39

of their children were lost to childhood diseases. Neither the reduction in child mortality nor the shortening of birth intervals was motivated simply by a need for laborers in the fields; nonetheless, the villagers did not respond to declining mortality with further reproductive restraint, even though it was within their capacity to do so. To the contrary, they relaxed the traditional cultural controls on fertility. The result was an increase in the supply of family labor at a time when it was needed.

The rise in fertility during the 1960s was reversed in the 1970s in conformity with a nationwide reduction in birth rate of 25 percent (table 3; see also chapter 3). Several factors were doubtless promoting lower birth rates in the country as a whole. In Tlayacapan a lowering of the rate of reproduction was part of the peasants' evolving adaptation to modern economic conditions. Tomato cultivation continued to play a part in the strategies of many families, but other tactics were becoming increasingly important, particularly that of putting one or two children through higher education with the aim of placing them in well-paying professions. Investment in education competed with the capital requirements of tomato gardens and so curbed further expansion of production and increasing demand for agricultural labor. Meanwhile, a punishing rate of inflation and changing standards of consumption further elevated the costs of rearing children. And for some farmers, at least, bad luck with weather and tomato prices also acted to deter any expansion of cash cropping.

Mother and Child

A corollary of the estrangement of husband and wife is a strong mother-child relationship, a distinguishing feature of the Mexican peasant family. Accordingly, women have a more positive image of the relationship between mother and child than of that between husband and wife. "A mother's love," they say, "is without stain." "There is no parent like a mother." Indeed, mothers of young children in Tlayacapan are nurturing and attentive. They breast-feed their babies on demand, usually for more than a year and, not infrequently, for two or three years; occasionally, a child is still taking the breast at age five or six. During infancy the child sleeps next to the mother at night and is often carried next to her body in her shawl during the day. One imagines that the first years of life are blissful for Tlayacapense children. The period may be equally pleasant for their mothers. Women describe the physical and emotional satisfaction of nursing and caring for babies as though nothing else in life were so gratifying.

Some children wean themselves. Mothers who become pregnant, however, take active steps to wean a child. If the child resists weaning, the mother may put bean paste on her breasts and tell the child it is the excrement of a dog or turkey, or she may smear Mercurochrome or lipstick on the breast and say that it is blood. Some women apply the juice of a bitter herb to their nipples to cause the child to reject the breast.

Following weaning, the child—unless the last one—is deprived of the mother's attentions. As the mother becomes preoccupied with the child *in utero* and then in her arms, the toddler finds himself or herself walking or crawling on the floor instead of riding the mother's hip and eating a diet of mostly carbohydrates instead of mother's milk. Moreover, the child's socialization may be relegated to older siblings, who are inclined to vent their envy and resentment toward the youngster. Within a few years, the regimen may become even more severe. Typically, the child is given little or no physical affection and, instead, may be scolded and punished. Irate parents may call the child a "pig" and say that they are going to "eat" him or her, a metaphor for physical punishment, which many fathers really administer to their boys. By age six or seven, the children are expected to contribute to the tasks of farming and housework. Boys begin to accompany their fathers to the fields and girls learn to make tortillas, care for younger children, and run errands.

The child, then, receives good mothering in the early years and less nurturing later. These experiences may have long-lasting effects on character and worldview. A general attitude of mistrust and an expectation of betrayal, which are commonplace among Tlayacapenses and other Mexican villagers, may have psychological roots in the transition at weaning. Floods and other forms of chaos are called *desmadres*. The word comes from the use of *madre* for "streambed," but it is also related to *desmadrar*, to wean an animal from its mother. The connotation may be that weaning is the prototypical disaster. In a classic paper, Bushnell (1958) described the transition from early to later childhood and the quality of mistrust in a central Mexican village and suggested that the early positive experience with the mother, combined with later disappointment and mistrust, lays an emotional basis for idealizing the Virgen de Guadalupe. In Tlayacapan two emotional disorders tend to give credence to Bushnell's interpretation.

Chipileza

Villagers say that pregnancy may make the nursing child *chipil*. (The word derives from the Nahuatl *tzipitl*, which also referred to a child made sick by a pregnant mother.) The nursling senses the change in the mother's milk and becomes sick with resentment of the unborn. Children who are not nursing can have the condition, however. Being aware of the unborn, the toddler sickens with jealousy. Some mothers explain that it is the hotness of the pregnant mother that causes the illness.

If the sickness is severe and persists, the child may become *ético*—he or she may develop diarrhea and lose weight. The mother can treat the *chipileza* before she gives birth by bathing the child in water mixed with ashes from the hearth and, after birth, by bathing the toddler in the bathwater of the newborn. One woman nursed her sister's infant to help cure its *chipileza*. The treatment for *etiqueza* implies an understanding that the symptoms are related not only to jealousy of the unborn, but also to poor nutrition following weaning. Some people decapitate a turtle and rub its blood on the toddler's joints. They then boil the meat of the turtle, bathe the child in the cooled broth, and feed the meat to the child. Others follow the same procedures using an iguana.

Chipileza also may affect young husbands who are about to become fathers for the first time. The husband with *chipileza* is touchy and irritable. The roots of his hair hurt, his body (especially the wrists and finger joints) ache, and he tires easily. Folk remedies may include the revealing symbolism of tearing strips of cloth from the hemline of the wife's dress and tying them around the husband's wrists, neck, or waist. A husband suffering from the illness is said to resent the unborn, and sometimes he is advised not to sleep with his wife, and even to find a girlfriend or visit a prostitute.

It is significant that only young husbands become *chipil*. We can surmise that their suffering arises from the anticipation of the change in the couple's relationship signaled by the arrival of the first child. Until a bride becomes pregnant, there is no restriction on lovemaking (other than the inhibiting effects of the extended-family situation), and the groom is the primary object of the bride's affection. All this begins to change when the wife becomes pregnant. Her pregnancy initiates the physical and emotional estrangement that characterizes the mature marital relationship. Older men who are more accustomed to abstinence from marital relations no longer experience emotional distress; for young husbands who are still sexually and romantically attracted to their wives, the prospect of marital continence is disturbing.

The emotional and physical separation from the wife may echo the early loss of the mother's concentrated attention. Yet, for the young husband, there may be compensations. He may lose the wife as a sexual object but, instead, find in her a facsimile of his nurturing, virginal mother. The wife continues to take care of her husband as a good mother would. She feeds him on demand and obeys his orders. Some men refer to their wives as "mothers." One informant even said, "When one is abandoned by the mother [that is, when the mother dies], one still has the wife, who is the true mother."

Negative as well as positive feelings about the mother may be displaced onto the wife. Wives are scolded and beaten precisely because they seem to fall short of the ideal of the virginal, all-giving mother: suggestions of infidelity bring beatings; so do failures to provide good food at the expected time; and, significantly, wives may be punished for what husbands construe as inadequate maternal behavior. Once when I arrived at Bengano's house, I encountered an uproar at the front door. The baby had just fallen off the steps, banging its head and raising an ugly bump. The baby was screaming, older siblings were yelling at younger ones, and the mother, obviously distraught, was blaming everyone. She wrapped the baby's head in a cloth and tried to comfort her. In the midst of the confusion, Bengano came home, half-drunk; he berated his wife and told her in no uncertain terms that she had better take care of "his child," or else.

One hears much testimony concerning ambivalence about wives and mothers in male slang. One expression affirms, "No es la misma cosa, madre pura que pura madre" (A mother who is pure and pure mother are not the same); the first is perfect, the other worthless. Similarly, *a toda madre* (all mother) expresses the strongest praise, but *vale madre* (it's worth mother) indicates unimportance. On the one hand, there is the figure of the virgin, sacred and inviolate; on the other there is the harlot, the woman of the street and ultimately any woman with sexual experience. One hears few references in slang to the Virgin, of course, but those to the Chingada, the violated woman, are many and various, as if being a "son of a so-and-so" were part of the human condition.

The father is also the object of ambivalent feelings. In many families there is genuine respect and even reverence for the father. Yet, he is the one most likely to apply physical punishment, and, what is more, he may be seen as a sexual aggressor. Some children witness their drunk fathers beating mothers, and they may hear their parents having sex. Children often sleep in the same room with their parents, if not in the same bed. What young children may make of parental intercourse is uncertain, but there is no doubt that older children are aware of it and understand its role in the procreation of younger rivals. Apparently, they resent the father's sexual demands on the mother. In one joke told by young boys, a clever boy manages to seduce his grandmother; the boy's father discovers the deed and asks his son why he did such a terrible thing. The boy replies, "But you make love to *my* mother!" In effect, both mother and child may view the husband/father as a sexual aggressor who interferes with the pure relationship between mother and child (or self).

Susto

In Tlayacapan a combination of sadness, loss of appetite, and fitful sleep is diagnosed as *susto* (fright). A frightening experience, whether brought about by a meeting with a ghost or supernatural being or by a natural event, is said to cause the *sombra* (shadow-soul) to leave the body or fall asleep. About two-thirds of all *susto* cases involve children.

Susto is probably a rubric for various ailments, especially among children, although the symptoms suggest that often it is a folk-medical category for depression and, possibly, anxiety reactions. As Freud noted, there is a similarity between mourning and depression, and modern psychiatry has accumulated evidence pointing to a link between loss and depression (Bowlby 1980). Information on fifty-nine cases of *susto* in Tlayacapan suggests that it may be variously a reaction to maternal separation, weaning,[10] bereavement, separation from loved ones, and threats to livelihood. Twenty-three percent of the fifty-nine cases were caused by deaths of loved ones; another 20 percent, by encounters with ghosts, usually those of relatives shortly after their deaths; a few, when the lives of family members seemed to be in danger; and occasionally by threats to or punishment of the self, sometimes by husbands or parents. Mothers not uncommonly experience minor *sustos* in response to *sustos* in their children.

As children are expelled from the protective mother-child symbiosis, they learn their parents' mistrust of people and of forces in the outside world and so, not unexpectedly, often suffer *sustos* when they leave the house to play. Within the family, the threat and practice of physical punishment also cause frights, especially in boys. When I asked one folk curer if thunder sometimes caused *susto* in children, her grown son, who was standing nearby, interjected, "And also the stick!" Because children tend to turn to their grandparents for affection when mothers are nursing infants and fathers seem to become less affectionate and more punitive, the death of a grandparent can be especially disturbing. The grief-stricken child "looks for the grandparent," as they say, seeing him or her in disturbing dreams or as a ghost.

Maternal overprotection may increase vulnerability to fright. Father Chavo, who performed many *evangelios* (readings from the gospels) as treatments for *susto* and kept written records of the circumstances of the patients, observed that the typical child suffering from fright illness is timid, melancholic, and overprotected by a mother who centers her life in her children. The effects of such overprotection may persist into adulthood. A man who was reared by an abandoned mother reported having frightening nightmares and lurid sexual dreams after he and his wife parted, more than ten years earlier; following the separation, he became a recluse and ascetic, living alone with his mother. Villagers say she has dominated him all his life.

The various treatments for *susto* evoke maternal presence in different ways. Mothers may offer afflicted children certain teas and food. An *agua de espanto* (fright water) may be purchased in pharmacies in nearby towns. Another common treatment is to seek out a woman who knows how to *poner la sombra*. For the latter ritual, which takes place in the home of the curer, the patient's mother brings red flowers and twelve or, in serious cases, twenty-four kernels of maize, preferably red. The curer places the flower petals in her *jícara*, which she has filled with water (the *jícara*, a gourd bowl, is always painted red and decorated with white birds). If the *susto* is thought to be severe, she also may light a candle and incense.

Apart from these preparations, each curer performs the *sombra* ritual somewhat differently, although most pray in Nahuatl and invoke the names of saints as they stroke the patient with the kernels. Doña Arnulfa begins the ritual by placing a maize kernel on the patient's right wrist with her own left thumb. She touches the patient's head, shoulder, and wrist with the *jícara* three times and calls on the Holy Trinity. She then takes the maize kernel and rubs the patient's arm with it from the elbow to the wrist while reciting a prayer in which she asks the *sombra* to return to its place, to its *petate*, and calls on San Miguel Arcángel, San Juan Bautista, and the Apostles. She repeats the procedure six times and then sips some water from the *jícara*, places her mouth over the patient's fontanel, and gurgles, repeating the action over the back of the head, shoulder, elbow, wrist, and palm. Thereupon she spits out the water to one side and, cupping the patient's head in her hands, blows on it and utters his or her name twice. Then she repeats the rite for the other side of the patient's body.

The patient's progress is revealed by the behavior of the kernels when they are dropped into the *jícara*. They stand on end if the patient is improving and lie down if the *sombra* is still lost or weak. Before the patient departs, the curer encourages him or her to drink some water from the *jícara*. She may suggest that the mother toast the kernels, flavor them with salt and lemon juice, and feed them to the child.

In the *evangelios* the patient is taken to a priest for prayers and readings from Matthew, Mark, Luke, or John. For this rite, special godfathers and godmothers are selected. At the start of the rite, the priest explains the rite's purpose and says a prayer, sprinkles the child with holy water, touches the patient with his hands, and gives the benediction. After he reads from the gospels, the godparents touch the patient.

This instance of godparenthood is remarkable in various ways. Six godmothers and six godfathers are considered ideal by some villagers, but the number may be fewer or greater. More than one hundred special godparents attended one rite. The godparents are selected especially for the *evangelios*. Having no lasting importance, they are called *padrinos de acahual*, implying that they are dried weeds or sunflowers. Curiously, unlike other types of godparents, who are generally chosen with moral qualities in mind, those for the *evangelios* are supposed to be persons of "strong character"—persons who are not altogether virtuous and respectable. Prostitutes and murderers are thought to be especially effective, although people ordinarily settle for adolescents, whose blood is presumably stronger than that of most adults.

In still another remedy a godmother or godfather of *escapulario* (scapular) gives a religious pendant to the ailing child. The scapular consists of two cloth patches joined by two ribbons so that they straddle the shoulders with one patch resting on the chest and the other, on the back. Sewn to one patch is an image of the Virgen de Carmen or Virgen de Rosario and to the other, that of a saint. The young patient receives both a new godparent and a token of the perfect mother.

The Family and Supernatural Representations

The nearly ubiquitous presence of an image of the Virgen de Guadalupe on family altars, the characteristics of the proper wife and mother, and the similarity between the home and church or chapel all speak to the salience of the Holy Family as a social model.

The woman does not conform perfectly to Mary's example, however. As Gudeman (1976a:52, 233) observes, differing facets of the woman are represented in Eve as well as in Mary; the one is a likeness of the woman as sexual partner and the other, as mother. These contrasting supernatural images, I would add, encode the cycle of reproduction within the domestic group. When a woman is nursing and sexually continent, she resembles the Virgin. When she submits to sex, she is more like Eve. This sexual mother may disappoint her children when she brings sibling rivals into the world, and she may be a disappointment to her husband, since she reminds her husband of the loss of his own mother.

The husband's role parallels the actions of supernatural figures in similarly ambiguous ways. During the time he "cares" for his wife, he plays the role of Joseph, the self-denying and dutiful husband. Men are not perfectly self-sacrificing, however, nor would they want to be: Joseph is a respected but somewhat emasculated figure; a man must reassert his sexuality toward his wife and his manliness in the street. To his wife, then, he may seem to play the part of Adam, or to the extent that he comes home drunk and feeling abusive, even that of the serpent. The male, in other words, takes the initiative in redefining the marital relationship in natural as opposed to spiritual terms.

5. Ritual Kinship

Religious symbols and meanings inform relations between families as well as roles within families. In this and the following chapters I shall consider the ways in which positive and negative sociality are construed and constructed in religious terms. In this chapter I show how positive relationships are reinforced and institutionalized in terms of what I shall call spiritual kinship, particularly godparenthood and the religious fiesta. My aim, however, is to go beyond the usual observation that these institutions establish social solidarity and to show that their social function is closely related to their religious meaning, something that has been all but ignored in the literature. A consideration of meaning argues forcefully for the inclusion of fiesta organization along with godparenthood under the rubric of spiritual kinship and, at the same time, makes the function of both customs within the entire culture more intelligible. Let us begin with a brief review of dogma.

Catholic theology traces the Devil's influence in human affairs to the Fall of Adam and Eve. According to the doctrine of Original Sin, the Fall left a stain on human nature and even the whole of nature. The stain, which is passed from one generation to the next, accounts for the human disposition to envy, greed, and lust and sinful acts that bespeak Satan's persistent influence.

There is then a continuing struggle between God and Satan. In this struggle God achieved a victory in Christ, but it is understood that the victory will not be complete until the end of time. Meanwhile, the sacraments and prayerful blessings of the church are viewed as the principal means for sanctifying and redeeming a fallen creation. They exorcise the influence of the Evil One and convey grace and benediction. In this manner the rites reincorporate persons and things into the spiritual family of the church.

Saint Augustine thought that the stain of Original Sin was transmitted in the act of sexual intercourse. Although this belief is no longer given explicit emphasis in church teaching, it is nonetheless implied by the rite of baptism, which cleanses the stain of Original and actual sin and effects spiritual regeneration through the instrumentality of godparents (see Gudeman 1972). If spiritual regeneration removes sin, the implication is that natural reproduction perpetuates it. Saint Augustine's attitude toward sex is still in evidence in Tlayacapan, where sex is a subject of shame and pregnancy is a matter of embarrassment, as though it were punishment for the weakness of the flesh. The notion, mentioned earlier, that the saliva of a pregnant woman is lethal to a scorpion is probably another expression of these sentiments. Since the Bible (Lk 10:19) speaks of both snakes and scorpions as manifestations of the Devil, the implication is that a woman's submission to sexual intercourse repeats the sin of Eve and involves her in Eve's conflict with the Devil.[1]

Baptism is said to cleanse and regenerate through the mysterious action of water and spirit. Water represents a feminine substance, and spirit, a masculine one. This symbolism is suggested by the traditional blessing of the baptismal font on Holy Saturday. The opening words of the rite's prayer mentioned the movement of the Holy Spirit on the water at the beginning of time and then the Deluge, as if to suggest that these events prefigured the cleansing action of baptismal water. The priest traced the form of a cross in the water of the baptismal font and prayed, asking that by a secret mixture divine power render the water "fruitful" for "regeneration" and that those who are sanctified in the "immaculate womb" of the font be born again as "heavenly offspring," whatever their age or sex, into the "same infancy." In addition, he asked that all unclean and evil spirits be banished from the water. Continuing to pray, the priest made the sign of the cross over the water, divided it with his hand, and tossed it to the four quarters. He then breathed on the water three times and plunged the paschal candle into the water three times, and holding it there the last time, asked that the Holy Ghost descend into the water. Breathing again on the water three times, he further asked that it make the whole of the water "fruitful for regeneration." After removing the candle from the water, he sprinkled some water on the people of the congregation and set some aside as holy water for the Asperges on Sundays, for blessings, and for use by the people in their homes (before use, holy water is blessed with salt). Last, he added oil of the catechumens and holy chrism (olive oil and balsam), singly and then together (Roman Missal 1951:288-290).

In the rite of baptism itself the priest meets the baptismal party at the church door, makes a sign of the cross over the child, and places a pinch of salt in the child's mouth. During the rite, the godparents and parents profess their rejection of Satan and his works and affirm their faith in the Holy Spirit, the Holy Catholic Church, the communion of saints, the forgiveness of sins, the resurrection of the body, and life everlasting.

The dogma of baptism holds that God is the father and the church is the mother in regeneration. These supernatural personages are represented by the priest and godparents, who serve as the instruments of God and church. The rite of blessing the baptismal font together with the actual rite of baptism, then, enacts a spiritual counterpart of natural procreation: godparents are to baptism what natural parents are to sexual reproduction. The rites help to transform the child from what the villagers call a *criatura* (creature) into a *cristiano*, a child of both the church and a specific set of godparents.

Spiritual regeneration through baptism incorporates the person into a spiritual family. Catholicism conceptualizes the church as both spiritual mother and family. God is the father, and Joseph, Mary, and Jesus compose the Holy Family. The church is both the body and bride of Christ, and lay Christians, in keeping with the metaphors, are members of the body and children of the holy union. In ecclesiastical organization, the pope and priests are "fathers," friars are "brothers," and nuns are "sisters." Religious societies are known as "confraternities." Priests in Tlayacapan refer to the villagers as "children."

Occasionally, one hears villagers invoke an inclusive spiritual kinship. Doña Pechi, pondering the egoism and arrogance of certain "rich people" when dealing with "poor Indians" like herself, asked, "How can they act that way?" Attempting to answer her own question, she allowed that the rich have "different physiognomies" and "another way of life," but then asked rhetorically, "Are we not all baptized in the same water?" Christians, she was saying, may be naturally or socially unequal, but spiritually they are members of the same community and therefore have a responsibility to treat one another with civility.

As this example also shows, however, the villagers are aware that social distinctions and divergent interests interfere with the realization of the ideal. The mere fact that a stranger is a fellow Christian may enjoin a measure of initial good will but it does not ensure trust or mutual support. The ideal of spiritual kinship works best at the local level, within spheres of familiarity and actual or potential mutuality of interest, which provides some basis for overcoming social and economic differences. The local level in this sense may be the village, the barrio, or a relationship between neighbors or kin. In ritual terms, the notion of spiritual kinship attains partial realization in Sunday mass, godparenthood, and ritual feasts. These local versions of spiritual kinship are less inclusive than the notion of a universal congregation and more germane to social life. The fiesta embraces neighbors and fellow villagers, whereas godparenthood establishes spiritual kinship with particular families, whatever their neighborhood or social station.

Both institutions suppress selfishness and lust, traits associated with the taint in human nature. In doing so, they establish a moral community that transcends the diverse interests of particular families. Villagers are acutely aware of who is involved in ritual kinship and who is not, and they are especially sensitive to the willingness of individuals and families to assume ritual responsibilities. Those who refuse to participate place themselves beyond the pale of the moral community.

Ritual sponsors mediate the transmission of divine grace to other villagers, either by functioning as instruments of the church in the ministration of the sacraments or by supporting the saints, who are themselves mediators and intercessors. In actual practice, ritual sponsors provide gifts of food for others and may extend to them various favors. In these ways they indicate their own positive, beneficent attitude toward the households of their godchildren or, if fiesta sponsors, toward other members of the neighborhood or community. In return, they receive, along with God and the saints, the respect of others (fig. 4).

The idiom of ritual kinship does not deny the negative side of human nature but presupposes the possibility of incorporating it into a higher order. Although sexuality and self-interest are suppressed in the context of ritual relations themselves, ritual kinship legitimates the economic self-interests

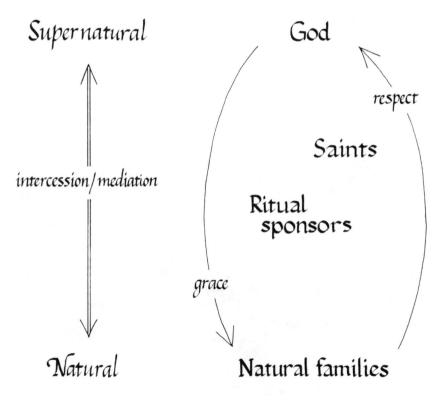

Fig. 4. Grace and Respect

and natural reproduction of individual families. To put it more precisely, the exchange of grace and respect is paralled by an implicit contractual relation in which reproduction and production in some families are sanctified in return for recognition of the higher social status held by others, the ritual sponsors.

Godparenthood

Many types of godparenthood are found in Tlayacapan. The most important are those of baptism, confirmation, First Communion, and marriage, which villagers say are *de sacramento* (sacramental). In addition, there are various nonsacramental types of godparenthood.

Godparenthood comprises two sets of relationships: *padrinazgo*, which links godparents and godchild, and *compadrazgo*, which links parents and the child's godparents. The godfather is the *padrino*, the godmother, the *madrina* (the words are etymologically related to *padre* [father] and *madre* [mother]). The godchild is the *ahijado(a)*, which derives from *hijo(a)* (child). The parents and godparents are compadres (co-parents) to each other, the men being known as compadres and the women as comadres.

The godmother and godfather of baptism present the infant with new clothes and accompany the father and infant to the church (the mother usually remains at home). The godparents carry the infant together, the godmother or godfather supporting the child's head, depending on whether the godchild is a girl or boy. After the ceremony, the godfather pays the priest and thanks him. Leaving the church, the godfather throws coins to children waiting on the steps.[2] Later, the parents hold a *mole* fiesta in their home for the godparents.

The baptismal godparents also accompany the parents and godchild to the *sacamisa* (churching, or blessing, of the mother at her first mass after parturition). The *sacamisa* may follow the baptism by a week or two, although there is no rule about the lapse of time; some people baptize a child and go to the *sacamisa* on the same day. The Virgin Mary's *sacamisa* is represented by Candelaria, which falls on February 2, or forty days after Christ's birth. Older informants say that the *sacamisa* used to occur six months after birth. The godparents also give new clothes to the godchild for the *sacamisa*. If the two events occur on the same day, the godchild's clothes are changed after the baptism. Sometime after the *sacamisa*, say a week or two later, the parents send the godparents a turkey as a token of their appreciation.

The godparents of confirmation and First Communion also buy special clothes for their godchildren. For both ceremonies only a godparent of the same sex accompanies the child to the church, although it is understood that the godparent's spouse is virtually a godparent. The godparents of these events are also invited to banquets in the homes of the godchildren's parents following the ceremonies.

Sacramental clothing is expensive, but even heavier burdens fall on the marriage godparents. They pay for the music of the wedding dance. The bride's and groom's godparents of baptism, confirmation, and First Communion participate in the ceremonial preparation by making gifts of turkeys for the wedding fiesta.

Several nonsacramental types of godparenthood begin with the blessings of persons and objects. The church as a matter of standard practice provides for the blessings of persons to mark stages of development or to aid recuperation from illness as well as for the blessings of ritual objects and edifices, homes, animals and seeds, and tools and machines. The rationale for such blessings is the belief that the Fall affected not only human beings, but the whole of nature. It follows that a Christian community depends on the sacramental redemption of both human beings and those things in nature that serve human purposes. According to church doctrine, the blessings do not confer sanctifying grace, but their function is clearly analogous and complementary to those of the Eucharist and the sacraments. Blessings are thought to provide remission from venial sin and freedom from the power of evil spirits. Almost invariably they use holy water, which ultimately derives from the baptismal font (Morrisroe 1907). The similarity between the sacrament of baptism and blessings in folk culture is implied in the custom of having special godparents sponsor blessings.

In Tlayacapan a special godparent is chosen to sponsor the blessing of a new house. The godparent brings the priest, pays him, and may provide rockets and music as well. (The adobe worker puts up the house cross on May 3.) Similarly, villagers seek godparents to sponsor the blessings of new trucks, tractors, and commercial mills and tortilla-making machines. For example, the godparent will decorate a new tractor with flowers, whereupon the tractor is driven to the church door for the priest's blessing. Afterwards there is a fiesta of *mole* or barbecued goat's meat at the owner's home.

Moments of transition in the life cycle apart from those marked by the sacraments also require godparents. A godparent is selected to sponsor a child's graduation from primary school, and a special godparent is required when a young woman turns fifteen—when she has "completed fifteen springs." A special saint's day celebration is held for her, for which a godfather *de quince años* (of fifteen years) is required. Following attendance at a mass, there is a *mole* fiesta in the parents' home and then a dance with music. The young woman wears a bright red dress, high heels, and new jewelry. She is accompanied by fifteen *damas* in red or blue dresses and a *chambelán*, or young man, who wears a dark suit or black cardigan sweater. The young woman advises her parents of her choice for the *chambelán*, and it is understood that he may become her fiancé and groom. Usually, the parents purchase the clothing and the godfather pays for the music. Godparents also play an important role during the final transition, death. A special godparent is selected to provide the wooden cross for the funerary ritual (see chapter 9).

Most forms of compadrazgo, especially the several types of compadrazgo *de sacramento*, entail expectations of enduring solidarity. Compadres address each other with the respectful *usted* (you), not the familiar *tú* (thou) used with friends and children, and they show their mutual respect in other ways as well. When compadres meet in the street they greet each other and often shake hands; noncompadres may or may not greet each other but they do not stop to shake hands. Favors and tokens of mutual regard are frequently exchanged between households linked by compadrazgo. Comadres send each other baskets of food, and men may help each other with fieldwork and house repairs, loans, and political favors. Compadres are always invited to family fiestas. Villagers themselves emphasize the importance of the mutual respect that compadres feel for one another. With compadres, they say, one has *confianza* (trust).

Since sexual relations between parents and godparents are considered even worse than adultery, compadrazgo ensures a degree of trust regarding sexual behavior. Men and women alike are less inclined to mistrust the sexual intentions of their compadres and comadres. Of course, it is possible that this trust may be used to conceal illicit sexual relations. Such transgressions, however, are subject to supernatural punishment. It is said that a comadre and compadre were enchanted—turned to stone—after having sexual relations during a peregrination to the sacred shrine at Chalma. Jokes are told about compadres and comadres who have sex together, but it seems unlikely that they reflect common practice. They are amusing because they describe outrageous departures from moral behavior.

Compadrazgo is sometimes sought to improve relations that are becoming strained. Men who abuse each other when drinking together in cantinas, for example, may become compadres to preserve their friendship. Compadres avoid drinking together in informal settings to avoid such abusive interaction, because it is incompatible with the canons of deference and respect in compadrazgo. Compadrazgo may be superimposed on employer-employee and store owner (creditor)–customer relations, making them more secure and harmonious.

Godparenthood in Tlayacapan brings into being an extensive network of positive, sacred relationships among separate households. Occasionally, parents ask kin who live in the same household to serve as godparents; parents and siblings are not eligible for the roles, but grandparents and aunts and uncles may be asked to serve. In most cases, nonrelatives living in other households are preferred. The multiplicity of bonds ensues not only from this preference for godparents who are outside the family but from the various types of compadrazgo and the many children in most families. There is also a tendency for the network of compadrazgo to ramify in conformity with existing natural and ritual kinship relations. Thus, the parents of the godchild's natural parents and the parents of the godparents may address each other as compadres, as though they were cograndparents. At weddings, all the godparents of the bride and groom become compadres to the marriage godparents, since they are godparents of the same people.

The size of a family's compadrazgo network is partly a matter of choice. People may elect not to serve as godparents in particular instances, and parents may postpone the sacraments for their children. Some compadrazgo relations may be allowed to languish, although usually those that do are nonsacramental. Moreover, redundancies are possible. Marriage godparents often sponsor the baptism of the first child of the marriage, and the baptismal godparents of one child may become baptismal godparents to other children in the same family. However, confirmation, First Communion, and baptismal godparents and the various kinds of nonsacramental godparents are usually different people. Even with redundancy, the compadrazgo networks of most families remain extensive.

Symbolic Asymmetry and Social Hierarchy

The formal relations established between two families through compadrazgo are conceptually and ritually asymmetric. The notions of spiritual parenthood and natural parenthood imply inequality (Ingham 1970b); spirit is higher and more perfect than nature (see also Gudeman 1972, 1975). In keeping with this categorical asymmetry, the obligations of godparents and parents are not the same. Mutual respect characterizes both *padrinazgo* and compadrazgo, but on balance more respect is accorded the godparents because they occupy the honored position in the two sets of relations. When greeting godparents, the godchild addresses them with the respectful *usted* and kisses their hands. This gesture of kissing the hand is even extended to the parents of the godparents. In addition, there is a subtle but discernible tendency for parents to show more deference to godparents than they receive in turn.

Material obligations are similarly asymmetric. In godparenthood, the godparent has the immediate obligation to buy clothing for the godchild and the long-term obligation to aid the child as he or she grows up. There is also an implicit understanding that compadres may be called on for favors, and such requests are usually directed at the one likely to be the wealthier of the two compadres in a compadrazgo relationship. Although the fiesta the parents give the godparents is costly, on the whole, the economic expenses of the godparents exceed those of the natural parents.

The asymmetry between the spiritual and natural parents is evidenced in a lack of reciprocal godparent selection. Choice reversal, in other words, is rare. When a couple agrees to serve as godparents for a child, they do not later ask the godchild's parents to be godparents to their children. Gudeman (1975) notes that choice reversal would confuse the distinction between spiritual and natural parenthood; each couple would be at once spiritual natural to the other. Of course, all parents are natural parents in relation to their own children, but this fact is conveniently forgotten in the context of godparenthood; what counts is that the relation between the two sets of parents be defined in terms of their relations to particular children.

The asymmetry in godparenthood is not merely a matter of symbolism or ritual. The distinction between spiritual and natural is projected on socioeconomic differences between families: spiritual parents are often wealthier than their natural counterparts.

This pattern is illustrated by a sample of baptismal godparent selections drawn from my 1966 census of the village. The sample includes 155 godparents of children three years of age or younger at the time of the census. (Of 186 children in this age group, 10 had not been baptized, and 21 others were excluded because it seemed desirable to include only 1 child per family.) The data show that compadrazgo is asymmetric regarding socioeconomic status between communities and within the community. Some Tlayacapenses have godchildren in nearby hamlets but the reverse hardly occurs. By contrast, 15 percent of the baptismal godparents selected by residents of Tlayacapan live in larger towns and cities, and many of these outside godparents are politicians, professional people, or owners of successful businesses. Table 5, which compares the status of godparents with that of the families that selected them, reveals the trend toward upward choices within the community. However, given that the poor outnumber the wealthy, the question turns not only on the percentage of upward choices but also on the difference between the a priori probability of a selection pattern (given the population's distribution by status), and the actual distribution of selection by status category. The comparison of the status distributions of godparents' households with the distribution of all village households demonstrates that choices are strongly skewed toward the higher categories (table 6; see Ingham 1970b).

Table 5
Socioeconomic Status of Parents and Godparents, Tlayacapan

Households of Parents	Households of Godparents				
	0-4	5-8	9-12	13+	Out-of-Town
0-4	6	28	13	2	10
5-8	5	29	19	4	9
9-12	2	9	11	1	5
13+	0	1	1	0	0

Source: After Ingham (1970b)

Table 6
Deviation between Status Distributions of Godparent
Selections and Households, Tlayacapan

	0-4	5-8	Status 9-12	13+	N
% of godparent choices	9.9	51.2	33.6	5.3	131
% of total households	38.0	42.3	16.5	3.2	503

Source: After Ingham (1970b)

Even though social hierarchy affects selection, many families choose godparents among their social equals or near equals. Some wealthy persons never ask to serve as godparents and refuse when asked (although such refusal adds to their reputations for being selfish), and many villagers try to limit their ritual obligations. For their part, poorer villagers say that entertaining wealthy compadres with humble resources can be embarrassing, and most villagers prefer to avoid indebtedness to more powerful persons, even though their patronage can sometimes prove helpful. The costs of fiestas that honor godparents also deter upward selection insofar as wealthy compadres deserve a special effort. Indeed, villagers adopt various strategies to reduce the costs and entanglements of compadrazgo. One strategy is to intensify previous relations, which, as a result, carry less additional burden; of those surveyed, 21 percent of baptismal godparents represent repetitions of previous selections, and 17 percent were described as relatives. To avoid expenses, parents may delay baptism, confirmation, and First Communion, since there is "not enough food in the house." Or, the child may be baptized and another confirmed on the same day, and both may be celebrated with one fiesta instead of two.

The Sanctification of Reproduction and Production

Much attention has been given to the relationship between co-parents in the literature on compadrazgo, but we should not lose sight of padrinazgo, godparenthood as such, since from the point of view of religious doctrine, it is fundamental.

The sacraments that godparents sponsor are rites of passage. Their common purpose is to promote the development of spirituality and to incorporate the person, despite his or her natural origin, into the spiritual community. Many ongoing godparental responsibilities are aimed at furthering this end. Above all, the godparents are supposed to be the moral guardians of and counselors to their godchildren.

Baptismal godparents have a duty to advise their godchildren on correct behavior, to encourage parents to send a godchild to school, and to make sure that a godchild is confirmed and receives his or her First Communion.

When a godchild is still young, the godparents should aid the parents if the child becomes seriously ill; and if the child dies, they are supposed to help with the costs of the funeral. If a godchild is orphaned, godparents should offer to become step-parents. Godparents of confirmation and First Communion, too, are expected to give good advice on manners and morals. Wedding godparents are charged with the responsibility of reminding their godchildren—the bride and groom—of their wedding vows when they quarrel.

The godfather of *quince años* performs a particularly interesting function in moral education. In various respects, the celebration of a young woman's fifteenth birthday calls attention to her sexuality. The jewelry, high heels, and bright red dress seem to signal her eligibility for courtship and marriage. The color red, which also figures in the curing of *susto*, may have a sympathetic relation to blood, a repository of a young woman's *naturaleza*. A birthday is at once a celebration of a natural event and a celebration of one's saint's day and a commemoration of christening. And indeed, the activities in the fiesta of *quince años* have both spiritual and natural connotations: the young woman and fiesta party first attend mass and later partake of a ritual banquet; following the banquet, the young woman dances with her godfather and father and then with the *chambelán*. The most important duty of the godfather of fifteen years is to take the young woman aside and to tell her about men and how she should comport herself (for example, she is a woman now and should act like one; she should be wary of men, for some are not gentlemen; she should not fall in love with just anyone). The birthday festivities acknowledge the young woman's natural readiness for marriage but also aim at moral preparation for courtship.

The association between godparenthood and moral education may explain the custom of selecting special godparents to sponsor graduation from primary school: graduation from school may be analogous to confirmation, a graduation from catechism class. Both graduation and confirmation mark stages in moral development, something that concerns godparents. In this respect, graduation and confirmation are themselves like baptism, which is the spiritual or moral counterpart of natural birth. The word *matriculación*, meaning registration for school, implies that entering school is like entering a womb. The Latin expression "alma mater" carries this same implication. Graduation, or leaving school, then, is a moral birth, and so, given the underlying logic of sacraments and godparenthood, it requires the sponsorship of special godparents.

This interpretation seems particularly plausible in view of the inclusion of civics and ethical instruction in the public school curriculum in Tlayacapan. School children learn to read, write, and do sums, but they also learn about patriotism and citizenship. Speeches during graduation ceremonies place great stress on the civic and moral responsibilities accompanying education.

Delivered by the village priest, civil authorities, and outstanding students, they emphasize that educated persons have a duty to use their knowledge for the good of the community and the nation. What is being hatched at graduation ceremonies, then, is a civil, moral person.

Persons who are often asked to be godparents are not merely wealthier than most villagers, nor are the motives for asking them strictly utilitarian. Wealthy persons with reputations for selfishness or immoral behavior are not popular choices, whereas wealthy persons who exhibit traits of good character are much more apt to be selected. The most popular choices in the 1960s included a schoolteacher, several enterprising truck farmers, a sober but friendly store owner, and a young man who was doing well as a university student.

It is thought rather tasteless to use compadrazgo solely for personal gain, and villagers are reluctant even to discuss the practical advantages of the institution. Explicit motives are more likely to focus on the idea of selecting persons who are models of civic responsibility, moral comportment, and industriousness. Apparently, the hope is that some of these qualities will rub off on the godchild. Another hope may be that successful godparents will be able to exert influence for the godchild by helping him or her to enter secondary school or college or to find stable employment. There are benefits for the parents, as grown children are expected to help their elderly parents, but consciously, at least, parents consider the welfare of their children when making godparent selections.

The obligation to adopt an orphaned godchild is taken seriously; my census uncovered an instance of such adoption, although, admittedly, few children are orphaned and even fewer are orphaned and left without relatives to care for them. Godparents also offer advice to godchildren, although less often than one might expect from the ideal formulations of their duties. The implicit understandings in godparenthood, though, may be just as influential as the actual behavior of godparents. The mere existence of godparents reminds parents of the importance of moral education. Children learn to show respect for authority when interacting with them and are taught to admire them. Godparents are social models, even when they do not actively intervene in a child's education. Moreover, there is some evidence that they are thought to exert a mystical influence on their godchildren. In the rite of *evangelios*, for example, godparents with "strong character" touch a patient, thereby conveying some of their strength to the patient.

Sacramental rites of passage, then, sanction natural and social reproduction. The sacrament of the marriage ceremony legitimates the offspring of a union, and the rite of baptism cleanses children of the taint of sin associated with natural procreation; later, the rites of passage requiring godparents mark the child's moral and educational development. It could be argued that the blessing of homes indirectly legitimates reproduction, as the marital bed is within the home. Indeed, the church has a special blessing for bridal chambers, although to my knowledge no requests for it are made in Tlayacapan.

Blessings also sanction production. Some productive activities take place in the home, so in this respect the blessing of a home sanctifies both reproduction and production. Moreover, specific blessings and godparents are sought for seeds, animals, and equipment (the blessings of seeds and animals do not require special godparents). The reasoning may be that such things are like newborn babies. By asking a fellow villager to sponsor their benediction and giving a small fiesta, as in other types of compadrazgo, the new owner legitimates objects that otherwise could become targets of negative social reaction.

The social significance of this legitimation must be understood against the background of the interests that divide families. Children represent a family's ability to mobilize labor in its struggle to survive and prosper. Along with land and the tools of production, children—especially sons—are the basis of a family's strength. The concepts of children and family are almost synonymous. It is hardly surprising, therefore, that children as well as material possessions are thought to be targets of destructive envy.

A family's network of ritual kin lessens the envy and resentments of others. Godparents often are socially important people, a characteristic that adds credibility to their roles as protectors of godchildren. Godparents need not covet their godchildren or their siblings, for they are in a sense the godparents' own children. When a man wants to tell his compadres that he is the father of a new baby, he may say, "Now you have another creature to order about," as if to say, "All my children are your children." Moreover, the fiestas held in conjunction with the sacraments offer the family an opportunity to show its generosity and thereby to invite the good will of others.

Baptism, blessings, and godparenthood compose a system that both legitimates the social status of spiritual parents—often high social status— and sanctifies production and reproduction by the natural family. The system, in other words, entails an implicit reciprocity between two households: the actual status of one is sanctioned in return for the sanction of production and reproduction in the other. The institution of godparent- hood validates the differences that set families apart yet bonds them together.

The Fiesta

Whereas baptism is the ritual device by which the young and the heathen are recruited into the spiritual family, the mass is the focus of worship within the church. It is the central event in the collective life of the spiritual family. The breaking of bread and drinking of wine commemorate the Last Supper and give thanks. They also signify Christ's presence: the wine and bread are thought to be the body, blood, soul, and divinity of Christ. Because this mystic body of Christ is at one with the church, there is a sense in which communion is established with both the rest of the congregation and the divinity.

From the earliest days of Christianity, ritual meals have been focal in religious celebrations. The agape, or love feast, in which members of a congregation took food together was a central custom in the first Christian communities, one with deep historical roots. W. Robertson Smith (1889) showed that among the ancient Semites and Arabs the sacrificial meal effected communion between the social group and its deity and signified the solidarity of the group itself. The sacrificial animal incorporated into the meal had a sympathetic relation to the blood of the group as well as to the divinity. These themes, Smith noted, persisted in the Eucharist, in which Christ's blood and body also are thought to represent a sacrifice that mediates between the community of believers and the divinity.

Some uncertainty attends the question of whether the sacramental breaking of bread and drinking of wine were part of or separate from the agape. In any event, the sacrament became a distinct rite performed in a church, whereas ritual commensality outside the church persisted, no doubt with the understanding that it was a nonsacramental commemoration of the Last Supper and, at the same time, a celebration of fellowship in the community (Deiss 1976).

The religious feast or banquet in Tlayacapan represents a continuation of this tradition. Fiestas are generally combined with the mass or Eucharist, but whereas the latter takes place in the church or chapel, the fiesta occurs in a private home. The fiesta meal has three courses: a plate of rice, followed by a bowl containing a portion of turkey in the reddish-brown *mole* sauce (made with chocolate, chiles, tomatoes, and many other ingredients), and then by a bowl of large brown beans garnished with lettuce, radishes, and cheese. Nowadays beer and bottled liquor are served along with the more traditional rum drinks. In the colder months these drinks include hot punches made from fruit juice and sugar. Throughout the year men may also drink *toros* (bulls), which are made of cane alcohol or rum, flavored with anise or lemon peel. Interestingly, people jokingly liken blood to *mole* sauce and they refer to all hard liquor, including rum, as "wine."

The sharing of the ritual meal is an emotionally moving and meaningful moment of communion and fellowship, noteworthy for its conviviality. The mood of enjoyment and togetherness is conspicuously different from the somberness and aloofness that tend to characterize demeanor at other times. When Tlayacapenses want to affirm that they are truly good friends with someone, they say that they know the person *hasta el mole*, to the point of sharing *mole*.

There are, then, two parallels between the natural and spiritual families. Both are reproduced through some type of generation and both are sustained through commensality. In one instance the generation is natural, whereas in the other it is mysterious; in one, ordinary food gives natural life to families, whereas in the other, ritual food gives spiritual life to the neighborhood or community.

Fiestas occur in conjunction with various events. Some memorialize saints' days (birthdays) or religious rites of passage in the family; others are more communal celebrations of saints, including images of Mary and Jesus. Some fiestas honor the patron saints of neighborhoods; others are more inclusive and honor saints that are supported by all or large segments of the village: San Juan Bautista, San Nicolás, the Señor de la Tres Caídas, the Virgen de Guadalupe, the Virgen del Tránsito, the Virgen de la Asunción, the Niño Dios, the Santo Entierro, the Santo de la Resurrección, and the Señor de Chalma.

Fiesta Sponsorship and Socioeconomic Status

Barrio and village fiestas are organized and funded by groups of men and women called *mayordomías* or *hermandades* (brotherhoods). These groups include several ranked mayordomos and various lesser mayordomos or assistants and their wives. The banquet, including the alcohol, is the responsibility of the principal mayordomos and is held in the home of the first mayordomo. The mass, music, and fireworks are organized by assistants in two or three committees called *comisiones* (some informants refer to these committees as *hermandades*). The committees solicit small supporting contributions from compadres, friends, and neighbors.

The costs of the fiesta are shared by the mayordomos, "by equal parts," as they say, but they are nonetheless serious for most villagers and even prohibitive for the poor. The expenses are especially heavy for the first mayordomo. Even though the mayordomos try to shoulder expenses evenly, the first mayordomo is expected to entertain his associates and pay for miscellaneous items, and so he contributes somewhat more. In a major village fiesta a first mayordomo contributes about thirteen hundred pesos (roughly a peon's wages for two months), whereas the others contribute about one thousand pesos each; and in barrio fiestas, a first mayordomo may spend about six hundred pesos and his associates, slightly less.

The most expensive ritual office is that of the mayordomo of the Niño Dios. The mayordomo contributes seven thousand pesos or more to the fiesta of Candelaria, which celebrates both the Virgen de la Candelaria and the Niño Dios. In contrast to the sponsorship of other fiestas, there are no supporting mayordomos for these. Many families, nonetheless, want to sponsor the fiesta, often to express appreciation to the image for help in curing an illness in the family. The mayordomo and his wife, the mayordoma, are said to represent the parents of the Niño Dios. The sponsorship of the Niño Dios is also unusual in that the image has a special godparent who purchases clothes for the saint and serves sherbet and pastries in his honor on Christmas Eve.

Assisting in the festivities associated with the Niño Dios are fifteen to twenty elderly women known as Tenanches (from the Nahuatl, *tenantzin*: a mother). They are known as the "grandmothers" of the Christ Child and are led by a *madre mayor* (senior mother). Together, they train the young people who play the roles of Joseph, Mary, the Angel, the Shepherds, and the Three Kings in the various processions. In addition, they solicit contributions to pay the priest for the masses that are held in honor of the Niño Dios. In keeping with the understanding that the mayordomo and mayordoma of the Niño Dios represent his parents, the godparents of the Niño Dios and the mayordomos address one another as compadres.

Mayordomos occasionally nominate a man who is reluctant to serve, although more often a candidate asks the current mayordomos for the privilege of serving the saint in the next term of office. Before making a commitment, however, the candidate consults with compadres and friends to make sure he can in turn enlist enough supporting mayordomos. Ordinarily, he asks six or more men to help him in this fashion. The mayordomos usually honor the first request as long as the applicant resides in their neighborhood. In barrio fiestas, this restriction is not so rigorously applied as formerly, though, and men are sometimes allowed to serve if they simply live in the same quarter of the village. The names of the mayordomos for the ensuing year are announced following the feast; nominees kneel and rockets are launched outside in their honor. Nominations for mayordomo of the fiesta of the Niño Dios are ordinarily made on January 6. In 1966 the waiting list held about twenty names, so people nominate their young sons, knowing that they probably will be fully grown when their turns come around.

The symbolic structure of sponsorship (see fig. 4) and the economic burdens entailed by mayordomos imply that they tend to have high socioeconomic status. According to my 1966 census, the characteristics of eighteen mayordomos of barrio- and village-level fiestas who served during 1970-1971 give only qualified support to this expectation, however. The mayordomos were average with respect to the scale of socioeconomic status (table 7). Yet, they were unusual in other ways. Seventy-eight percent had ejido or communal land in 1966, in contrast to 52 percent of other heads of households, and 78 percent were involved in tomato planting, in contrast to 45 percent of other household heads. These data suggest that mayordomos have more disposable income than their homes and household durables would seem to indicate and they imply that mayordomos depend more on communal resources and positive labor relations than do other men.

Table 7
Mayordomos and Socioeconomic Status, Tlayacapan

	0-4	5-8	Status 9-12	13+	N
% of mayordomos	33.0	61.0	0.0	6.0	18
% of households	38.0	42.3	16.5	3.2	503

Meanwhile, the wealthiest stratum of Tlayacapan is underrepresented in the sample. Many of the wealthy households have invested in land and large tomato gardens and even in trucks and tractors, not to mention household durables. Given their stronger economic position, the wealthy can use more purely economic means in competing for labor. For them, the social and economic returns on ritual expenses are less compelling.

This aloofness of the wealthy from the *mayordomía* system is not a recent development. Members of the pre-1910 elite occasionally served as godparents to the poor villagers, and the shopkeepers among them gave Christmas posadas; otherwise their participation in the system of ritual redistribution was limited. My oldest informants were sure that the "people of the plaza" ordinarily did not participate in the *mayordomías*. The one exception to this rule was the *mayordomía* of the Señor de las Tres Caídas. The elite viewed this saint as their special patron and regarded his fiesta as their exclusive preserve; they expressed their disdain for Indian fiestas by serving Spanish cuisine in place of turkey *mole*, an Indian food.

The egalitarian and communal character of fiesta organization may be rooted in its Hispanic predecessor, the cofradía (confraternity), a voluntary sodality organized around a patron saint (Foster 1953). On the eve of the saint's day the members of the confradía gathered in the house of the mayordomo. Carrying lighted candles and their cofradía standard and accompanied by music, they walked to the church for the saying of creeds. On the day of the feast a mass was held at which the saint was eulogized as an exemplar worthy of emulation by all the members of the cofradía. The costs of the feast were met by the levy of periodic assessments and fines on members for infractions of various and sundry confradía rules. Members also assisted the families of deceased brothers with funeral expenses.

Although *mayordomías* throughout rural Mexico derive at least in part from the Hispanic cofradía, some retain more of its features than others. Those of Tlayacapan seem to have changed little, despite the effects of syncretism and changing social conditions since the conversion. Aid to bereaved families and widows within the sodality is no longer a feature of the institution, but otherwise both the ritual and the organization of the *mayordomía* retain a strong likeness to the cofradía. Membership in the Hispanic cofradía was for life and entailed an enduring and, presumably, somewhat exclusive loyalty to its patron saint. Similarly, *mayordomías* are formed within barrios whose members have an ongoing fealty to their patron saints. Even saints revered by more than one barrio often draw most of their support from particular major barrios or wards. In these respects, the system in Tlayacapan seems to differ from those found in some Mexican communities in which men advance through a hierarchy of religious offices, each associated with a particular saint.

The *mayordomía* system in Tlayacapan further resembles the Hispanic cofradía in that financial support for the fiestas is broadly based within the barrio or ward. The burden of a fiesta is borne not merely by one or two mayordomos, as in some communities, but by several mayordomos and, to a lesser degree, by many other families. As in other parts of Middle America, the trend is toward an even broader sharing of ritual responsibility; where six to twelve mayordomos were sufficient in 1965, by 1984 some *mayordomías* had as many as thirty-five (see Brandes 1981a).

There is an informal stratification of religious offices in Tlayacapan. Village-level fiestas are more elaborate and costly than the barrio fiestas, and the offices of first mayordomo, secondary mayordomos, and helpers in the *hermandades* vary in prestige and responsibility. Even so, the offices are not explicitly ranked and entry into them occurs at every level.

If the parallels with the Hispanic cofradía are clear, it nonetheless seems plausible to argue that the fiesta system is rooted in pre-Hispanic practice. *Calpultin*, wards, and communities had patron deities, which were honored in annual festivals. These were organized by the nobles or elders, yet the costs of the festivals were borne at least in part by the commoners, who paid tribute to the *calpulli* chiefs to defray the expenses of organizing the festivals. Indeed, the colonial custom of granting usufruct to house sites and fields in exchange for tribute in support of the barrio fiesta seems to derive from the pre-Hispanic arrangement. The institution of chapel lands worked under the direction of the mayordomos apparently has both pre-Hispanic and European origins.[3]

Ritual

Fiestas celebrating a person's saint's day or birthday are called *cuelgas*. The guests bring necklaces of small circles of bread called *rosarios*. Large pieces of bread are also given. Traditionally, guests come with their gifts (usually bread, and possibly small bottles of perfume for girls or a bottle of liquor if the celebration is for adults) on the eve of the saint's day and are served hot chocolate and bread. The next day they either return for a *mole* fiesta or are sent portions of *mole*.

At dawn on the morning of the saint's day itself friends and relatives sing

"Las mañanitas," the traditional birthday song. In the afternoon there is a *mole* fiesta. Following the meal, the birthday person is seated in front of the family altar, while others gather around. One or two men play their guitars and sing "Las mañanitas" and other songs; the guests step forward and place crowns of flowers on the head of the honored person, sprinkle colored confetti, and place the *rosarios* around her or his neck. They may also present a bouquet of flowers. In one *cuelga* I witnessed, not only the honored man but his spouse and a relative were lavished with this treatment. Later, guests may again be served hot chocolate and bread.

The mayordomos' activities begin with a ritual called the *recibimiento* (reception), which usually occurs in May. In it the *santitos* (little saints) are brought to their new homes. The large images of the saints are housed in the main church or their respective chapels, but smaller, doll-like images are kept in places of honor in the homes of the first mayordomos, each in its own small wood and glass catafalque. These *santitos* are said to "walk among the houses," to travel from year to year from the house of one mayordomo to that of the next. After gracing the house of a first mayordomo for one year, the *santito* is carried in a procession to the home of a new first mayordomo. The procession is made up of the actual mayordomos and mayordomas, a boy or girl, members of the committees and spouses, a band, and the *santito*. The women lead the way in two files carrying censers and candles; they are followed by the *santito*, which is carried by a boy if it is a male saint or a girl if it is a female saint or Virgin; the mayordomos and musicians bring up the rear. Among them are men who fire off exploding rockets from time to time. Outside the house of the new first mayordomo, the mayordomos set up a table where the *santito* will be placed. When it arrives the first mayordomo hands the catafalque to the new first mayordomo, who places it on the table. One by one the new mayordomos cross themselves and place chains of *cacalozuchil*, a sweet-smelling yellowish flower, on the catafalque while their wives hold lighted candles. When this reception is over, the mayordomas blow out their candles and place them on the table, which is then brought inside, where all the principals and guests who have gathered for the ceremony are served homemade sherbet and pastries. Men are served rum as well.

Following the liturgical calendar, a fiesta is held in honor of the saint once a year. The actual day of the feast is preceded by nine days of rosary in the chapel or church. The *santito* is taken to the chapel for the last of the rosaries and placed on a pedestal before the altar.

In the morning and again at noon on the day before the saint's day, a band gathers in front of the chapel or church to play the *serenata*. In the evening, band members climb to the roof of the chapel or church to play. Afterward, the band retires to the first mayordomo's house for a meal of white beans and dried fish in green *mole* sauce. Throughout the night young women sing *alabanzas* (praises) at the chapel or church, and in the early morning the band returns; at dawn, the young women sing "Las mañanitas" to the accompaniment of the band. Later in the morning there is a mass. In the afternoon people congregate at the home of the first mayordomo for the three-course fiesta banquet. The guests include members of the band, former and incoming mayordomos, their families, and perhaps compadres and friends and their families. All these people may bring their own compadres and friends, ensuring a large gathering and necessitating a prodigious amount of food and beverage.

Formerly, comic risqué dances were performed by Tenanches and Retores ("teachers," old men who knew the traditions and collected firewood, *metates,* and contributions for the fiestas) following the banquet and the nomination of new mayordomos. In the most notable of these dances, the Xochipitzahua, a woman carried a tray that held red flowers and a turkey head with a peso in its beak as her male partner offered flavored rum or *toros* to the spectators. The bystanders in turn placed coins on the tray to help defray the mayordomos' expenses.

My informants remembered only the first two stanzas of the accompanying song:

> Xochipitzahua del alma mía,
> ¿adónde me llevas, a la tierra fría?
> Xochipitzahua de mi corazón,
> ¿adónde me llevas, a la oración?
>
> Cuando era yo muchacho,
> que sombrero con toquilla.
> Ahora que soy un viejito,
> un sombrero de a cuartilla.
>
> (Xochipitzahua of my soul,
> where are you taking me, to the cold country?
> Xochipitzahua of my heart,
> where are you taking me, to the prayer?
>
> When I was a boy,
> I had a hat with trim.
> Now that I am old,
> it's worth mere pennies.)

Xochipitzahua, the lyrics imply, is a sirenlike figure who takes a man to perdition. The references to the man's hats in the second stanza probably allude to youthful virility and elderly impotence; in men's street language, "hat" is a standardized metaphor for the male organ.

In another dance, la Sarna (the Scratch), the Tenanches and Retores scratched at each other's bodies:

¡Ráscale, ta lan, ta lan!
¡Ráscale, ta lan, ta lan!
¡Ráscale las barrigas!
¡Ráscale las barrigas!

(Scratch, ta lan ta lan!
Scratch, ta lan ta lan!
Scratch the stomachs!
Scratch the stomachs!)

Yet another song played on the word *pan* (bread), a euphemism for the female sex organ:

Estos son panaderos,
que bien saben trabajar.
A las once de la noche,
tienen que entregar el pan.

(These are bread makers,
who well know how to work.
At eleven at night,
they must deliver the bread.)

Several fiestas embellish this pattern in peculiar ways. Some include bull riding. Because Santiago is a mounted warrior, displays of horsemanship accompany his fiesta. Young men on horseback charge down the main street of the barrio and attempt to lance with pencil-sized sticks some small rings that hang by little ribbons from a taut rope. The ribbons bear the names of young women who trade large ribbons for captured rings. The youths also try to decapitate a rooster that has been hung from a line by its feet. Traditionally, the fiesta of the Señor de la Exaltación included the Dance of the Santiagueros, the Dance of the Pastorcitas, and the Dance of the Vaqueros, although in recent years the usual practice has been to combine the Dance of the Pastorcitas with Aztec dancers. Vaqueros have also been known to appear in the fiesta of the Virgen del Tránsito.

The Saints

According to church doctrine, the saints are persons who led virtuous lives and went to Heaven. Devotion to them should consist in part in the emulation of their virtues, just as the saints themselves followed in the footsteps of Christ. The saints, intercessors between Christ and human beings, complete Christ's work. Devotion to them, then, is also expressed in pious appeals for their assistance and in expressions of praise and gratitude. In the peasant cultures of Hispanic America, these orthodox ideas are reflected in a multiplicity of local images and customs. Saints are patrons of all manner of social groups, the givers of extraordinary favors and makers of miracles, and the objects of pilgrimages, honorific masses and feasts, and votive offerings (see Gudeman 1976b).

Since its inception, anthropological research in Mexico has focused primarily on their roles as patrons and advocates of persons and social collectivities. Saints, it has been repeatedly observed, are the patrons of neighborhoods, villages, regions, and entire countries. The names of communities often include the names of their saints, and individual persons are christened with saints' names. As there are four or five saints for every day in the year, the effect is a partition of time by the names of saints and a distribution of socially relevant festivals throughout the year. The saints, in effect, are symbols of social entities—persons and groups—and, viewed as a system, are a means of modeling social solidarity and diversity.

In addition, the saints are exemplars of moral behavior. They serve as models for ideal behavior for all villagers, but it is the ritual sponsors who most closely emulate their example. Like the saints, ritual sponsors provide for others and receive respect in return. The structure of the saint-feast sponsorship complex, then, is a variant of the sacrament/benediction–godparenthood complex; like sacraments, the saints mediate God's beneficent influence; and like godparents, mayordomos serve as instruments in this process. What is more, the blessings that are mediated by the saints are similar to those that are mediated by benedictions and blessings with holy water: most saints can be invoked to help the sick (usually children), and many are known to contribute to agrarian fertility in one way or another.

The role of the saints in curing illness is mentioned earlier in this chapter and in chapters 4 and 9. A few examples of their part in promoting the well-being of plants and animals will be presented here; still others are given in chapter 8.

Prayers to the Virgen de Rosario are thought to ward off plagues in the tomato patches (de la Peña 1980:275). Seeds for the next planting are blessed by the priest on Holy Saturday, a day when the Santo de la Resurrección, an image of the resurrected Christ, is carried in procession to symbolize Christ's rebirth. The Virgen de la Asunción decides who is going to have a good crop.

Santa María Magdalena, Santiago, and Santa Ana are thought to offer protection against strong winds and hail (ibid.:273-274). Mountaintop crosses and those in the barrios are thought to provide protection during the rainy season. It is believed that the cross of Altica can be carried in procession to end drought but it will be effective only if a priest participates; otherwise, the cross will be too heavy to carry. One of the two images of the crucified Christ kept in the chapel of Exaltación has a special power to bring rain. When the rains had not arrived as usual in the early summer of 1968, a procession was organized for this saint; scores of men and women joined in and thousands watched as the saint made the circuit of the entire village, passing by the main church and the other three major chapels before returning to the chapel of Exaltación. The rains began within hours of the procession and remained reliable throughout the remainder of the season. It was a "miracle," but the villagers, although pleased, were hardly surprised; the saint's miracles are commonplace, the expected quid pro quo of favors they do for him.

On January 17, the day of San Antonio (the saint who recovers lost animals), people take their animals to the church, where the priest sprinkles them with holy water and pronounces a benediction to protect them from harm. Tiny metal figures of animals are pinned to pictures of San Antonio on family altars. When an animal is lost, villagers put his picture in a box and tie a string around it. When the animal is found, its recovery is considered a "miracle," and the incarcerated saint is released and rewarded with the miniature image of the animal he has found.

The Fiesta as Ritual Kinship

Godparenthood and fiestas for the saints have been treated as separate phenomena in the anthropological literature and, in fact, they differ from one another in various respects (see Foster 1953). In this chapter I have suggested that the two institutions are complementary components of a system of ritual kinship: along with baptism and blessings, compadrazgo is an instrument for recruiting individuals into the spiritual family; ritual commensality is the principal activity within the spiritual family.

Some of the evidence favoring the inclusion of fiestas within a category of ritual kinship is linguistic. All the various sponsors of a fiesta are sometimes referred to as a brotherhood. Historically, fiesta organization derives from the Hispanic *cofradía*, a word that means "confraternity." *Mayordomo* means "steward" or "head of a great household."

Those who participate together in fiestas are often compadres. The mayordomos of a *mayordomía* are sometimes compadres to one another, and compadres are among the first to be invited to a fiesta. The close connection between godparenthood and the fiesta is apparent, too, in the fiestas parents give for sacramental godparents. A fiesta is to a considerable extent a gathering of compadres and comadres, and the initiation of compadrazgo occasions a fiesta.

The fiesta is similar to the Eucharist or Holy Communion, the central ritual of the church. The latter is clearly conceptualized as a spiritual family. It makes sense, therefore, that groups within the spiritual family that sponsor and share fiestas should be described in an idiom of spiritual brotherhood. At the same time, the fiesta is analogous to mundane commensality, which occurs within the home. More than any other activity, the taking of food from a mother or wife and the sharing of it under a common roof symbolize the togetherness of a family. In a fiesta, a mayordomo and mayordoma invite others to share food at their table and in their home, as if the invited guests were truly members of their family. For a special moment, they incorporate others into their home and family.

We can discern, moreover, a system of symbolic affinities that links fiesta participants, saints, and the members of the Holy Family, the nucleus of the spiritual family. One series of connections joins individuals (the honored subjects of birthday fiestas), saints, and the Niño Dios: individuals are identified with saints, and saints are identified with Jesus. Individuals are named after saints and celebrate their birthdays on those days of the ritual calendar that are dedicated to their namesakes. The images of the saints, in turn, recall persons who modeled their lives after the example of Jesus. Family fiestas honor individuals on their saints' days. Fiestas for the saints seem to commemorate their birthdays, whatever their actual birthdays may have been, and Christmas marks the birthday of Jesus. Fiestas for the saints are preceded by nine days of rosaries. Similarly, Christmas follows nine nights of posadas (see chapter 7). The similar periods of nine days before the celebrations probably correspond to the nine months of gestation preceding birth. Indeed, Catholic scholars have traced novenas (nine-day periods of ritual observance) to commemorations of Mary's pregnancy (Hilgers 1911). On the morning of their fiestas, the saints are greeted with "Las mañanitas," the traditional birthday song. It is sung for the Niño Dios on the morning of the first posada. The Niño Dios is itself a "little saint," the diminutive or infantlike version of the various adult images of Jesus Christ in village ritual.

Meanwhile, in a second series of linkages, ritual identifies the sponsors of the fiestas with Joseph and Mary, the parents of Jesus. The mayordomo and mayordoma of the Niño Dios are said to represent the image's parents; in keeping with this conception, the mayordomos and godparents of the Niño Dios as well as his grandmothers are all understood to be compadres to one another. Clearly, the mayordomos of the other saints act as parents toward the *santitos*. They receive and keep the latter as members of their own families, much as the mayordomos of the Niño Dios receive and keep his image. Parents may play the roles of Joseph and Mary when they stage a saint's day fiesta for their own child.

In addition, the identification of individual families with the Holy Family is repeated throughout the village insofar as every household has its own Niño Dios and nativity scene. By setting up a nativity scene, each family expresses commitment to the values symbolized by the Holy Family and Virgin Birth and indicates a willingness to participate in its more costly realizations.

Finally, we may note that Christmas ritual helps to inculcate the values of ritual kinship in general. Children play the parts of Mary and Joseph and the shepherds in the processions, and when they participate in the construction and enjoyment of nativity scenes and serve as godparents for the images of the Niño Dios in nearby households, they take their first step toward playing the roles of mayordomo and godparent.

6. The Faces of Evil

Unless they are couched in the idiom of ritual kinship, relations with others are commonly seen in negative terms, that is, as exemplifying the influence of the Devil. "Others" are variously said to be "shameless ones," "witches," "egoists," "wastrels," "drunkards," "chicken thieves," or troublemakers who stir up difficulties "with the tail of the Devil." What is more, the Devil and the various beings that make up what villagers sometimes call the "Devil's family" have a palpable presence, as though they too were members of local society. Unlike the saints, who have a beneficial effect on production and reproduction and support communality, the Devil and his servants harm production and reproduction and mock equitable exchange and positive patterns of reciprocity and redistribution. In short, they undermine the foundations of peasant existence and invert the symbolic and ritual content of spiritual kinship. In these respects, actions of the Devil and other evil beings may be said to symbolize threatening behavior and qualities of other persons.

Barrancas and Caves

Although church and chapels, homes, and fields enjoy the protection of crosses, there is the ever present danger that the evil forces lurking beyond may breach supernatural defenses. In the dark of night, witches may enter to suck blood from babies or cast spells on the houses themselves (the houses become "salted"). Fields also are vulnerable to evil influence. When they do not produce as expected, villagers may say they are "salted" and "lacking the benediction of God." They are also subject to harm by evil weather spirits and even the Devil himself.

Evil beings may frequent the streets outside homes but their abodes are barrancas, caves, sinkholes, and anthills. Barrancas in particular are often mentioned in tales about encounters with evil beings. Barrancas are intrusions of unruly wilderness amid an otherwise civilized landscape. Their banks are laced with thickets and underbush that make them notorious rendezvous for sexual liaisons. Moreover, the villagers believe that they harbor snakes and anthills. They are dumps for garbage and, sometimes, animal carcasses. During heavy rains they suddenly overflow with turgid, fast-running water, which erodes the adjacent topsoil and endangers livestock and even people. Pigs root in the garbage and wallow in the stagnant pools left by rains. These, however, are superficial characteristics. Ultimately, it is the phantasmagoric qualities of the barrancas that make them truly foreboding; they are asylums for miasma and monsters, passageways to the underworld.

Dreams about the barrancas illustrate their negative connotations; invariably the dreams are disturbing and terrifying. Typically, they concern loss of love, bodily injury, or death. For example, Doña Petra dreamed that she came upon an owl when walking in a dark barranca (the owl is an omen of death). Oscar dreamed that the barranca's water swept away his mother and sister. A young man recalled a dream in which he was suddenly attacked by a hideous snake as he paused to look at dirty water in a barranca (a portent of death in the family). Doña Juana recalled a dream about two snakes that slithered out when she lifted a box in her house; her husband killed one but the other escaped in the direction of a nearby barranca.

Tlayacapenses do not believe just anything. The traditional beliefs about supernatural beings become more credible with personal confirmation. People listen with interest to accounts of spooks and ghosts but they weigh them against their own experiences. Many people have encountered evil beings, usually near one or another barranca, and some have had such experiences repeatedly. When asked to describe evil beings, the villagers oblige by reiterating customary beliefs, but they warm to the topic when they begin to recollect what they themselves have witnessed.

Their tales show that certain situations and mental states are more conducive to demonic visitations than are others. The perception of evil figures, unlike perception per se, is facilitated, not diminished, by darkness. Women walking along unlit paths without the protection of menfolk are alert to suspicious shapes and sudden movements in the shadows. Drunk men staggering home through dimly lighted side streets or following pitch-black barrancas after a night of revelry have a special propensity for stumbling, as it were, into supernatural danger of one sort or another.

In keeping with their social roles, men and women react differently to these situations. Both may be frightened, but men tend to react aggressively, women passively. Men may follow an apparition or even try to threaten it, whereas women, after seeing something unnerving, are apt to hurry home, maybe to ponder ways of reinforcing the home's magical defenses. One can sense in accounts of experiences with evil figures that cultural conceptions of maleness and femaleness are being expressed and confirmed. Women more often than men are the victims of evil spirits, as befits women's view that suffering is inherent in their role; men, who are expected to be more aggressive than women, tend to assume a more militant posture against evil. A confrontation with evil may be a moment of truth that a man will recount to friends and relatives, even years later, as a token of his faith and courage.

Although caves, barrancas, anthills, and sinkholes—the demonic counterparts of church, chapel, and home—are primarily associated with harmful and evil beings, there are exceptions to this rule. During the fiesta of San Juan Bautista, for instance, the barrancas become invocations of the River Jordan. Another ambiguous place is the Cave of Alcaleca, located on the side of Popocatépetl, which is the abode of both sinister and beneficent weather spirits. The meanings of openings in the earth's surface, like the meanings of the street, fluctuate according to context.

The Devil

Known by various names in northern Morelos, the Devil is often called Moxicuani, from the Nahuatl word for "envy." The name may allude to a distinguishing characteristic of the Devil. According to long-established theological thinking, the Devil envies God and resents his love for human beings, which explains why he tries to corrupt human affairs with his pride, envy, and lust and by snatching souls away from God. He is also called the Devil, Lucifer, the Second God, the Demon, Caesar, the Malignant One, and the Enemy. Many of these terms are more on the order of allusions than actual names. The Devil's real name is "Satan," but people are reluctant to use it or even some of his other names lest their owner suddenly appear.

The Devil may appear in various guises. When he meets with witches or negotiates the exchange of money for souls, he is seen usually as a handsome charro (horseman) with eyes burning like live coals, dressed in a well-tailored riding coat, tight pants, and golden spurs. It is said that once when the Devil was seen on his way to the house of a local witch, he was dressed in an elegant manner and puffed on a big cigar, and his horse's hooves gave off sparks on the cobbled streets. Agents of the Devil, called *pingos* (devils), also appear on horseback dressed as charros. In Tecospa, men who have sold their souls to the Devil are said to become *pingos* (Madsen 1960:133). In addition, the Devil may appear on foot dressed like a gentleman in a black business suit and carrying a briefcase full of money. The image of the Devil on horseback is reminiscent of the hacendados, who were fond of donning riding finery and going on horseback when visiting their estates, whereas the Devil on foot suggests a merchant. In either case, the Devil is clearly a wealthy Spaniard or Creole, not an Indian.

Alternatively, the Devil may be said to have horns, long eye teeth, red skin, spines on the backs of his hands, a tail, and flaming breath, a form more reminiscent of the Red Dragon of Revelation. This is how the Devil appears in Carnival and the Dance of the Santiagueros (see chapter 7).

According to informants, some of the Devil's other metamorphoses are La Muerte (Death), a noisy clanking human skeleton sometimes riding in an oxcart; a ghostly black or white shroud called the Mala Hora (Evil Hour; see below); a goblin; and animals, for example, a goat, dog, or turkey, which are seen near bridges. The curer Don Lucio told of being brought in to heal a seventeen-year-old boy who was suffering from "a complication of Caesar." As Don Lucio studied the young man, he gradually began to see, hovering close by, a shape with horns and ears like those of a bull. Hunters have trailed wounded deer and rabbits for some distance only to find on running them down that they had turned into toads and snakes. The coyote, something of a thief and trickster, is said to be the Devil's dog.

Other manifestations of the Devil are whirlwinds and violent weather. Whirlwinds may originate in the Devil's cave or anthills, according to the villagers, and they are said to cause ague, pains, and even death. They also damage crops, particularly on or about September 29, the day of San Miguel Arcángel. On this day the Devil wanders loose, spoiling for another fight, and vents his anger on the villagers with destructive winds.

The Devil's association with the day of San Miguel suggests that another of his manifestations may be a dragon called the Canícula. In Tlayacapan, the Canícula causes diarrhea and vomiting in children during the rainy season or summer. It arrives on July 16, the day of the Virgen del Carmen, and lasts through August 24, when San Bartolomé de las Casas runs it off with his lightning. The Canícula returns in less virulent form, however, and lasts until September 29, the day of San Miguel Arcángel (Madsen 1960:168).

Although the world is the Devil's dominion, his stronghold is the earth's interior. He inhabits the Cave of Tezonclala, which is located in a cliff of red rock a short distance to the northeast of the village, and he often appears near a bridge on the road to Tlalnepantla, to the north. Indeed, the Devil has a close association with bridges in general. Bridge builders are thought to kidnap the weak and vulnerable—women, children, and drunks—perhaps as sacrifices to reinforce construction. In the summer of 1968 many parents refused to send their children to school because they feared that the teachers would turn the youngsters over to the engineers and workers who were building bridges for a new rail line a few kilometers away.

The Devil, seeking to enlarge his following, takes souls away from God, sometimes by contracting with living persons to provide money and worldly success in exchange for their souls; in other cases he steals them at the moment of death. For example, he may foment terror and confusion to provoke accidents, often near bridges, and then abscond with the souls of the victims before last rites can secure them for God.

Stories about contracts with the Devil abound. Wealthy villagers, like the hacendados, often are suspected of being parties to such agreements. The belief that hacendados or the owners of sugarcane refineries obtained their money from and collaborated with the Devil, a belief found in many parts of Latin America, is widespread in northern Morelos (see Woods 1959:85). In Hueyapan it was once thought that the tainted nature of the Devil's ill-gotten money explained why it was sterile or incapable of multiplying once paid in wages to humble Indians (Warman 1976:65).[1] In Tlayacapan people think that the hacienda at Oacalco was built with the Devil's help: how else can one explain the presence of the boulders near its main gate? Francisco Vélez, the refinery's first owner, is said to have given his soul for the hacienda. Although the haciendas were greatly reduced in number and the political influence of their owners was curtailed after the Revolution of 1910, there is a lingering apprehension that the Devil is scheming to restore the power of the hacendados; at least this is the implication of a tale about the ruined hacienda of Pantitlán:

José, his brothers, and a friend heard that there was buried gold in the ruins of the hacienda of Pantitlán, so they decided to try a little digging. While José was shoveling dirt, a man appeared; unusual for the Devil, he was dressed just like the villagers, in the work clothes of a campesino. He warned José that the gold did not belong to them (the other treasure hunters never saw or heard the man). José ignored him and continued digging. The man then reappeared to José and told him he would disclose the location of two buried chests of gold if José would deliver a life and vow to restore the hacienda. José, the Devil said, would become the new hacendado. But José could not bring himself to hand over a brother or friend to the Devil; moreover, he was worried that the gold would not suffice to complete the restoration and, as a result, he would look like a fool. José said he would think about it. A week later he felt "very bad." He had *susto*. He recovered only after confessing himself and receiving the *evangelios* from the priest.

Wealthy landowners in the uplands sometimes are accused of having sold their souls to the Devil. According to one tale, the Devil gave a man a large chest of coins that permitted him to hire many peons and thereby increase his fortune. When he died, four black dogs entered his house during the wake and caused the four large funerary candles at the corners of the casket to go out. After the mourners left, the wife peered into the casket and discovered that the corpse was missing; to avoid suspicion, she filled it with rocks. The ruse did not work, however, because her husband was later seen horseback riding near a barranca, his eyes glowing like embers and his horse frothing at the mouth. It was apparent to everyone that he had become a *pingo*. A priest was hired to say a mass at the site of the appearance, and a cross was placed there to keep the ghost away.

One does not necessarily have to seek out the Devil or even voice his name to get his attention and cause his appearance. It suffices to work on Sunday, the day set aside for rest and devotion to family and religion. Presumably, working on a holy day represents acquisitiveness and so sends the Devil a signal.

The Devil, then, personifies an unmitigated expression of the profit motive. He uses money and a parody of contractual relations to appropriate a person's soul, his or her essence. In this respect, his behavior mimics that of the Spaniard who appropriated the labor of Indian peasants and took advantage of them in commercial transactions.

The image of the Devil and the structure of demonic contractual relations suggest a metaphorical similarity between soul and labor. The hacendado receives money from the Devil and then gives it to the peon; money exchanged for a soul is exchanged for labor. The hacendado is to the peon what the Devil is to the hacendado, but since the Devil appears as a Spanish hacendado, it follows that the hacendado is playing the role of a Devil in his relationship with the peon. It may be going too far to suggest that the soul is merely a symbol for labor power, but clearly both allude to essential parts of a person, which are vulnerable to appropriation.

Virility in the male and fecundity in the woman, as we shall see later, are also subject to demonic appropriation. Moreover, it will become evident that sexual nature, the force in the blood that makes labor possible, and soul are related phenomena in traditional belief. In short, the contract with the Devil reifies illicit appropriation of the peasants' labor and reproductivity, the two fundaments of their security. By selling their souls for material wealth, peasants trade the real sources of security for the mere appearance of security. They engage in activity not unlike that of the poor farmer who sells maize in advance or the worker who bought from the hacienda's store on credit.

The villagers are not altogether helpless victims of the Devil. Life is a continuing struggle in which the Devil wins at times and loses at others. Jokes and stories are told about men who have even tried to defraud the Devil by using religious amulets for self-defense. On one occasion, several young men, heavily armed with rosary beads, crucifixes, and holy water, went to the Cave of Tezonclala, intending to bamboozle the Devil. For better or worse, he was not home.

A joke is told of the Devil's coming to a sick man and offering health in return for his soul; but the man asks the Devil for a special medicine to make him "feel good," which the Devil takes as a veiled request for a sexual favor at his own expense—that is, as an appropriation of *his* masculinity. So the two engage in an exchange of abusive repartee until the Devil withdraws, averring that the man would be too much of a troublemaker in Hell.

In some tales and jokes the Devil is portrayed as a pathetic fool who is more a victim of his own myth than an exploiter, as in the following supposedly true story.

Pablo, being poor and deep in debt, decided one morning that he would try to sell his soul to the Devil. He went to a certain cave known to belong to the Devil and sure enough encountered a well-dressed man there. The poor villager greeted him as "brother"; the Devil, in turn, politely answered that he was there to "serve him." Well, the man said, he needed a loan. The Devil replied that he was sorry but he was unable to oblige. Pablo protested, promising that he would pay back the loan and even give his life. Again the gentleman said "no" but allowed that Pablo might try at another cave over yonder. The morning being still young, the villager thought he would give it a try. After hiking through the underbush, he came to the spot and there met another well-dressed gentleman. But it was the same damned man! Pablo received the run-around all over again. Apparently, the Devil was poor. So many people had defaulted on their loans that he was flat broke!

The representation of the Devil as victim inverts his more typical aspect as sinister victimizer and makes him a martyr. It parallels the image of the fighting saint, an image that transforms the martyrdom of the usual saint into a far more active posture. The struggle with the Devil may modify his image, but it may also, to anticipte later arguments, affect the character of those who struggle against him.

The figure of the Devil in northern Morelos closely resembles his counterpart in the folk cultures of Europe. The Devil's fiery eyes and other aspects of his appearance, his market mentality and association with wealth, his victimization, and his association with dogs, other animals, whirlwinds, and bridges, among other things, are all common themes in European lore. So too is the belief that working on Sunday will cause the Devil's appearance (Woods 1959).

Nonetheless, he also recalls various pre-Hispanic supernatural figures, especially Tezcatlipoca. A punitive and fear-inspiring god, the latter was known as Yoalli-Ehecatl (Night Wind) and Necoc Yaotl (Enemy, Sower of Discord; Sahagún 1956:1:44, 52-53). He was thought to be responsible for drought, famines, and plagues (Durán 1967:1:47). He gave and took away riches and fame (Sahagún 1956:1:44), and when he walked on earth he quickened vice and sin (Sahagún 1950-69:Bk.1:5). His body was black, draped with a red mantle bearing skulls and crossbones, and he carried a shield and spear (Durán 1967:1:47). Like some versions of European devils, he had only one foot and walked with a limp. He could also transform himself into a coyote (Serna 1953:224).

Tezcatlipoca, it should be remembered, was a patron of warriors and hence closely affiliated with nobles. The mythical cycle about the defeat of Quetzalcoatl by Tezcatlipoca, Huitzilopochtli, and other gods of war was a charter for conquest and human sacrifice but also for the domination of commoner farmers and artisans by warrior-nobles: Quetzalcoatl and other gods closely associated with him were patrons of farmers and craftsmen (see Ingham 1984). Like the Devil, then, Tezcatlipoca was a symbol of power and wealth.

Also like his European counterpart, Tezcatlipoca was a hunter: recall that he transformed himself into Mixcoatl, the god of the hunt, to make fire.

Tezcatlipoca was the principal god of the North, a region that merged with Mictlan, a hell-like abode of Mictlantecuhtli, the god of death. In contemporary ritual, Death appears along with the Hunter, devils, and impersonators of the pagan. Moreover, the Devil is said to assume the form of Death.

The Harlot

All through central Mexico stories are told about a wicked woman, a female personification of evil. In Tlayacapan and vicinity, as in many other parts of the region, this figure is called la Llorona (the Weeper). In some communities she is said to be la Malinche, the Indian mistress of and interpreter for Hernán Cortés, the Spanish conquistador. This identification of la Llorona with la Malinche was once present in Tlayacapan as well; one informant recalled her grandparents' saying that the two were one and the same.

In Tlayacapan la Llorona is a nocturnal figure usually seen near a barranca. She is sometimes called the Mala Hora because she appears at midnight. One person recalls seeing her washing clothes in the barranca at midnight, although in most of her apparitions she wanders along the edge of the barranca, crying and calling out for her children. It is said that she was a prostitute or mistress who threw her children into the barranca, aborted them, or fed them to pigs. She carried out these abominations either because she did not want to be bothered by the burdens of motherhood or because, having been rejected by her lover, she wanted to take her revenge on the children: if she could not have their father, she would not have them. After her death, God punished her by condemning her to wander the earth in search of them.

La Llorona typically is seen in a white dress, which some informants describe as a bridal gown with veil. Less often she is seen wearing black. Her hair is long and seductively unkempt. She is like a spirit or wind: she floats along without touching the ground with her feet. Sometimes she appears simply as an amorphous white cloud and at other times she is not seen, only heard. One young man heard her call out his name as he was crossing a bridge. Looking around, he saw nothing but asked, "What?" and then heard her answer, "For the flesh, stupid!" Others have heard the sound of someone or something pouring broken glass when crossing this same bridge. A group of drunk men once saw la Llorona enter a vacant house on the plaza and leave by its back door, reappearing near the bridge at the back of the house. When they took a closer look, they found that the front door to the house was shut and padlocked as usual.

La Llorona lures men closer only to frighten them. In the distance she seems tall and beautiful, and her movements are teasing and seductive. She appears and disappears, luring men on, reappearing farther away and closer to the barranca. When her voice is loud she is far away and when it is soft she is close by. If, by chance, men get close enough to remove her veil, they see a horse's face. According to Don Lucio, she has the power to turn into a snake; indeed, she is la Diabla, the female Devil (see also Hunt 1977:103).[2]

Various students of la Llorona–la Malinche have noted her similarity to the pre-Hispanic goddess Cihuacoatl (Snake Woman; see Horcasitas and Butterworth 1963; Hunt 1977:100-105). Cihuacoatl was closely associated with Quetzalcoatl, principal god of the West. Taking a clue from her name and the belief that she helped Quetzalcoatl to create the human race, Sahagún likened her to Eve. She is said to have had long hair and ferocious teeth and to have dressed entirely in white. She could be heard wailing and raging in the night air. Her face was half red and half black, like Quetzalcoatl's. She caused adversity, poverty, and discouragement. A mother of the commoners, she nonetheless intimated the opposite of motherhood: she had a habit of abandoning her cradle in the marketplace; even worse, when concerned women looked into the cradle the only baby they found was a stone knife, the instrument of sacrifice (Durán 1967:1:125; Sahagún 1956:1:46-47).

Cihuacoatl was related to the *cihuapipiltin* or *cihuateteo*, the ghosts of women who had died in childbirth. Their faces and legs were tinged with white and they wandered in the air like clouds, bringing sickness to children and causing twisted mouths, paralysis, trembling, and loss of sensation. The days on which they descended were associated with the West and tended to augur ill. Boys born on the day 1 House, for instance, grew up to become ill-fortuned and adulterous; girls born on this day were likely to become ignorant, promiscuous, and lazy, and even unable to grind maize on the *metate* (Sahagún 1956:1:49-50, 334, 349, 354-355).

Xochiquetzal and Tlazolteotl, the love goddess, were also associated with the West. Tlazolteotl was a temptress, an eater of filth, and an ally of women who had a talent for lovemaking. She may have been associated with Cihuacoatl and the *cihuapipiltin* (ibid.:54); like Cihuacoatl, she was known as Our Mother, and her carnality placed her in Tamoanchan, the mythic realm of mist and water and the setting for sexual reproduction (ibid.:4:301-302). The hymn to Xochiquetzal places her in Tamoanchan also (ibid.:1:259).

There is, then, evidence for continuity between la Llorona and Cihuacoatl. In addition, Cihuacoatl was apparently conflated with the historical la Malinche. Yet, la Llorona is also a variant of several related Old World figures. One is Eve, another, Lilith, and still another, the Schalangenjungfrau, the Enchanted Lady. Tales about the latter were widespread in Europe at the end of the Middle Ages. John Mandeville, for example, recorded one version in his *Travels* (ca. 1366), which he said he had heard on the Mediterranean island of Cos (English, Latin, and German versions of his book were available by 1372). In the tale, a lady dressed in white is enchanted into animal form. A youth must kiss or hit her in order to release her and take her as a bride and to free a treasure guarded by a black dog; in some versions she turns into a snake or some other animal (that is, the Devil) at the moment of the disenchantment attempt (Woods 1959:123-132).

The Beasts of the Water and the Earth

Other than the Devil, the most powerful wind spirit is Yeyecatl. He clears the way before storms. A related spirit is the Acoatl or Culebra de Agua (Water Serpent), a water spout or black cloud, shrouded in white, which hangs down from the heavens like a snake, lashing and blasting the earth with wind and rain.

According to Don Lucio, another destructive weather spirit is the Torito (Little Bull), which is said to assume the form of a destructive squall. He can rampage through a cornfield, uprooting and knocking down plants like real bulls when they stray into fields. In Amecameca, the Torito is said to be in charge of the spirits of hail (Bonfil Batalla 1968:112). Don Lucio explained that the Torito and the Culebra de Agua are just two variants of the same being.

The connection between the water serpent and Quetzalcoatl deserves further discussion, for it has implications for the interpretation of their significance. Sahagún (1956:3:266-274) mentions several types of snake that may have been associated with Quetzalcoatl in ancient Nahuatl culture. One was an *acoatl* (water snake), a large creature that inhabited caves and springs. With powerful inhalations, it drew animals and persons into the water, drowning them. The *mazacoatl* (deer snake) had deer antlers on its head and, like the *acoatl*, was large and dark, lived in caves, and captured victims with its breath. The meat of a smaller *mazacoatl* allowed a man to have multiple ejaculations in quick succession, but when taken in excess, it caused a permanent erection and even death. Another snake was called the *ehecacoatl* (wind snake). A *quetzalcoatl* (feathered snake) was about the same size as the water snakes. In Tecospa, the leader of the rain spirits is called Yeyecacoatl (Wind Serpent) or, in Spanish, Culebra de Agua (Madsen 1960:130-133). Around Amecameca, to the northeast of Tlayacapan, he is called Ehecatl (Wind) and is credited with the power to move hail-bearing clouds away from fields (Cook de Leonard 1966:298). Farther to the south, in Oaxaca, the Culebra de Agua is a sinister, winged, horned serpent, which causes floods and droughts. According to one tale, a similar female serpent called Mother of the Water lived in the Lake of White Water; when it was accidentally killed, the lake dried up. These horned serpents live in the Devil's cave. A tale about one such horned devil describes how he drove away rain clouds but was killed by Lightning (E.C. Parsons 1936:223-224). Among the Totonac, a *mazacuate* (deer snake) is associated with wind; it lives in water and is apparently identified with the Water Snake (Ichon 1973:139-140).

Horned snake masks and costumes are used in ritual in various parts of Mexico. They have long, caimanoid snouts, remarkably similar to some of the renditions of the pre-Hispanic Quetzalcoatl (Cordry 1980:54, 125). A dramatic example is a step-horned snake and horned mask combination once used in Nahuatl Guerrero (ibid.:194; see fig. 5). Its similarity to Quetzalcoatl is unmistakable (see fig. 6). Still other evidence identifies Quetzalcoatl with the deer. In ancient Mexico, deer-hunting incantations invoked Cihuacoatl, Chicome Xochitl, the *tlaloque*, and the four winds (Alarcón 1953:76-87). Chicome Xochitl (Seven Flower), the deer god, was a manifestation of Piltzintecuhtli (Serna 1953:294). A hymn situates Piltzintecuhtli with Xochiquetzal in Tamoanchan, a mythic realm of mist and rain in the West, and refers to him as the priest of the god of wind (that is, Quetzalcoatl; Sahagún 1956:1:259).

Various tales told in ancient Mexico link Quetzalcoatl with Cihuacoatl and Xochiquetzal and portray him as a fertility god who succumbs to incontinence and drunkenness. As priest in the ancient city of Tula, Quetzalcoatl was a virtuous and penitent figure who instructed the Toltecs in the arts and crafts of civilization, but the tales also say that he was humiliated and forced to leave Tula by Tezcatlipoca, Huitzilopochtli, and their allies. According to one account, Quetzalcoatl was tricked into getting drunk with his sister (Codex Chimalpopoca 1945:10), whereas another says that he was maneuvered into the same room with Xochiquetzal (Durán 1967:1:14). After a long flight from the city, Quetzalcoatl was overcome by sadness. He threw himself into a fire, and his soul became the morning star, or Tlahuizcalpantecuhtli. In this guise, he wore the red and white body stripes that were typical of Mixcoatl and representations of victims of human sacrifice (Seler 1963:1:190-198).

In a tale about the origin of aromatic flowers, it is said that Quetzalcoatl touched his penis while bathing, causing himself to ejaculate. His semen landed on a rock, thereby engendering a bat. The gods then sent the bat to visit Xochiquetzal. Finding her asleep, the bat bit off part of her genitalia. The bat took the offensive-smelling part to the gods for a bath, but when it continued to smell, he took it to Mictlantecuhtli, who washed it again, turning it into aromatic flowers (Codex Magliabechiano 1970, plate 62).

According to another story, Quetzalcoatl traveled to Mictlan to recover the old bones with which to fashion a new race of human beings. When he arrived, Mictlantecuhtli gave him a conch shell and challenged him to blow it as he walked around Mictlan four times. Mictlantecuhtli expected Quetzalcoatl to fail in the task because the shell lacked holes, but worms

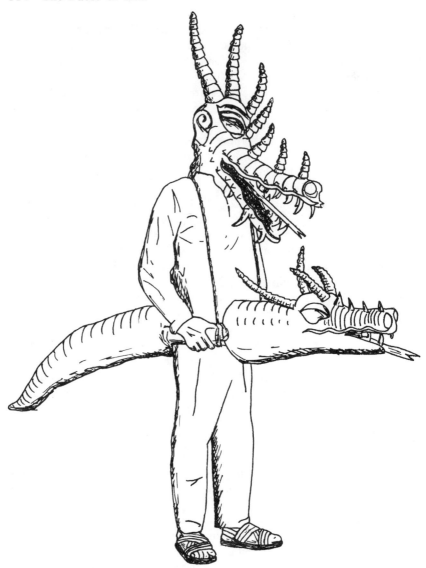

Fig. 5. Horned Snake, La Parota, Guerrero (after Cordry 1980:194)

came to his aid and made some holes for him. Grudgingly, Mictlantecuhtli gave up the bones, although not without putting a pitfall in Quetzalcoatl's path, which caused him to trip and scatter the bones. The hero's *nagual* (animal companion spirit) gave him encouragement and so Quetzalcoatl gathered up the bones and took them to Tamoanchan. Cihuacoatl ground

Fig. 6. Quetzalcoatl (after Codex Magliabechiano 1970:plate 61)

them up on her *metate* and they placed the bonemeal in an earthen tub, whereupon Quetzalcoatl dripped some blood from his penis over the meal, engendering the human race (Codex Chimalpopoca 1945:120-121).

Quetzalcoatl's lapse into drunkenness in Tula was consistent with his sexual incontinence; both alluded to his animality. In this respect, he was closely associated with the gods of alcohol, who, like him, were often painted red and black. Patecatl, one of these gods, resembled Quetzalcoatl even more closely: his headdress bore the same hummingbird-flower arrangement as Quetzalcoatl's and his weapon and shield were similar to those of Quetzalcoatl (Codex Magliabechiano 1970, plate 53).

The bone-flower-hummingbird arrangements in the headdresses of Quetzalcoatl and Patecatl evinced their common association with fertility. In her intriguing essay on Mayan demonology, Blaffer (1972:63-67) observes that the hummingbird and bat compete for the nectar of flowers. She suggests that the hummingbird is a symbol for the sun, light, and fire and that the bat is a symbol for the underworld, night, and darkness.

Flowers, she thinks, may represent blood and eroticism, an interpretation that agrees with the Nahuatl tale about the origin of aromatic flowers. In present-day Zinacantan, a man may carry a dead hummingbird to ensure sexual prowess in courtship (ibid.:67). Similarly, in Tlayacapan a dried, swallow-tailed hummingbird may be wrapped in red ribbon and carried as a love charm, and it is said that one can eat the heart of a hummingbird for luck in love. The bone in Quetzalcoatl's headdress was no doubt one of those he brought back from Mictlan. Bone, flower, and hummingbird were, then, a complex symbol for procreation.

Quetzalcoatl and his companion Cihuacoatl/Xochiquetzal were no doubt identified with Adam and Eve following the Conquest. They were also identified with Cortés and la Malinche, who played a role not unlike that of Adam and Eve in founding the mestizo race. There were, however, yet other refractions of the Adamic couple. The most sinister of these—the Culebra de Agua, the Torito, and the Llorona—are also reminiscent of the beasts of the land and sea and the Harlot mentioned in Revelation.

Los Aires

Various lesser spirits inhabit the ground. Called *los aires* (the airs) in Spanish and *yeyecame* (the winds) in Nahuatl, they are pictured as dwarflike beings who dress in the traditional Indian attire of the region. Although some reside in the ground under houses or wander loose in the streets, most dwell in or around barrancas, particularly in anthills associated with *cuatalatas*, or large red ants. Both *los aires* and the ants are said to live in the holes with the coral snake, the queen of the ants.

The Rainbow is another dangerous spirit. Thought to leave and reenter the earth by way of caves, anthills, and sinkholes, it is said to cause *susto*, dropsy, headaches, and fever chills. If pointed at a rainbow, a finger may dry up and whither away. (In chapter 9 I describe *los aires* and the illnesses they cause in greater detail.)

Goblins

Duendes (goblins) are smallish, childlike figures who inhabit the *amate* and mesquite trees in or near barrancas. They taunt passersby with funny faces and mock them with laughter. Occasionally, they enter homes to steal brooms and other household goods from women. Male goblins carry money on their backs, which they use to bribe women for sexual favors. The goblins are a type of *pingo* and are said to be the ghosts of children who died before they could be baptized. They are condemned to "walk in darkness."

The Witch

Witches, the agents of the Devil, are called *brujos* or *hechiceros* (doers, makers). They are people who know how to do *cochinadas* (piggish things). Having made pacts with the Devil, they can make people sick or poor and they can encourage or destroy relationships by stimulating sexual desire.

Instances of witchcraft are much talked about, although witches themselves are rather elusive. Almost everyone can identify a witch or two, yet the people so accused do not admit to working on the side of darkness. To the contrary, they see themselves as well-meaning folk curers whose profession is one of undoing the actions of witches; for this task, they may know what witches know, but any insinuation that they themselves practice witchcraft is nothing more than slanderous gossip (this is not to say, however, that sometimes the supposed witch would not take a somewhat different line if one were to allow, in the strictest confidentiality, that one were willing to pay a considerable amount of money to return an unjust injury). Putative witches invariably are socially distant. Rarely if ever are the evil ones members of one's circle of relatives, compadres, or friends. Indeed, most witches seem to live in "another" barrio, and often they live in "another" village (ironically, the accusations are reciprocal). The person who lives next door or across the street is simply Don Graciano, who cures *aire* illness, or Doña Arnulfa, who knows how to cure *susto* and the evil eye. People who are accused of being witches are likely to be marginal in still other ways: some are immigrants from other villages who lack kin or compadres in Tlayacapan, and some are reputed to be sexually deviant. Alleged female witches often are spinsters or widows who are said to be "merry," and one elderly male witch supposedly had many lovers in his day; rumor has it that he did not charge female clients for his services if they agreed to go to bed with him. Another male witch was purportedly more interested in sexual relations with men than with women.[3]

Frequently in witchcraft cases a seductive sexual attraction disrupts a legitimate relationship or prevents one from developing. When a married man or woman runs off with a lover, one or more persons in the triangle may be accused of having hired a witch. And when parents, despite repeated remonstration, cannot dissuade a son from eloping with what to them is an unsuitable partner, they may conclude that the young woman has had their son bewitched.

Villagers also assume that witches are enlisted by greedy persons who wish to improve their economic position at the expense of other villagers. Storekeepers often suspect persecution by witches, particularly when a business is failing; they complain that they are the targets of envy by either the poor or other storekeepers. A storekeeper who lived across the street from me began her day with a prophylactic sweeping of her doorstep; bad people, she said, were putting salt on it. Another store owner claimed that her family's business was ruined by a concoction that someone had thrown onto her doorstep. She suspected that a witch had been hired by another storekeeper to do the job.

Witches are said to carry out their evil deeds on Tuesdays and Fridays at midnight. They may transform themselves into *vampiros* (that is, buzzards, turkeys, or large black moths) or balls of fire to fly through the night air. While everyone sleeps, they sneak into homes and suck blood from the necks of infants. They also can harm people at a distance by sticking pins into rag dolls that are made of pieces of the victim's clothing or by hurling evil air against a person. One woman was supposedly blinded because a witch placed salt in the eyes of a toad and then threw it into a barranca.

The *Nagual*

The *nagual*, another type of transforming witch, has the power to change into an animal by reciting evil prayers and incantations. However, *naguales* transform themselves only into domesticated animals (usually pigs, donkeys, dogs, or sheep) and, on the whole, are somewhat less sinister than witches per se. Their actions range from innocuous, even comic, mischief to serious crime; more often than not they merely scare or bump into people on side streets and paths after dark, commonly near barrancas. *Naguales* also pilfer corn, chickens, and kitchen utensils, especially *metates*, which, curiously, they do not keep but simply drop in the street. Along with performing such pranks, *naguales* can prove destructive. If a *nagual* pinches the arm or leg of a sleeping person, lassitude and even death may follow; if he pinches a nose, it will bleed profusely the next day. What is worse, *naguales* are said to kidnap and kill babies, and their erotic impulses may lead them to rape young women. Men are known to change into animals to intimidate rivals for young women's affections. When the naked body of a woman was found in a barranca, it was said that she had been murdered by her jealous lover, a *nagual*.

Obviously, *naguales* pose a special threat to women who leave their homes at night or who are unfaithful to suitors. They also pose a threat to children who are not being well cared for and, by implication, to women's reputations as mothers. Attacks by *naguales* seem to imply that the victims are not blameless. In this respect, the *naguales* of Tlayacapan perform a function similar to that which Blaffer (1972) attributed to the Black-man of Zinacantan, the winged demon with a long penis who attacks women who are careless in performing domestic duties.

This role of the *nagual* as the scourge of the negligent homemaker suggests a reason for his otherwise curious penchant for stealing kitchen utensils and, especially, *metates*. Kitchen tools belong to women and are essential to the proper performance of their principal domestic chore— preparing food for the family—and since they spend much time using the *metate* to prepare food, it naturally is closely associated with the female role. Stealing kitchen utensils in general and the *metate* in particular, therefore, is an appropriation of a woman's means of productive activity and, perhaps, a metonymic representation of the appropriation of her labor as such.

Not so obvious is the parallel between the theft of kitchen utensils and the sexual appropriation of women. Various riddles link foods and kitchen tools to female sex organs and activities. Grinding corn and other foods on the *metate* and making tortillas are timeless metaphors throughout Middle America for sexual reproduction; Cihuacoatl used her *metate* when she helped Quetzalcoatl in the creation of human beings. In Tlayacapan, the *nagual* is not the only male who goes about gathering up *metates*; Retores, the men who dance with the Tenanches, also collect *metates*. This connection between female sexuality and the *metate* is even more explicit in a kitchen riddle:

Tú boca arriba, yo boca abajo.
Te repego las bolas y te trabajo.
(You mouth up and I mouth down.
I hit you with the balls and work you.)

Although the rhyme alludes to sexual intercourse between a man and a woman, the correct answer is "the *metate*," not a woman, and "the hand stone" and "corn dough or tomatoes," not penis and testicles.

A variety of defenses are employed against *naguales*. If a cross of lime is painted on the bottom of a *metate* it becomes "too heavy" for a *nagual* to carry. A man can defend himself against *naguales* by holding his hat down by his side, turning his clothes and hat inside out, or placing a cross of holy water on a new hat. Pinning an upside-down hat to the ground with a knife fixes a *nagual* where he stands and prevents him from turning back into a "Christian" in the morning. A *nagual* can be fought with the left hand, a cross of bamboo moistened with holy water, or the excrement of a black donkey; the right hand, knives, and guns are ineffectual. When defeated with the appropriate measures, a *nagual* may confess his true identity and beg for forgiveness. The person who changes into a *nagual*, in other words, has an ambiguous moral character; by day he may be an ordinary Christian who turns into a sinister animal only by night.

Among the ancient Nahua, the thief-*naguales* transformed themselves into various types of animal. A gang of fifteen or twenty such witches would dance through the streets, carrying an image of Quetzalcoatl and the forearm of a woman who had died in first childbirth. Arriving at the victim's house, they would beat the arm on the ground of the patio outside the house and then again on the threshold, thereby enchanting the persons inside. As the latter stood speechless, the thieves would eat the food, take the valuables, and rape the women of the household. If any of the witches stopped to rest, he would not be able to move until the morning and would then lead the way to the other culprits (Sahagún 1956:1:357-358).

Summary

Evil assumes various manifestations in Tlayacapan (see table 8). Whatever its guise, the underlying characteristics are the same. Evil is associated with envy and greed, and inclination to appropriate what belongs to others, especially their essence. The excessive appetite of evil beings is often economic but it may be sexual as well; evil beings appropriate the sexual powers of others and covet babies, the products of sexual fertility. In

Table 8
Evil Beings

Evil Being	Manifestation
El Diablo	Charro, Hacendado Gentleman, City Slicker Red Dragon (anthropomorphic) Whirlwind Snake, Goat, Turkey, etc. Death Ghost Goblin Canícula (?)
Pingo	Charro Goblin
La Muerte	Human skeleton
La Llorona	Woman in White Woman in Black White Cloud La Malinche
Culebra de Agua/Torito	White-black cloud Wind Squall
Los aires	Dwarf Invisible spirit, wind
Cozamalotl	Rainbow
Duende	Childlike ghost
Brujo	Buzzard, Turkey, Black moth, Ball of fire
Nagual	Domesticated animal

summary, the essence that evil beings would appropriate is variously the soul, a person's virility or fecundity, or his or her labor. In these respects, the Devil and his demons are the antithesis of God and the saints, who give strength to the soul and support to economic production and biological and social reproduction.

7. The Ceremonial Cycle

The domains of good and evil—what theologians sometimes call the two cities or kingdoms—are represented in the moral topography of the villagers by particular social spaces and features of the natural landscape. The two domains—and the struggle between them—are represented too by moments in village festivities and fiestas. Whereas conceptions of space compress an entire Christian cosmos into the local environs, the ceremonial cycle replicates within a single year major moments in biblical time, past and anticipated.

So viewed, the year begins with Advent, the period before Christmas, when the villagers celebrate the Virgin who will bear the Christ Child. The fiesta of the Virgen de la Concepción, which commemorates the Virgin's own Immaculate Conception, occurs on December 8, and on December 12 the major fiesta for the Virgen de Guadalupe is held.

Traditionally, there were two images of the Virgen de la Concepción, one in the chapel by that name and another, also known as the Virgen del Apocalipsis, in Altica. The latter is a statue of a woman standing on a seven-headed serpent and a globe. In the past, the villagers hung paper lanterns on the fronts of their houses throughout the month of December, and the Virgen del Apocalipsis was carried in procession through Altica on the morning of her fiesta.

For the mass of the Virgen de Guadalupe, little boys and girls are dressed in the traditional Indian attire of the community: white pajamas for the boys and dark blue wrap-around skirts with white trim near the waist and embroidered blouses for the girls. The boys are called Juan Diegos, after the Indian who is supposed to have witnessed the miraculous visitations of the Virgen de Guadalupe shortly after the Conquest, and the girls are called las Malinches.

Between December 16, when Mary and Joseph begin to look for lodging, and February 2, or Candelaria, when a feast celebrates Mary's purification, ritual activities focus on the Niño Dios. Nativity scenes, each with its own replica of the Niño Dios, are set up in homes, and posadas are held in the homes of various storekeepers and in the church for the nine nights before Christmas.

Of all the saints, the Niño Dios ranks among the most miraculous. On request, his mayordomo brings him to a home where his clothes are used to cleanse a patient of illness. In gratitude, the householder may promise to give the Niño Dios a mass, rosary, or new dress, or to serve him as mayordomo or godparent.

On the morning of December 16, villagers gather at the house of the mayordomo to sing "Las mañanitas" and to greet the Niño Dios with flowers and rockets. In the past, the older women known as Tenanches danced to Carnival music outside the mayordomo's home.

In the afternoon, the Niño Dios is taken to the church in a procession that includes Joseph, Mary, and the Angel, and then he is returned to the mayordomo's house. In the evening, the first of the nine posadas is held in the church. The pilgrims sing praises at the door while inside a group of women sing the response: they cannot give lodging, there is no room in the inn. Eventually, the doors open and the procession passes inside. Following prayers, the children break a piñata in the monastery courtyard. At the same time, posadas are held in the homes of the mayordomo, godparents, and various families.

On December 23, the mayordomo and godfather go to the hills in the company of their compadres and friends to gather pine boughs for the nativity scenes in their homes and the church. The following morning, the Niño Dios is taken to the godfather's house in a procession that includes Joseph, Mary, and the Shepherds. In the evening, after the godfather of the Niño Dios dispenses sherbet and pastries, the image is carried to the church for the mass of the Rooster.

Meanwhile, throughout the village, the images of the Christ Child in the homes are "lulled" so they will "go to sleep." Usually, a boy and girl from a nearby household offer to serve as "godparents" to a Niño Dios: they place the naked image on a scarf and, holding the ends to form a cradle, they take the image for a walk along the street and sing lullabies to it.

The principal Niño Dios remains in the church until Epiphany, January 6. In the morning before the mass the Three Kings and the Shepherds travel the main streets of the village. Afterwards, the Shepherds, Mary, Joseph, and the Angel, who holds a papier-mâché star, and the godparents, who carry the Niño Dios, continue to the house of the godparents. The image remains there for the rest of the month, during which rosaries are said every evening.

On February 1, the Niño Dios is returned to the church. The mass of the Virgen de la Candelaria is offered the next morning. It is understood to be the *sacamisa* of Mary and the Christ Child. During the mass, the Niño Dios is placed in the arms of the life-sized image of the Virgin. The young women who act the parts of godmothers of the images of the Niño Dios in separate households bring their "godsons" as well. As in an actual *sacamisa*, the godmothers supply their godchildren with new clothing, although interestingly, the images are dressed to represent various images of Christ or several saints (for example, Niño de Atocha, San José, San Martín de Porres, Sagrado Corazón, la Virgen de los Milagros). Some people take advantage of the February 2 mass to baptize and observe the *sacamisa* for their own infants. The babies are baptized before the mass and then changed into their new clothes for the *sacamisa*.

After the mass the Niño Dios is removed from the Virgin's arms and carried to the mayordomo's house for the fiesta banquet. Like the *santitos* of other fiestas, the Niño Dios remains in the mayordomo's home until May, when it is transferred to the home of the new mayordomo.

In the past the Tenanches and Retores danced the Xochipitzahua, Sarna, and other comic dances following the banquet (see chapter 5). In contrast to la Virgen de la Candelaria, the Tenanches would seem to represent natural motherhood; their dancing with the Retores alludes to carnal relations. The Tenanches are said to be the grandmothers of the Niño Dios, which structurally places them in the position of Eve, the mother who precedes Mary. The lyrics of the Xochipitzahua seem to link the sex act with aging and death, and indeed the Tenanches are older women, as the Retores are usually older men, often former mayordomos.

The evocation of pagan times in the dances of the Tenanches is even more apparent in the pre-Lenten Carnival, which follows soon after. Carnival is a time of exuberance and license, a period when, to all appearances, normal Christian values are suspended. Pagan figures dance in the streets, formal balls are held with music provided by orchestras, and bull rides are staged in the plaza. There is also whoring and much drunkenness. In effect, the profane values of the street predominate over the sacred values of home and church.

The principal figures of Carnival are masked, costumed, male dancers known as Chinelos. They wear ankle-length dresses of white cotton with horizontal blue stripes and grotesque pink masks that have green eyes and pointed, upturned black beards made from horse hair. The Chinelo speaks in a high, falsetto voice and dances a distinctive jumplike step.

The most striking feature of the Chinelo's costume is the hat. Its peculiar shape—an inverted cone, wider at the top than at the bottom—is achieved with an up-turned brim. The hat (made with wire and woven palm) is covered with velvet and decorated with beadwork. Glass fringes dangle from the top edge and several large, dyed peacock feathers are attached. Traditionally, eagles, Apache warbonnets, and flowers and laurel leaves were favorite motifs, but when Angel borrowed one of my books about the Aztecs and copied the Aztec calendar and Tezcatlipoca onto his new hat, his innovation was quickly adopted by others. Angel and his friends were improvising, nonetheless, on established themes. The parade of the Chinelos is said to commemorate the wanderings of the Aztec tribe before its arrival in the Valley of Mexico: the dance groups, remember, are named Azteca, América, and Unión. The group flags variously display Aztec queens, Aztec war gods, heads of Apache warriors, eagles, and suns; otherwise, they resemble the Mexican national flag, which, as a symbol of independence from Spain, has strong associations with Mexico's indigenous past. The Chinelos represent pagans in other ways. Some villagers relate that they portray Moors or Arab pirates who preyed on Spanish ships or that they represent Arab merchants.

Informants say that until the end of the nineteenth century Carnival dancers also included men who costumed themselves in jackets and pegged pants, presumably in imitation of Spaniards. They carried bats or sticks, like the Chinelos in those days.

The approach of Carnival proper is heralded by each dance group with an "invitation" or mini-Carnival. Each of these little masquerades is staged on a separate Sunday, two or three months before the actual Carnival. An invitation begins before sunrise when the group's band goes into the street to play Chinelo music. In the afternoon, the band takes to the street again, now with the company of Chinelos and with other figures, most notably, men representing Hunters and Deer.

The Hunters wear tattered old vests and blue, black, or brown suit coats covered with black and blue patches, and they have dead snakes and lizards tied to their belts. Padding gives them the appearance of being hunchbacked or having large bellies, and they purposely limp as they walk. In the past, they wore pink Chinelo masks; today they tie scarves over their faces and wear sunglasses or rubber masks. They carry muzzle-loading shotguns with which they fire blanks at the Deer—men who wear antlers and deerskins. The masquerade also includes big and little devils, Death, a Doctor, a Charro, a Photographer, a Shoe Shiner, a Coyote, and a Gorilla, although the variety and number of figures varies from group to group and year to year. The devils, dressed in red, cavort about, poking tridents at people and forcing embraces upon young women. Death dresses in white with black skeletal markings. A Doctor, wearing dunce cap and white smock, gives fast-acting "injections" to wounded Deer. The Photographer pretends to take pictures of female onlookers and passes out their "portraits" (that is, photographs of nude women cut from men's magazines). The parade begins in the barrio at the home of the group's principal official, moves upon the plaza, then tours the rest of the village, to reappear in the plaza for a rollicking finale of music, flag waving, dancing, and comic mischief-making, much to the delight of the hundreds of children and their parents who make up the rest of the crowd. From start to finish the spectacle is most impressive, but the beginning is particularly so for the sheer explosiveness of its commotion: what is usually a peaceful street becomes a montage of swirling color, dust, and gunsmoke, and a cacophony of jabbering devils and demons, gun blasts, exploding rockets, and band music. It is as if the creatures of Hell have been loosed on the world. In the evening the group holds a ball for young men and women, and late at night its officials deliver its flags to the new, incoming officials.

In Tlayacapan Carnival per se begins with several days of bull riding. A few days before the first *jaripeo* a corral is set up in the central plaza and men begin to dare each other to ride bulls. The animals usually arrive the day before and are kept in a pen adjacent to the corral. Sometimes the bulls, closely followed by a band and men sending off exploding rockets, are run through the streets on the morning of the *jaripeo*. Later in the morning, one or two young bulls are mounted by adolescent boys who are learning to ride. Shortly thereafter the crowd goes home for the afternoon meal. In the late afternoon, when the *jaripeo* is held, the populace gathers again in swollen numbers. Men sit on the corral fence or press hard against it, and women and children hunt out safer vantage points. When a bull is sent into the corral, charros bring it down with their lassos and the rider's companions cinch a rope around the animal to give the rider a grip. The rider (called the *novia*, fiancée or bride), walks to the animal with an assistant who helps him to mount and gives him a puff on a cigarette and some last words of encouragement and advice. When everything is ready, the bull is released and the band strikes up a lively tune. As the bull charges around the corral, charros and their horses scatter for safety and the men on and behind the fence grab at the bull's tail and horns and taunt it with insults. *Toreros* with capes try to protect the rider if he is thrown or, if the bull is listless and played out (which is often the case), they coax what action they can from the tired animal, and the charros dare the bull to "enter" and berate it with insinuations of femininity.

The last of several *jaripeos*—the one held on the Sunday before Lent—is the most impressive. It has the fiercest bulls, which are garlanded with paper wreaths. Riders may have "godmothers," young women who embrace them and toss confetti before the ride and present them with colored ribbons afterward. Even the corral may be decorated with colored paper.

When the Sunday-afternoon *jaripeo* is finished, the dance group bands, accompanied by a few Chinelos, march into the plaza, where group officials distribute printed invitations to the festivities. In the evening there is a ball at which the young men and women, chaperoned by their mothers, dance. Meanwhile, the men drink and enjoy the "old ladies" in the makeshift cantinas and whorehouses that have been set up in the plaza area for Carnival. On Monday and Tuesday, during the day, the Chinelos of the rival groups dance through the streets, sweeping spectators—especially females— into the general commotion whenever possible. Each Chinelo takes a young woman on his arm and dances lively steps descriptively called the "jump." The band's music, which alternates between 2/4 and 6/8 time, includes more than fifty variations of the basic tune, and dance steps, though less numerous, vary accordingly. From time to time the Chinelos and young women enter homes in the neighborhood to dance and receive refreshments. It is said that the Chinelos are like the agents of Herod who wore disguises to enter homes in search of the Christ Child. The Chinelos insofar as possible try to conceal their identities from non-Chinelos, whom they like to tease, particularly about not entering into the fun. At about four o'clock in the afternoon the throng converges on the house of the group's principal official for a banquet of turkey *mole*.

Don Modesto, an old informant in 1966, said that long ago the Chinelos danced in the fiesta of Candelaria on February 2. I was unable to confirm this information, but it does seem plausible, since there is evidence for an affinity between the Tenanche dancers and the Chinelos; as noted earlier, the Tenanches danced to Chinelo music on the morning of December 16.

According to Don Ramón, a devil occasionally accompanied the Chinelos in the streets. Dressed in red and wearing a tail and horns, he carried a little notebook. Acting as seductively as he could, he asked young women to dance with him. If they refused, he wrote their names in his notebook and said that he would get them later; if they agreed, he gave them a lusty grin and wrapped his tail around them. He also carried play money with which he bought people's souls; whenever he found a taker, he wrote his or her name in his book, too.

The most extravagant balls are held on Tuesday night of Carnival. The rich no longer organize their own ball apart from those of the three dance groups, but in the past theirs was by far the most elegant. They wore formal evening attire and discreet half-masks and they hired the most expensive orchestra available.

The last event of Carnival is the "goodbye" on the morning of Ash Wednesday. The Chinelos dance in the street one last time and the group officials distribute printed farewells to Carnival. Among other things, the witty verses may thank the young women who have danced with the Chinelos for honoring the groups with their lovely presence and voice regret that some will not be back the following year because they will be married and tied to the dreary duties of the hearth. And there may be a reference to a certain married man who fell in love and so went the way of the Devil, or mention of the drunks who will have to go off and drink some more just to cure their hangovers. Pride is expressed in the squandering of so much hard-earned money, and the contributions of peddlers of booze and pleasures of the flesh are duly acknowledged. Last, the verses note that joy has given way to sadness and express the hope that, God willing, all will gather again a year hence for another Carnival. Exhausted and badly in need of sleep, participants walk to the church for the Mass of the Ashes, which marks the beginning of Lent.

Redfield (1930:111) speculated that the word *chinelo* derives from *chino* (Chinese), a word that functioned in sixteenth-century Spanish, like the word *moro*, as a metonym for "pagan" or "heathen." This is not an implausible etymology. As we have seen, the Chinelo is explicitly linked with the Arab or Moor in Tlayacapan. In Guerrero, Chinelo-like performers wear Moro Chino and Moro Pasión masks, which, like their counterparts in Tlayacapan, are colored red and sport black beards (Cordry 1980:37). Moreover, Redfield's suggested etymology is consistent with the indigenous associations of the Chinelo. Among the prominent deities in the pre-Hispanic pantheon, one is indeed similar to the Chinelo: the figure of Huitzilopochtli, the patron of the Aztec tribe, manifestation of the sun, and the one god that more than any other epitomized Aztec paganism for the sixteenth-century friars (figs. 7, 8).

These indigenous nuances, however, probably represent accretions to what is essentially a European figure. In a footnote to his discussion of the Chinelo in Tepoztlán, Bock (1980:147) mentions that Chinelo-like performers in the Brussels Carnival are called *punchinelo*. The *punchinelo*, it may be added, is a variant of Punch or Pulcinella, a character in the commedia dell' arte, the popular and ribald dramas performed in courts and at fairs and carnivals by traveling troupes of professional actors in sixteenth-century Europe. Not only the Chinelo but many of the characters in the masquerades of northern Morelos derive at least in part from the commedia dell' arte.

Members of the cast in the commedia were nearly always the same. First among them was Harlequin or Arlecchino, who wore a black half-mask with tiny eyeholes, warts, and a chinstrap of coarse black hair. He also wore a suit with many patches, either blue and black or blue and yellow, and he carried a bat. Niklaus (1956:33) described Harlequin as brutish, cunning, Negroid, sly, atavistic, and feline. His brother, Brighella, had a great hooked nose, fearsome beard, and carried a sharp dagger. More clever than Harlequin, he was a confidence trickster, a stealthy and sinister figure.

Pulcinella, another main character, wore a black half-mask and had a hunchback, potbelly, and limp. He walked with a henlike hop and talked with cheeplike sounds (Madden 1975:12); indeed, one representation shows a little Pulcinella being hatched from a gigantic turkey egg (Bragaglia 1953:33). He carried a wooden sword and a large wallet.

Pantalone was an elderly, amorous merchant. He wore a reddish-brown mask with a hooked nose and long pointed beard (Madden 1975:4-5) and dunce cap. Other characters included the Doctor, a university professor and physician; Pedrolino, a country bumpkin; and Columbine, the sometimes innocent sometimes lusty object of Harlequin's and nearly everyone else's

Fig. 7. Chinelo, Tlayacapan

Fig. 8. Huitzilopochtli (after Codex Magliabechiano 1970:plate 61)

lascivious interests. Harlequin, Pantalone, Pedrolino, and others in the cast were hunters (Niklaus 1956:192).

The similarity between the Hunter in Tlayacapan and Harlequin is striking and needs no further comment. Other commedia dell' arte figures, however, have become confused in the masquerade in Tlayacapan. The Hunter has Pulcinella's hunchback, potbelly, and limp, although Pulcinella's chickenlike movements and cheeplike vocalization suggest the dance step and high-pitched voice of the Chinelo. Most artistic representations of Pulcinella bear little resemblance to the Chinelo, but occasionally the upturned brim of his dunce cap was sufficiently wide to make it very similar to the Chinelo's hat, and when he wore this hat style with a coat, the result was something remarkably like the Chinelo indeed (see fig. 9). The Chinelo, however, wears the mask of Pantalone, whereas Pulcinella's mask is worn by the Huehuenche Carnival figures in other parts of the Nahua region. In Tlayacapan the role of Pantalone was once played by the performers who wore pegged pants.

Fig. 9. Pulcinella (after Bragaglia 1953:12)

Some historians trace the commedia dell' arte to a sixteenth-century Italian version, which in turn is said to have derived from early Roman adaptations of popular Greek comic drama, mimes, and pantomimes. According to this reconstruction, the Young Satyr developed into a series of clowns, especially in the Italian town of Atella. Atellan comedy contained a variety of gluttonous and animalistic clowns, which wore ugly masks and the exaggerated leather phalluses of the Greek farces.

Tne Italian troupes enjoyed widespread popularity and did much to elaborate the commedia dell' arte, but their productions were not grounded merely in Italian culture. What seems more probable is that Italian and other troupes drew on local folklore and masquerades for at least some of their dramatic material and comic characters. These, in turn, were enriched by the performances of the professional troupes.

Harlequin was a widely recognized figure in European folk culture. Driesen (1904), for example, demonstrated that the comic Harlequin was none other than the French devil Herlequin. The Herlequin tradition preceded the arrival of the Italian troupe in 1585 by at least six hundred years. Niklaus (1956:30), who tended to emphasize the originality of the Italian troupes, also admitted that the figure had roots in folklore:

There is in it [Arlecchino] perhaps a trace of the *harle*, a little darting bird with bright plumage, and more than a trace of *Alichino*, legendary demon who rose from the infernal regions at the head of a diabolic throng, to haunt and ravage the countryside, riding the night wind and striking terror in the hearts of those who saw or heard him.

In the French tradition, the "Herlequin Family" was an army of dead, condemned souls wandering in the night and making a tremendous noise (Driesen 1904:24ff). This army included dwarfs with big heads (interestingly, big-headed figures appear in some Spanish carnivals). Driesen argued that the Italian troupe adapted the Italian *zanni* tradition to the French Herlequin. He noted the conspicuous hairiness of Harlequin's face and pointed out that the term *hure* was regularly applied to men with heavy beards and animals and devils (ibid:58). In a provocative essay that drew on Driesen's book, psychologist David McClelland (1964) noted that *herle* and *harle* were old English roots for hairiness.

The theme of the Wild Hunt or Furious Host, a rampaging horde led by the Devil in the guise of the Wild Hunter, was found throughout Europe. Its leaders and principal participants were variously Herne, Herla, Herlichen, and Holda.

Following Carnival, two fairs are held in Tlayacapan, one on the first Friday of Lent at the chapel of Exaltación and another on the fourth Friday, at the chapel of La Villa. They are part of a series of Lenten fairs that occur in various communities in Morelos and the town of Amecameca in the State of Mexico. An intriguing mixture of sacred and profane elements, the fairs are the occasion for religious fiestas and peregrinations, commercial activities, masked dances, and vice (see Bonfil Batalla 1971).

In Tlayacapan the first Friday of Lent is dedicated to the Señor de la Exaltación, the saint kept in the principal chapel at the southern end of the village. Pilgrims returning from their peregrination to Chalma may stop to enjoy the fair. An open-air market is installed in front of the chapel where people vend food and craft products. The foods include boiled and sugared peanuts, breads, cooked bananas, popcorn, enchiladas, sweet tamales, and ice cream. For the most part, these foods are not typical cuisine either in the home or at fiestas; instead, they are foods that are eaten outside the home. With the fair's commercial activities and drunkenness, they indicate its association with the street. These profane aspects, however, are counterbalanced by the mass and the ritual meal.

The juxtaposition of secular activity and sacred ritual is further illustrated by the Dance of the Santiagueros, which, traditionally, men from Tlayacapan staged at the chapel on Friday, Saturday, and Sunday. Although Tlayacapenses no longer stage the drama, dancers from Casasano or other towns are sometimes invited to perform. In the traditional rendition, the dancers formed two groups, the Santiagueros and the Moros, or Mahometanos. Santiago dressed in green and arrived mounted on a horse. The other Santiagueros were dressed in black and wore black hats with one side pinned up to which a mirror and a large black feather were attached. The capes of the Santiagueros were decorated with large crosses. The Moros, dressed in red, were led by a character called Pilato, who wore a red suit and cape and a grotesque wooden mask with movable mouth, mustache and beard, and two long horns. His two little sons also were dressed in red and wore horns on their heads. The Moros themselves wore tin helmets and capes decorated with crescent moons, suns, skulls, and animals. Individual Santiagueros and Moros recited lines and fought each other with long machetes. On Friday and Saturday, the Moros were gradually defeated, and on Sunday, the Pilato and his children were subdued. As the Pilato faltered, he said to a son, "Son, I am going to leave you an inheritance, so you can maintain yourself—a field of rocks!" Finally, the pagans were baptized.

The Dance of the Pastorcitas (Shepherds), a traditional part of the fair, is still regularly performed. In one recent fair, the Pastorcitas danced along with Aztec dancers from Totolapan, who took the place of the Santiagueros and Moros. The Pastorcitas, girls ages three to seven or eight, wore white dresses and scarves and carried staves with bells attached. In the late morning the fifty or so children lined up in two columns before the chapel, older ones to the front. At the head of the columns was a girl dressed in white with a blue cape, representing the Virgin, and a boy holding flowers, dressed in green with a yellow cape, representing Joseph. Tapping their staves and occasionally twirling around, they sang their praises:

El Señor de la Exaltación,
te damos tus mañanitas.
Echar tu bendición con tus sagradas manitas.
De lejos caminos te venimos a cantar.
Ya las pastorcitas van a comenzar.
Hace la visita en este santuario.
Ya tus hijos llaman la reina del cielo.
Adoremos al oriente y vendimos este día.

(Venerable Lord of Exaltación,
we sing you your birthday song.
Give your blessing with your sacred hands.
From distant roads we come to sing to you.
Now the little shepherdesses are going to begin.
Make your visit in this sanctuary.
Now your children call upon the queen of heaven.
We adore the east and arrive this day.)

After their songs a mariachi band sang and played "Las mañanitas" and other songs and a village band played as well. At noon there was a Pan American mass with mariachi music inside the chapel at which four priests officiated. The Pastorcitas and the Aztecs crowded the aisle. When the mass was finished, the Aztecs chanted and beat their drums in the chapel for a while and then, on leaving the chapel, were surrounded by the Pastorcitas, as if they were being herded by them. Later, the Aztecs danced in the atrium of the chapel. Half naked and wearing *yoyote* shell rattles for leggings, they danced to drum and flute and the sounds of conch shells.

The fair on fourth Friday is observed jointly by Tlayacapenses and pilgrims from Tepoztlán. Together they celebrate the fiesta of the Virgen de Tránsito. The story is told that she was originally located in Tepoztlán but was brought to Tlayacapan for refurbishing by local painters. When she was returned to Tepoztlán she came back to Tlayacapan on her own accord, leaving foot and knee prints on the trail between the two villages. Alternatively, it is said that when she was being returned to Tepoztlán she became so heavy that she had to be left at the site of the chapel of La Villa, whereupon a spring issued forth. Nowadays there is no spring near the chapel but there is a large cistern. Believing that its water has miraculous curative properties, Tepoztecans carry jars of it home with them.

As usual, rosaries and vigil precede the fiesta. On the day of the fiesta a mass is said in the chapel and a ritual meal, supported by mayordomos from the two villages, is provided. Outside the chapel people set up food stands. When Guillermo Bonfil Batalla (1971) observed the fair, prostitutes plied their trade in makeshift cantinas. According to his information, the proprietors and prostitutes of these little establishments were itinerants who usually operated in towns along the Pacific coast.

The Dance of the Vaqueros is part of this second fair. Some twelve men dance to the music of a violin. One man, the Amo (Boss), wears a large scarf on his head and carries a long machete. Together with his foreman, the Caporal, he leads the Vaqueros into the atrium of the chapel. The Vaqueros wear spurs but otherwise their attire is ordinary peasant clothing. The men dance in two lines and the Little Bull moves about between them. The Little Bull is played by a boy who wears on his head a bull made of wood and leather.

The Little Bull dodges and hooks between the two rows as the men recite witty verses and pretend to poke the Bull with their lances. These routines begin on Friday and resume the following day. On Sunday the Bull escapes and the Caporal goes looking for him. A Vaquero prays,

> Ay, San Antonio the miraculous,
> make one of your marvels,
> so that the bull will appear,
> by the hill of Tetillas.

Shortly thereafter, another responds,

> My Señor Amo, it seems that
> I see a shape;
> I think it is my Caporal!

The others together exclaim, "It is!" And the Vaquero cries, "A little lower I see another!" (the Bull), and others again shout, "It is!" The Caporal brings the Little Bull back, leading it with his lasso. The Little Bull is freed again, and again the men take turns fighting it. Then a Vaquero places the *banderillas* and the Caporal lassos the Bull (just the hat) and drags him off the boy's head to the ground. The men then gather around for the slaying of the Bull. They pretend to skin and butcher it and offer the various cuts to onlookers, not without double entendre:

> ¡Costillas para Lucía!
> ¡Esta costilla para mi tía!
> ¡La cola para Doña Lola!
>
> (Ribs for Lucía!
> This rib for my aunt!
> The tail for Doña Lola!)

In the past, a pyrotechnic Little Bull and Castle were burned as part of the celebration and recently, at least, there have been *jaripeos* on Saturday and Sunday. Informants say that it was once the custom as well for Santiagueros and Pastorcitas from Tepoztlán to dance.

During Holy Week the struggle between Christians and pagans persists and the Last Supper, Passion, and Resurrection are reenacted. On Monday a mass is held for the Señor de las Tres Caídas. Traditionally, on Tuesday there was an elaborate dance called Las Doce Pares de Francia, featuring a battle between Christians and Moors. On Thursday a morning mass is followed by a reenactment of the Last Supper in the afternoon. The priest plays the part of Christ and twelve village men play his disciples. Meanwhile, the Pharisees ride through the village looking for him. Eventually, they find him with the Apostles and bring him to trial. Pilate tries to defend Jesus, but the Pharisees insist that he be punished, and Judas receives the money that burns his hands.

The following morning a soldier rides through the village announcing the crucifixion of Jesus. His ordeal is portrayed by a young man who, bent with the enormous weight of a huge wooden cross, carries the cross on his back around the atrium of the church, encountering along the way the three Virgins: Magdalena, Soledad, and María Cleofás. The figure of Santo Entierro is attached to the cross and the cross is raised. The priest recites the rosary of the Sermon of Solitude, after which Santo Entierro is taken down and placed in a casket. In the evening, a long procession accompanies the casket and the images of the three Virgins to the northern chapel of Santa Ana, passing through the barrio of Altica on the way. When the procession approaches the chapel of Santa Ana, it passes under an arch adorned with *pirú*, camphor, and cactus thorns; here the new mayordomos receive the casket from the out-going mayordomos. The procession then continues to Santa Ana, moving slowly and arriving there at midnight. Santo Entierro and the three Virgins are returned to the main church when most villagers have gone to bed.

In the evening on Holy Saturday, the Santo de la Resurrección, dressed entirely in red, leaves the chapel of Santa Ana in a procession that follows a clockwise course through the barrios of Santa Ana and Altica. With the completion of the procession, which represents the resurrection, the mood becomes festive, almost fairlike. Men drink heavily and shoot off fireworks, a Little Bull and Castle. The Little Bull, made of a stick frame and paper and worn by a young man, launches erratic, tailless rockets as the man charges through the streets. Pandemonium breaks loose as the missiles careen and ricochet off the cobbled streets and the sides of houses. Most people scatter but the bravest young men dash toward the Little Bull to try to touch it. The Castle is an even more spectacular display of fireworks. Mounted on a pole and surrounded by four model "ships" some fifty feet away, the Castle and ships exchange rocket fire.

Beginning just after Easter and running through the end of September, the ceremonial calendar recollects the founding of the Church and the continuing struggle with evil. Pentecost, the seventh Sunday after Easter, recalls the descent of the Holy Spirit upon the Apostles and Disciples. The Santa Cruz is celebrated on the third of May. The mountaintop crosses are carried to the village, and for nine days before the fiesta there are rosaries for them as well as for the principal crosses in the chapels of Exaltación, Tlaxcalchica, and Altica and the cross in a small shrine in Santiago. Masses are held on the eve of the fiesta, and, traditionally, a pyrotechnic Little Bull was burned in Santiago. After the fiestas on the third of May, crosses are returned to the mountaintops. Corpus Christi, observed eleven days after Pentecost, celebrates the Holy Eucharist and the Church, the body of Christ.

The fiestas of San Juan Bautista (June 24) and the Virgen de la Asunción (August 15) mark the summer. The summer months are also the time of Canícula, the dragon who is momentarily defeated by San Bartolomé de las Casas and bound for good on September 29, the day of San Miguel Arcángel. From this moment on, ritual turns to the representation of the final days, symbolized in part by All Saints' and All Souls' Days.

The various fiestas honor particular saints. All Saints' and All Souls' can be described as a fiesta for all the dead, including the saints. As November 1 approaches, villagers say, "The spirits of the dead are coming," and they go to work cleaning and painting the grave markers in the cemetery. During the afternoon of October 31, each household prepares for All Saints' Day by placing on the family altar an offering for the spirits of the family's dead children. Their spirits are remembered on the day dedicated to all the saints because baptized children are considered innocent; after death their spirits go directly to heaven where, like the saints, they join the Virgin Mary. The offerings include sweets, chocolate, chayotes, jícamas, special breads, oranges, peanuts, green *mole* with fish, flowers, tamales, and figurines. Some of these small, multicolored dolls represent angels; for the spirits of little girls, some represent women holding children or working the *metate*; for the spirits of dead boys, some depict men on horseback, lions, bulls, and donkeys with whistles attached. The figurines of angels and women are usually painted red, pink, blue, and white, and those for boys are red and yellow. In the home, a line of marigolds leads from the front door to the altar, where the offerings are placed.

On the morning of November 1, after a mass for the spirits of children, the families go to the cemetery to decorate the graves of their dead children with large and small marigolds. In the afternoon the offering for the children is removed from the home altar and is replaced by another offering for the spirits of adult dead, who visit the living on November 2, All Souls' Day or the Day of the Dead. The offering includes *mole poblano*, chicken, bread, candles, fruits, alcohol, incense, and flowers. Baby's breath and small marigolds may be used to decorate the altar, but the customary flowers are large marigolds and amaranth. The bells of the church and chapels are rung from three in the afternoon until the next day. On the evening of November 1, boys, organized into groups according to barrio membership, go from house to house asking for *mole* and a candle for the spirits. Formerly, they were led by a youngster who was dressed as a skeleton or carried a lantern in the shape of a skull. The candles are taken to the chapels and lit on the altars, and at least some of the *mole* is shared with the bell tollers. Men gather in the cemetery to drink "a few cups for the cold" as the band plays funeral music. Later, the men too may visit homes to share some *mole*. On the afternoon of November 2, godchildren take bowls of *mole* to their godparents; in the evening, candles are lit in the cemetery and the priest reads the responsory for the dead. It is the moment when the spirits depart from the village for another year.

The Roman Missal gives Revelation (7:1-17) as the lesson for the Feast of All Saints' Day. The passage describes John's vision of a great multitude of nations, tribes, peoples, and tongues standing before the Lamb. The vision evidently anticipates the eternal blessedness at the end of time and, perhaps, the great messianic banquet that will celebrate Christ's marriage with the church on the eve of the final victory over evil (see Rev 19:9; Lk 13:29). Indeed, the celebrations of All Saints' and All Souls' compose a commensal reunion of all the faithful: the living, the saints and little angels in Heaven, and the souls in Purgatory. In family fiestas and fiestas for the saints, *mole* is shared by a particular group of people. During All Saints' and All Souls', by contrast, *mole* is shared by the living and the dead and it is freely and spontaneously given and received by many people.

As the winter solstice approaches, the year turns full circle to Advent, a period that signals the beginning of the Christian Era but also alludes to the Second Coming.

8. The Struggle with Evil

I have suggested that ritual kinship represents a folk cultural version of essentially Catholic values and ideas. Some elements of the fiestas, however, are problematic for this contention. Moreover, there are moments in the ceremonial round that seem to flatly contradict the valuation of spirituality. What, we may ask, do risqué dances, heavy drinking, bull riding, cock fights, gambling, whoring, and pagan masquerades have to do with the teachings of the church? In this chapter I shall address the problem of moral paradox, showing that it is related to contradictory tendencies in the actual lives of villagers. More precisely, I shall consider the way in which the mimicry of nature and evil follow from the struggle with them.

Gudeman (1976b), writing about rural Panama, connects the problem of festive vice with men's street behavior in general. He notes that men prefer working in their fields or relaxing in the street to passing time at home. Work in the fields, however, is often prohibited during fiestas, and since the house and church are predominantly female domains, Gudeman reasons that men engage in drinking, gambling, and other vicelike activities during fiestas to avoid too close identification with the feminine sphere. "Males," he writes, "oscillate between two poles, the fields and the street, and these are not only set in opposition to one another but in opposition to the syndrome of femininity, domesticity, the family, and the church." The difference between work in the field and behavior in the street during fiestas is described as one of opposition and complementarity: work in the field is individual, productive, and oriented toward future provisions; the fiesta, including men's vice, is collective, extravagant, and present oriented.

As we have seen, there is a parallel between home and church/chapel in Tlayacapan. The home is strongly associated with femininity, and church and ritual kinship are inflected with this same quality; many of the male saints are passive, martyred, asexual figures, and clerics wear feminine clothing and, ideally at least, are celibate. Other observations fit Gudeman's argument. The behavior of men in fiestas is often both conspicuously masculine and manifestly unorthodox, and there is evidence that this type of behavior is related to a male need to distance the self from the feminine.

Nonetheless, there are problems with Gudeman's formulation, at least insofar as it applies to Tlayacapan. The church and fiesta, symbolically speaking, are neither simply nor primarily feminine. Ecclesiastical organization is predominantly masculine, and fiestas are organized mostly by males. As we have seen, the fiesta has other meanings and implications, and these suggest that festive vice is more than a reaction to femininity. And since the same men may simultaneously support the sacred aspects of the fiesta and yet engage in festive vice, we can infer that the latter is not quite as antithetical to the former as it may at first appear. Indeed, it can be argued that men's vice, albeit in paradoxical fashion, supports the moral order even as it opposes it.

The most salient semantic feature of the fiesta is its connection with spirituality. This very quality, by a kind of dialectical logic, may elicit an inclination to reaffirm the importance of natural reproduction, the precondition for spiritual relations. In the fiesta, spirituality is juxtaposed with the dances of the Eve-like Tenanches. And Holy Week and festivals representing the establishment of the church are preceded by invocations of pagan times in Carnival and the fairs.

The sponsors of the fiestas identify with the saints, that is, with martyrdom and self-sacrifice. Although there is virtue in this identification, there is also vulnerability, which, of course, gets associated with femininity and passivity. The mayordomos and their associates spend time and wealth in support of the banquets, masses, music, and fireworks; various households in the barrios or community make small contributions; and friends, compadres, and neighbors gather cooking utensils and help in the preparation of food. All these acts of sociability promote the success of the fiesta and are duly appreciated, but they are not performed without misgivings. Tlayacapenses believe that goodness—as in generosity—is desirable in principle but risky in practice. Any number of jokes and proverbs express the expectation that others will take advantage of those who are too good or who do not defend themselves. According to one popular saying, for example, "un bien con un mal se paga" (a good turn is repaid with a bad one). An overly generous person is deemed naïve and foolish; by contrast, a person who is less than saintly is likely to seem less naïve. One informant allowed that a man should be "neither good nor bad"; another said, "To ask for too much is greed, to ask for too little is foolishness, so it is better to be quiet." The fiesta, in other words, is associated with spirituality, asexuality, passivity, and femininity, characteristics that may motivate heterodox behavior in different but related ways.

It is suggestive that in Zinacantan the former mayordomos of the fiesta of San Sebastián impersonate pagan, and in some cases, clearly evil, beings during the fiesta. The impersonators entertain with obscene jokes and mime, poking fun in particular at those men who have not properly fulfilled their ritual and social duties, often accusing them of having too much sex with their wives and squandering money on them (Bricker 1973:46-67). Former mayordomos, it should be obvious, are precisely the ones who can be expected to take a special interest in making sure that other persons carry out their obligations to the fiesta. The implication would appear to be that the vulnerability associated with the fiesta encourages militant opposition to the forces of evil and, ironically, even identification with them. A similar logic seems to underlie ordinary male behavior in the street and heterodox elements in the ceremonial cycle in Tlayacapan. The expression of virile demeanor in everyday life informs other men that a man is willing and able to defend himself and thus, presumably, aims at deterring them from acting in an abusive manner, but it also implicates a man in morally questionable behavior. Similarly, displays of virility and manly courage in conjunction with spiritual kinship may be a means of underscoring moral norms and discouraging abusive behavior even though they also seem to compromise spiritual values. The message is directed at members of other barrios or members of one's own barrio, lest they mistake the celebration of a saint or Virgin or perceive the generosity of the sponsors and participants as signs of weakness.

Gudeman notes that men's activity in the field is informed with a sense of struggle. As in Tlayacapan, Panamanian peasants say that one has to struggle (*luchar*) for a living. I would add, however, that this sense of struggle has a moral connotation and that it carries over into other contexts. Tlayacapenses say that one must "know how to defend oneself in life"— that is, one must know how to make a living but also how to protect oneself against natural and human adversity. Struggle in this sense coheres with the struggle between the forces of good and evil. Natural adversity in the fields and abusive and exploitative behavior in the social sphere are often thought to be motivated by the Devil. In keeping with the metaphor of struggle, the Devil is commonly called "the Enemy."

In struggling with the Enemy, however, the villager is drawn into moral paradox: it becomes necessary to use evil to conquer evil. The church itself has rationalized militancy and moral compromise in dealing with the problem of evil. The papacy has its own soldiers, and the church often gave its blessing to so-called just wars against heathens. In these holy wars, images of saints were carried as standards and patrons and, with the approval of the clergy, acquired or enhanced the crusaders' reputations for bellicosity. The notions of holy war and fighting saint seem inconsistent with Christ's admonitions to love one's enemies and turn the other cheek, yet they have been part of Christianity since the earliest days. The acceptance of militancy is evident in Revelation, particularly in the personage of the Archangel Michael, the New Testament prototype of the fighting saint.

Several fighting saints figure in the folk religion of Tlayacapan. San Miguel Arcángel himself is the patron of a now-abandoned chapel in the major barrio of Santiago. People still believe that he fights the Devil and the Canícula on September 29; and he is the patron of the *graniceros*, who view themselves and their spiritual allies, the rain spirits, as Christian soldiers. Santiago, the patron of the main chapel at the east end of the village, is the image of the saint who led the Spaniards against the Moors. He carries a sword and sits astride a white horse, as befits his reputation as a warrior. Both San Miguel and Santiago are images of virility, more suggestive of strength and courage than of Christian charity.

A similar moral ambiguity is apparent in the figure of San Martín Caballero, the patron of a chapel in the major barrio of Rosario. Interest in San Martín is not localized to one barrio, however, since his picture is present among others on family altars throughout the village. He is shown mounted on horseback as he cuts his large cape in half with a sword. One informant explained that he was a gambler, drinker, and woman chaser. Eventually God resolved to determine whether he was as bad as he seemed. Assuming the guise of a naked mendicant, God placed himself in his path and begged for alms. The gambler, having just lost his fortune in a card game, had no money to spare but he still had his clothes. So he cut his fine cape in two in an act of saintly generosity.

The villagers' image of well-rounded manliness is not unlike that of San Martín. It admits the importance of both natural and spiritual qualities. The positive valuation of the natural or testicular component is evident in various expressions. The real man is said to be *muy macho* (very male) or *bien gallo* (a real rooster). Above all, he has *huevos* (eggs). Natural virility is evident in the successful courtship and wooing of women, the fathering of children, the physical exertion of work, and self-defense. It is further apparent in wit, musical ability, and almost any manly talent or skill.

Virility in these senses is admired, but masculine bravado per se is not given unqualified approval. The natural component of masculinity, desirable and irrepressible as it is, should be tempered by cultural and spiritual qualities. According to one traditional saying, for example, a man should be *feo, fuerte, y formal* (ugly, strong, and formal); that is to say, he should be natural and unassuming, physically strong, and well mannered and dignified.[1] When combined in proper proportions, virility and virtue are as much complementary as antithetical. Without the mitigating influence of culture and spirit, a fallen human nature would lead only to vice and sin; nonetheless, villagers appreciate that human nature such as it is has a proper role to play. Without nature there would be no human beings and people of good will would not have the strength to defend their families and the moral order.

Many beliefs and customs illustrate the apotropaic properties of *naturaleza* and sinister objects. Black cats are kept as protection against witches. *Naguales* are fought with the left hand or the excrement of a black donkey (the left hand carries sinister connotations; a black donkey may be a manifestation of the Devil). As noted earlier, people also protect themselves against *naguales* by turning their clothes inside out so the more natural side is presented in opposition. *Naguales* themselves assume animal guises to defend their lovers against other males. Weak blood makes one more vulnerable to *los aires*, which is why people fortify themselves by eating a pinch of salt or onion or by drinking rum before exposing themselves to them. Similarly, men drink rum for protection against ghosts when digging graves in the cemetery. Curers with bad temperaments are said to be better able to deal with evil spirits and to avoid the illnesses they cause, and men who have "strong blood" are thought to be better equipped to defend themselves against social adversaries. As mentioned earlier, according to folklore, people trick and cheat the Devil or discourage him by being more abusive than he is.

In the remainder of this chapter, the value of natural and even sinister attributes in the struggle against evil is examined in more detail. It should become clear that the customary behavior of men in the street and festive situations, whatever its underlying social and psychological motivation, constitutes a symbolic acquisition and assertion of natural power and an attitude of defense against the forces of evil. In this respect, the symbolic meanings of men's activity in the street are basically congruent with the contribution they make in their fields, at least insofar as their street behavior occurs in moderation. Obviously, there is a point at which sociable expressions of virility become mere vice or worse.

There are, of course, differences between the two spheres. Unlike the struggle in the field, which is hard and serious, the struggle with evil or the menace of the other in the street can be humorous and histrionic. It often occurs in what might be called a subjunctive mode; men simply *pretend* to struggle with the forces of evil. The masculinity expressed in the street may be largely theatrical, but it nonetheless entails real dangers and has detectable social consequences. Drinking can lead to fighting and killing; men have been gored in bull riding; and the swordplay at fairs, although rehearsed, has led to accidents. Moreover, men who remain aloof from the arena of the street may undermine the credibility of their masculinity in those contexts where it really counts.

Abuse and the Horns of the Male

The standard insults in male circles question a man's masculinity or impugn his mother's virtue, thereby suggesting the importance of virility for the defense of family honor. The expression "Soy tu padre" (I am your father) implies that the speaker had sex with one's mother. Telling a man that he is an *hijo de la chingada* (son of a bitch) casts similar aspersions; "Chinga tu madre" (Fuck your mother) compounds the affront to the mother with an invitation to incest. A less serious insult is the epithet *buey* (ox) or *pendejo* (pubic hair; figuratively, fool); if the terms follow the word *pinche* (kitchen boy), they are given more bite, as in *pinche buey*, a usage that clearly implies that masculinity is associated with getting out of the house. The insult "Pélame la verga" (Peel my penis) and its variants order the victim to submit to sodomy.

Serious as these insults appear to be, and sometimes are, the response to them can vary depending on social context and tone of voice. Insults, whether in jest or earnest, often gain in effectiveness when they are concealed in ostensibly inoffensive innuendos called *albures*. The *albur* is a pun, quibble, or double meaning, often combined with others in what may strike the outsider or slow-witted person as normal conversation or harmless verse. One hears *albures* in cantinas and on street corners where men gather in the evenings. *Albures* often begin when a man approaches the group and, perhaps, grabs the buttocks of someone in the group to suggest that he wants to sodomize him, saying, "Lend yourself to so-and-so! He can use you like an animal." A friend named Zacarías may be greeted, "¡Hola, Sacamocos!" (Hello, snot remover), which has the hidden meaning, "You make me ejaculate" (Zacarías sounds like *sacar*, "to take out," and *moco*, or "mucous," is a metaphor for semen). A friend named Martín may be greeted. "¡Hola Martín Cholano!"—the significant syllables being *in-cho* (I swell) and *ano* (anus). When a friend refers to another as *vale* (pal), the other may say, "No me digas vale porque mi leche se me sale" (Don't call me pal, because my milk will come out). In a typical exchange, Carlos approached Miguel and grabbed his buttocks, quipping, "What is happening, butt?" Miguel protested, "I am decent, don't be screwing with me," whereupon Carlos grabbed Miguel's chest and wisecracked, "Ay, little mother, what nice teats you have!" Carlos next intimated that Miguel was a homosexual, and Miguel responded by saying, "But I don't sleep with Manuela" (a woman's name but an allusion to masturbation because *mano* means "hand"); the response was telling, since Carlos was a bachelor and Miguel was married.

Performance of natural functions, such as sneezing, breaking wind, or even laughing out of control, renders one susceptible to verbal barbs. Sneezing may incite *albures* because mucous has a double meaning, and a mere innocent sneeze, then, may be taken as an insult that calls for a reply. If *albures* cause one to laugh, as they often do, someone may say, "Entre la chanza y la risa se va la longaniza" (Between the joke and the laugh there goes the sausage). One who breaks wind is especially apt to elicit a response, such as "Te saludo buen anciano, con el sombrero en la mano" (I salute you old man [*anciano*=*ano*=anus], with my hat [penis] in my hand), or "Te chispo un ojo y te acomodo un huevo" (I adorn you with an eye [penis] and furnish you an egg [testicle]).

Casual comments about bodily conditions sometimes draw ribbing. When Felipe innocently complained that he had a headache, Carlos remarked, "Yes, I can smell it." Once when Juan asked Julio to go drinking with him, Julio declined, saying he was sick; thereupon Juan claimed that Julio was not really sick but just having his "period" (playing on the use of the word "sick" for pregnancy) and had been giving himself douches. Julio, pointing a finger at Juan's truly formidable midsection, retorted that it was Juan, not he, who was "sick."

Usually such verbal jousting among men is not overly abusive and often is taken in good humor, each man giving as much as he gets while being careful not to go too far. However, when insults are directed toward one's mother or when one is cuckolded, exploited, or cheated, then abuse is not a laughing matter.

The truly abusive male is known as a *cabrón* (he-goat). He is tough and mean; he dominates and exploits others. He makes a cuckold of another man by seducing his wife so that she "puts the horns" on her husband. However, calling someone a *cabrón* does not always have weighty implications. At times, the word is bandied about so frequently in male conversation it suggests that every man is a *cabrón*. In Spain the word has the same connotations of abusiveness but it also refers to the *cabrón*'s victim—the cuckold. Commenting on this double meaning, Pitt-Rivers (1961:116) suggested, "The horns are figuratively placed upon the head of the wronged husband in signification of his failure to defend a value vital to the social order. He has fallen under the domination of its enemy and must wear his symbol." In Tlayacapan the sense of cuckold has been assumed by the word *buey* (ox). The imagery is the same, however, since the victim wears the horns. The ox, of course, is a castrated bull, an animal that has been robbed of its masculinity and made to serve others.

Besides turning other men into cuckolds, the *cabrón* may make them look like fools by exploiting them economically, as the following anecdote illustrates:

There are two compadres, one rich and the other poor, but the poor one is greedy. So the poor one says, "Listen compadre, you are rich, where did you get it?" The other, not wanting to share the secret of his wealth, says, "Why do you ask? I know how I got it." The poor one says again, "Look, compadre, don't be mean. I'm broke, and, well, I need money." The rich one says to himself, "To get rid of this *cabrón*, I'm going to screw him." So the poor one says, "Then what, compadre, do you say?" And the rich one says, "Well, you know, I have this money because I made a pact with the Devil." "Yes?" "Yes, I went to the barranca at midnight and waited for the Devil and exchanged my soul for money." So the poor one says, "Well, tomorrow I am going there."

And since the rich one knows which barranca his compadre will go to, he goes first and waits for him. The other arrives, calling, "Diablo! Diablo!" So his compadre says, "Yes, at your service, what can I do for you." "I want to make a pact with you." "Well," says the Devil, "with regard to souls, at present I am more interested in your anus." The poor compadre says, "Me, when was I ever a homosexual?" and goes away. But farther along he stops and says to himself, "But he is going to give me money. I'm going to return." He calls the Devil again and says, "I want to exchange my soul for money." But the Devil replies, "I told you I want your ass." The poor compadre goes away again, but returns, thinking, "I am going back, no one will see me." He calls the Devil and again the Devil says, "Yes, what can I offer you?" "I want to exchange my soul for money." The Devil says, "But I told you what the terms are." "Well, are you going to make me rich?" "Well, take off your pants." And he takes them off. The Devil grabs him and says, "Move, *cabrón!*" And the poor compadre says, "*Pendejo*, I am no queer!" And his compadre says, "*Cabrón*, nor am I the Devil!"

The anecdote says in effect that it is sometimes necessary to be a *cabrón*—in this instance, like the Devil himself, the greatest of *cabrones*—to defend oneself against the *cabrón*.

The Bull

The bull is a recurrent figure in the theater of masculinity. A Little Bull appears in the Dance of the Vaqueros and as a fireworks display on Fourth Friday; the pyrotechnic Little Bull appears again on Holy Saturday. Bulls are mounted in *jaripeos* and men drink "bulls" in fiestas and in *cantinas*. A similar fascination with bulls can be found in other regions of rural Mexico.

Some of the bull's meanings may derive from the Indian's relations with the Spaniard during the colonial period. The bull was an alien creature introduced to Mexico by the Spaniards. From the moment of its introduction, it posed a menace to the Indian community. Throughout central and southern Mexico bulls invaded Indian cornfields and destroyed crops; indeed, Spaniards repeatedly ran their herds into Indian lands with the aim of driving Indians away. Villages and entire regions were depopulated in this manner (Chevalier 1963:92-103). Colonial law restricted the ownership of cattle to Spaniards and limited Indian ownership and use of horses, which were needed to manage large herds. Although exceptions to the law occurred, in general cattle raising was a Spanish concern. Haciendas near Tlayacapan had cattle herds, as did wealthy Spaniards living within the village itself. Albino Salazar, the wealthiest man in Tlayacapan in the period preceding the Revolution of 1910, is said to have had more than a thousand head. As elsewhere in Mexico and Guatemala, beef butchers were Spaniards as well.

Ownership of cattle and the selling of beef, then, were instruments of Spanish hegemony, a social fact that was reflected in folk religious images of the Devil and the supernatural Little Bull. In the Dance of the Vaqueros, the owner of the Little Bull is a Spaniard. The supernatural Little Bull, which takes the form of slashing squalls that destroy crops, has its counterpart in the rampages of real cattle. Recall that the Devil is personified as a charro, a cowboy or hacendado in riding finery, and that villagers believe that the hacendados acquired their working capital from the Devil. A story told about a cattle-owning family of pre-Revolution Tlayacapan suggests that it too got its start through a contract with the Devil. According to the tale, a cattleman sold a mule to another villager. When the mule wandered off into the mountains, the new owner followed it, only to be led to a cave that belonged to the Enemy. Inside he discovered the cattleman tied up, in bondage "body and soul" to the Devil.

Bulls for *jaripeos* were traditionally lent to the village by the nearby hacienda of Pantitlán. The custom is described in a document dated 1765, a series of depositions regarding the boundaries of the village's communal lands. According to the recorded testimony, the hacienda contributed bulls, money, sugar, and honey for the *"fiesta titular"* in appreciation for the right to graze its cattle on the village's communal lands. The bulls and mules bearing the gifts were decorated with flowers and were led to the village by mulattoes on horseback and afoot. The custom was cited as evidence that the land belonged to the village, not the hacienda. The bull, in other words, was both a metaphoric and a metonymic expression of Spanish power. The bulls represented the Spaniard but also belonged to Pantitlán, an hacienda well positioned to make inroads on village lands.[2]

In Tlayacapan *los aires* are said to cause nightmares about bulls. In Tecospa bad dreams about bulls imply that a witch is trying to harm the dreamer (Madsen 1960:139). In Atla, another Nahuatl-speaking village, a dream about a bull portends the death of a friend (Montoya Briones 1964:177). Real bulls are dangerous and potentially destructive. A mature bull, head lowered, snorting, and pawing at the ground as if preparing to charge, can be an unnerving spectacle to anyone who is too close for safety. Once when Oscar and I were in such a predicament, he contemplated the animal with a wary eye and declared, "Doña Petra would say, 'Now the *demonio* has entered him!' "

Danger is a notable feature of *jaripeo* and, to a lesser degree, the tag-play with the pyrotechnic Torito. It is considered manly to mount bulls. Riders ridicule men who refuse to ride by questioning their manliness: "Why don't you mount one? Come on! Are you afraid? Aren't you a man?" Rival groups of riders tease each other when anyone procrastinates: "Ay, ay, shrimps, there are bulls, but you don't mount them—you are fearful shrimps!" When asked about the risk of injury and death, bull riders may say that riding a bull is a *gusto* (pleasure) even if it ends in death.

The Bull is not simply an evil figure. Don Lucio explained that the supernatural Little Bull is an instrument of evil but is not in itself diabolical. Ordinarily, the Torito does harm only when commanded to do so. Similarly, villagers see real bulls as potential vessels for demonic spirit but they also recognize that they perform a useful function by inseminating cows. Both the popular image of the bull and the innuendo in the Dance of the Vaqueros testify to the animal's association with sexuality and fertility. There are other indications of the bull's association with sexuality as well: the rider's position on the bull is sexually suggestive; the bull is urged to enter and otherwise assert his masculinity; the rider is called the "bride."

Awareness of the sexual connotations of the bull may begin early in life. Young boys imitate *jaripeo* in their play, one boy riding a "bull" (a stick with a bull's horn attached for a head) while another tries to distract the bull with a cape and still another, riding a "horse," tries to lasso it. The "bull," its upturned horn protruding from between the boy's legs, charges aggressively at available targets, including any giggling girls who happen to be nearby.

I once suggested that the classic bullfight is a symbolic act of courtship, which ends in sexual intercourse and death: the bullfighter begins wooing the bull from a passive, feminine posture but gradually assumes a masculine one, thereby inverting his first relation with the bull and proving his own virility at the expense of his male rival (Ingham 1964). I continue to think that this interpretation has merit, although I now suspect that McClelland (1964) better described the cultural meaning of the bullfight. In his view, the bullfighter is a demonic, underworld figure who seduces the feminine bull and kills it, an act that conflates sexual seduction and death. Indeed, he argues that the bullfighter is modeled after Harlequin, the demonic character in the commedia dell' arte who seduces young maidens; as McClelland notes, there is a strong resemblance between the bullfighter's hat and "suit of lights" and Harlequin's hat and colorful outfit, and like the bullfighter, Harlequin carries a sword and performs acrobatic movements.

In various parts of Spain, mock bull and heifer sacrifices occur in connection with the fiesta of San Sebastián or during the days before Carnival. The animals are "shot" and people consume large amounts of wine, said to be the blood of the bull or little cow. In the province of León young men wearing oxen horns charge toward young women and then are allowed to sleep with them without opposition from parents. In one community in Extremadura it was thought that the appearance of a fireworks cow and a boy masquerading as a little old lady represented Adam and Eve in paradise (Caro Baroja 1965:243-247). Douglass (1984) shows that the contemporary bullfight in Spain is metaphorically related to the male-female relationship in marriage. Idiom likens the bull to a female; there is, for example, a saying that "toro muerto, vaca es" (the dead bull is a cow). Although Douglass emphasizes the femininity of the bull and the masculinity of the bullfighter, her data are consistent with my argument that the bullfighter begins in a passive (feminine) position and finishes the bullfight in an active (masculine) one. In the *jaripeo* in Tlayacapan the rider is called the "bride" and the bull is a masculine figure, but the pattern may be essentially the same, since a willingness to ride bulls is considered a mark of masculinity.

The demonic, Harlequin-like qualities of the bullfighter are evident in the Dance of the Vaqueros in Tlayacapan. In the dance the bull is killed by the hacendado and his workers; the hacendado, we know, is closely associated with the Devil. Among the Totonac, Carnival ends with a bullfight. The Mulattoes and Malinches (Eve-like figures) dance but are interrupted by Tigers and Bulls. The latter cavort about in a scandalous manner while the Tigers make obscene sexual gestures. Finally, a Mulatto shoots the animals with a wooden gun and invites the spectators to drink the "blood" of the Bull (unfermented sugarcane juice). Ichon (1973:436-441) says that the Mulatto, or hacendado, who kills the animals is a variant of an indigenous fire god and a manifestation of the Devil.

The bullfighter's association with evil and the folk practice of drinking the "blood" of the bull are probably rooted in the pre-Christian origins of the bullfight. Bull ritual apparently spread to Spain from Italy, where it was well established in ancient times. The Greeks as well as the Etruscans worshiped bulls. The Itali worshiped the bull-god Mars, lord of battle. When the Roman armies conquered them, the bull hunts and fertility rites of rural Italy were reworked into Roman victory celebrations. Among the mystery religions that flourished in this context was Roman Mithraism, a mixture of local bull ritual and beliefs and cult practices borrowed from Persia and Asia Minor (see Conrad 1957:145-147). In time, the cult achieved popularity throughout the Roman Empire, particularly among the legionnaires. Remains of Mithraea have been found along Hadrian's Wall, in the Near East, and in Spain. Bas-reliefs, wall paintings, sculptures, and graffiti found in the Mithraea imply that Mithra and Sol, the sun god, were allies. They depict Mithra killing the Bull with a dagger while a snake and scorpion approach the Bull's testicles, perhaps attacking them. Corn can be seen emerging from the Bull's tail. In yet other scenes Mithra is an archer or mounted hunter. Recruits to the cult apparently partook of cakes and bread and a cup of wine in a rite of initiation, whereas the regular members consumed ritual meals of meat and wine.

A. D. H. Bivar (1975) has suggested that Mithra, the killer of the Bull, may have represented an evil, underworld figure. He notes, for example, that in Zoroastrian myth Ahriman (The Evil One) attacked the Bull. Moreover, a "lion-headed personage" in the cult may have derived from Ahriman and related Middle Eastern underworld deities, including the Babylonian Nergel, a god of death who was associated with hunting, warfare, plague, and the sun in its nocturnal, underworld phase. Nergel was apparently a variant of Gilgamesh, the slayer of the Bull in Babylonian myth. Ahriman was also a hunter.

The popularity of Roman Mithraism was an obstacle to the spread of Christianity during the first few centuries after Christ and, for the early Fathers of the Church, an outrage; to them, the sacrifice of the bull and the ritual consumption of beef and wine in Mithraism were a mockery of the Crucifixion and Communion and a work of the Devil. Yet it is clear that the folk, at least, have assimilated the bullfight into Christian categories. The bull was associated with Adam and Eve, and the bullfighter with the Devil. The bullfight thus complemented the story of Jesus. Just as Christ's death makes spiritual life possible, the death of the bull is associated with the propagation of natural life by Adam and Eve. The faithful share Christ's spiritual life through the Eucharist; the spectators of the mock bullfight receive parts of the bull or drink the bull's "blood."

Syncretism in sixteenth-century Mexico enriched this imagery in bullfight ritual. Pohl (1981) observes that the bull replaced the deer in post-Conquest Maya culture. The same thing happened in central and northwest Mexico. In Tlayacapan the Deer and Harlequin-like Hunter lead the Chinelos in the masquerades of the mini-Carnivals or invitations, just as several days of *jaripeo* anticipate the arrival of the Chinelos in Carnival proper, again suggesting a similarity between deer and bull. In pre-Hispanic culture, the deer was associated with Quetzalcoatl and Cihuacoatl, a god and goddess who created the race of commoners. Quetzalcoatl was also Adam-like in that he succumbed to immoral temptation (that is, drunkenness and incest). Mixcoatl, the hunter, was a god of the north and a guise of Tezcatlipoca, a maker of fire. As noted earlier, Quetzalcoatl and Cihuacoatl merged respectively with Adam-Cortés and Eve–la Malinche, whereas Tezcatlipoca-Mixcoatl was incorporated into the images of the Devil and Harlequin.

The ritual killing and consumption of the bull, then, alludes to the value and dangers of natural, libidinal energy. The bullfighter excites the bull and kills him, implying that evil and death are necessary conditions for both the positive and negative manifestations of the libido. There are interesting ambiguities, however. Since the bull is a vessel for evil and variously masculine and feminine, it may represent the influence of the Evil One in the form of either Adam or Eve. Thus the bullfighter may be more Adamic than demonic; and indeed there are places in Mexico where the killers or companions of the bull are "grandfathers" or "old men" (Bricker 1973:12-67; Parsons and Beals 1934:502).

The bullfight, thus, may represent the seduction of Eve by the Devil, and through her the Fall of Adam, but it may also symbolize an attempt to control and appropriate demonic power. In the Dance of the Vaqueros the bull belongs to the hacendado but his peones (that is, Indians) participate in its killing and dismembering. In colonial Tlayacapan the bull of *jaripeo* was again the property of the hacendado, and even today it comes from outside the community. The rider, meanwhile, is an ordinary villager, formerly an Indian. In mounting the bull, he symbolically asserts his power and that of his community vis-à-vis the hacienda or another community.

Animality and Drunkenness

As a mark of participation in the milieu of the street and as a somewhat backhanded compliment for possessing the attributes of primordial virility, many men in Tlayacapan are known by *apodos* (nicknames). Sons may inherit nicknames from their fathers, but more often, they get their own names in recognition of amusing habits, idiosyncrasies, facial features, or natural impulses. The Coyote was named for his prurient interest in the legs of young women; Do-Not-Move used to say, "Don't move!" before a fight; la Jitomate (a feminine version of *el jitomate*) is a tomato planter who once indicated the size of his ripe tomatoes with a gesture lewdly suggestive of female genitals; and Angel was dubbed the Devil by his teacher because even as a schoolboy he was notorious for his pranks and off-color humor. Since I wore a black hat when a white one was customary, I was called the Black Charro, a likely allusion to the Devil. Other men were known as the Drunk, Hare, Goat, Parrot, Heron, Bird, Pig, Parakeet, Old Lady, Badger, Gypsy, Fly, Rat, Climate, Fat One, Cow, Silvered One, Scorpion, Snake, Toad, Monkey, Squirrel, Scythe, Cheese, Indian, Eyebrow, and Screw. Women usually are not given such epithets unless they participate in the "merry life" of the street. A prostitute in a nearby town, for example, was called the Delicious One.

As these names imply, there is something uncivilized about men. For many women, the most scandalous thing about them may be their penchant for heavy drinking. Not a few women describe men sarcastically as "pure drunkards." To be sure, drinking is a typically male behavior. Women may drink a little at fiestas, but rarely to intoxication, and what sipping they do usually takes place apart from their menfolk. Men, by contrast, may drink heavily at fiestas, during Carnival, on weekends, or just about any time, for that matter.

Currently, beer can be purchased in about a dozen stores in the village; hard liquor is available in only a few. Any of these stores can serve as a cantina simply by providing a folding table and a few chairs, although excursions to real cantinas and houses of ill repute in other towns and cities are not unusual.

Generally, a group of drinkers forms in an impromptu fashion. Men in a cantina's doorway signal to passing friends to join them, posturing annoyance if they detect any reluctance; or en route from one drinking spot to another, the inebriated men gather recruits. When several men are planning a trip to another town, they may spend considerable time persuading others to join them. Some men are not always eager to drink, and when they do, it is often in response to these social pressures. If a sober man knows his friends are drinking in a certain cantina, he may take a long way around to his destination to avoid encountering them. When invited to drink, unwilling men may make excuses such as "I have work to do" or "I'm sick, the doctor said no alcohol."

Drinkers, though, wise to these ruses, continue to coax the demurrers, pleading, "Just one, just one for the thirst"; and one inevitably leads to many. When a man has emptied one bottle of beer, his companions persuade him to have another, intoning, "One is none, two are half, and three are one," or, "Three is the rule." They try to win over the most stubborn holdouts by appealing to their masculine pride, chiding, "They beat you," implying that the nondrinker is dominated by his wife or mother. Men may resist such needling for as much as an hour before they agree to drink. Declining an invitation is considered a breach of etiquette, at least by those who offer it, and the man who declines is seen as rude and unfriendly. The person whose invitation is rejected often takes offense and, at the very least, will put on a display of hurt feelings as a further persuasion to the abstainer.

The pace of drinking is set by the group, not by individuals. All raise bottles or glasses simultaneously, often with the toast "¡Salud!" (health), and tapping their bottles or glasses together. The pattern of toasting keeps everyone drinking the same amount, which is important, since often there is an element of competition in drinking. Concern with not "lasting" surfaces in arguments over whose turn it is to drink when a bottle of rum is passed from hand to hand. As the drinking progresses, men who doubt their capability to last may claim falsely that they already have had their turn, but such duplicity, too, can lead to altercations.

Because alcohol may make some men less respectful, there is a tendency to avoid drinking in the presence of respected persons, except at fiestas. Sons rarely drink with their fathers, and compadres either do not drink with each other or do so with conscious restraint. Adolescent boys sometimes drink, but not in the presence of older men. Inebriated men put their arms around each other, their speech becomes maudlin and effusive, and their tempers flare easily. They may engage in profane repartee that can lead to face-saving fights. People say , "Little by little drunks become brave," and the "braver" they become the more they hanker for a fight. Even normally friendly men may become belligerent when they are intoxicated. Friends try to restrain the contentious drunk whose anger may stem more from a desire to maintain self-respect than from any long-standing grudge. On occasion, however, passion rules, and since men carry knives, machetes, or pistols, intentions sometimes go astray, with tragic results. More than half the homicides in the community occur during fights between drunk men.

At home drunks are more apt to beat their wives, and in the street they are less likely to show respect for women. In the past, groups of drunks were known to gang-rape women. The victims were usually unattached women or outsiders who had come to the village as prostitutes or sellers of liquor for Carnival or fairs. The idea may have been that such women do not deserve respect and may even deserve punishment, as a lesson to others.

The association between drunkenness, animality, and sexuality, which is extremely old in central Mexico, may account for the characteristics of the *nagual* in Tlayacapan. The Aztecs used to say of the drunk that he had become his rabbit—that one of the four hundred rabbits of drunkenness had entered him (Sahagún 1956:1:325). Quetzalcoatl, a god who was seduced into drunkenness and incest and who was affiliated with the gods of alcohol, was the patron of the thief-*nagual* (see chapter 6).

In present-day Tlayacapan, men who see *naguales* often are drunk at the time, and *naguales* seem predisposed to attack drunks. In one instance, what was thought at first to be a *nagual* turned out, on closer inspection, to be nothing more than another drunk. Indeed, drunken men and *naguales* are suspiciously alike. Both undergo temporary transformations, usually at night. *Naguales* rarely are women, and women rarely drink to excess. Drunks and *naguales* both roam the streets, posing a potentially serious but usually inconsequential threat to others; both inflict bloody noses; both are unable or unwilling to inhibit erotic urges; and both are known to apologize for their offenses, once they are again sober, or human, as the case may be.

Idiomatic expressions and humor further attest to a cultural association between intoxication and animality. According to a joke villagers tell about the origin of alcoholic beverages,

The first alcohol, although it made one slightly drunk, left much to be desired. So the brewers added the blood of a parrot, and this second batch interfered with the power of speech. It was getting better, but the people thought that something was still missing, so they added the blood of a lion. It made drunks aggressive. Thinking that an essential ingredient was yet lacking, the brewers added some monkey blood, an addition that brought success. Ever since, drunks have been utterly shameless!

To be half drunk is to be *medio chile* (the chile pepper is a common metaphor for penis); to be fully drunk is to be *bien bruto* (really brutish), *bien burro* (like a donkey), *bien pedo* (really farted), *bien meco* (like a wild Indian), or *bien cuete*.[3] A hangover is called the *cruda* (rawness). To visit a house of prostitution—where drinking is part of the protocol—is *ir al burro* (go to the donkey). A mixed drink made with rum is called a "bull." Both drunks and animals lack "reason" and "judgment," according to villagers. Yet another similarity between a drunk and *nagual* is suggested by the following riddle:

Agua de las verdes matas,
me tumbas pero no me matas,
y me haces andar agatas.
(Water of the green plant,
you knock me down but you don't kill me,
and you make me walk on all fours.)

The answer is "pulque," the maguey beer. The *nagual*, it may be noted, is a domesticated animal, an animal that participates in human society. The drunken male is an ordinary "Christian" who, from time to time, becomes animalistic. Each is a somewhat liminal creature, operating somewhere between nature and culture. Villagers sometimes say that the person who becomes a *nagual* is *travieso* (flighty, mischievous), implying, perhaps, that the person has insufficient control over natural impulses.

The traditional recipe for making a "bull" was to flavor rum with anise or lemon juice. When soft drinks first entered Tlayacapan, "bulls" were made by mixing rum with any blood-colored soft drink. The bull drink, in other words, represents the blood of the ritually sacrificed bull. Like the ritual bull, the drink has sinister connotations. Villagers say that rum is a "vice" brought to the New World by Spaniards. Rum is made from sugarcane and was distilled on the haciendas; the haciendas were owned by Spaniards and, according to popular belief, were sponsored by the Devil. Similar associations between rum and the Devil occur elsewhere in Middle America. Among the Totonac, the Devil is the true owner of the sugarcane refinery, and rum is said to come from the Devil (Ichon 1973:212).

In the highland Maya community of Atchalán in south-central Guatemala, a Ladino- or Spaniard-like Judas figure is said to be the patron of the *parranda* (drunken, sleepless revelry). Judas is the hated outsider and the manager of the plantation; he is also the butcher who monopolizes the sale of beef and the owner of bulls. In addition, the Judas figure, it seems, is the patron of young men who are serving their first year in the ritual system of fiesta sponsorship. They get drunk in honor of Judas and even dance with his image, although, ironically, their task is one of breaking up drunken brawls and patrolling the community against the *tronchador*, a tall, thin Ladino who sneaks up behind people and breaks their necks under cover of darkness; later, he devours his victims or sells their flesh as beef. The *tronchador* is similar to Judas (Moore 1979:69-70). In other words, the young constables consume alcohol and identify with the enemy of the community so as to protect the community against drunkards and the forces of evil.

The cultural meaning of heavy drinking in Tlayacapan evinces similar themes. Alcohol enhances the subjective sensation of natural power, yet, since in large quantities it also makes one weak, drunkenness is at the same time an experience of struggling with the forces of evil. The struggle begins even before the first swallow, as men attempt to avoid drinking in the first place. In this respect, the meaning of drinking is precisely the same as that of bull riding. In fact, village men are aware of the similarity between trying to stay atop a bull in *jaripeo* and the struggle to stay upright when imbibing rum.[4]

This interpretation of the cultural significance of alcohol accounts for many ethnographic details, but it also poses a puzzle: how can the consumption of alcohol represent communion with both Adamic beings, on the one hand, and Christ and the saints, on the other? A general solution to the puzzle may be found in the complementarity—discussed earlier—between virility and virtue. A more specific explanation may lie in the Christian concept of blood and particularly Christ's blood, of which the wine of Communion is supposedly a transubstantiation. Christ's blood—and presumably that of the saints—has an ancient ancestry that includes both good and evil persons. According to Matthew, Christ's ancestors included Ruth, who had offspring by an alien being; Tamar, who played the part of a prostitute in order to have children; Rahab who was a prostitute; and Bathsheba, an adulteress. Ultimately, Christ's blood derives from Adam and Eve, the couple that brought sin into the world. According to the theologian Lucien Deiss (1976:152-153), the faithful commune with the entire history of Israel in the Eucharist. The villagers may not be aware of all the details of Christ's ancestry, but they know that his ancestors were pagans; the Tenanches, they say, are his "Grandmothers."

Carnival and Fairs

Carnival and fairs are occasions for heavy drinking, whoring, and bull riding as well as for explicit identification with pagan and evil beings. In the fairs, the themes of struggling with evil and dominating and appropriating the primordial animal—the bull—are explicit. They are hardly less so during Carnival, although that of struggling with evil is more ironic and more clearly illustrates the principle that I have been discussing here, namely, identifying with evil to defeat evil.

Antagonism is evident in Carnival along both horizontal and vertical axes. Fights are more apt to occur between individuals during Carnival than at any other time of year. Even more evident are frictions between major barrios. In the past there were occasional donnybrooks between rival dance groups as they encountered each other in the streets, and even today there is a strong sense of rivalry between them, each vying to present more dancers with more impressive costumes and flags. It seems likely that this competition is related to secular political competition between the barrios. We have already seen that village politics is structured in part by barrio affiliation. This is apparent in the way in which village officials are nominated and elected, and it became especially evident in the conflict surrounding Father C. Since most of the major barrio of Santiago sided with Father C., and most of the major barrio of Santa Ana opposed him, these sentiments were also reflected in the respective groups of la Unión and América. A handful of pro–Father C. families in Santa Ana felt so alienated that they denied their natal dance group affiliation and joined the group of la Unión. In this connection it may be significant that the masquerades and parades of Chinelos converge on the plaza in front of the town hall. It is in the plaza that political assemblies are held and the commissioners of communal and ejido lands are nominated and selected. Ritual, in other words, may be a means of kindling enthusiasm for collective political action in the plaza.[5]

There is in addition on the vertical axis an undercurrent of hostility toward the Spaniard, whether as hacendado or member of the local elite. People say that in the colonial period the Spaniards gave the Indians only three days of rest during the entire year, and they add that the Indians were so happy when the rest came that they would "jump for joy like animals released from a corral." The Chinelos' masquerade and dance, however, were a ritual rebellion against, as well as a release from, Spanish authority. By dressing as Chinelos, visiting prostitutes, and becoming intoxicated, the Indian made a mockery of the Spaniards' stereotype of the Indian, becoming in play what the Spaniard imagined them to be in essence: drunken heathens. Indians did not, by participating in this ritual drama, cease to regard themselves as moral persons, however. To the contrary, we know that they were inclined to suspect that the Spaniard was the one who had closer ties with the Devil. The Chinelo mask may assert as much, since its protruding beard and green eyes are European, not Indian, characteristics. One informant explained that the Chinelos wear dresses and speak in high voices to suggest that the Spaniard is a homosexual. What is more, when the Indians donned their disguises and converged on the center of the village—the residential neighborhood of the local elite—in a militaristic show of force, they not only teased the rich but conveyed something about the potential for actual rebellion.

Carnival, fair, and the fiesta are symbolic constituents in the structure of ritual time. Each represents a different moment in the moral progression of history. Carnival is an evocation of pagan times, beginning in Eden and lasting until the Christian Era. The fiesta, I have shown, represents spiritual kinship, the reintegration of nature into the sphere of God's grace. The fair is an ambiguous event. It represents both the pagan and the spiritual—that is, the real condition of the world. Whereas Carnival celebrates the profane values of the street and the fiesta the sacred values of the home and ritual kinship, the fair combines elements of both.

Doña María explained that Lent commemorates the time when Jesus walked on the earth, which is to say that the Lenten fairs represent his visits to various communities. In other words, during Lent the sacred makes its appearance in a fallen world. The fairs allude to both pagan times and Christian society and dramatize the struggle between good and evil. In Carnival, all the performers play the parts of pagan or evil beings. In the fiesta, at the other end of the spectrum, allusions to nature and evil persist, as if to say that in this world tainted nature must continue until the second coming.

Saint Michael, Mary, and the Rain Spirits

The *granicero* cult in northern Morelos also illustrates the theme of struggling with evil. According to the *graniceros*, good weather spirits are led by San Miguel Arcángel. He is said to be a *lucero* (star, probably Venus), and he assumes the form of a benevolent white cloud. He is thought to work on the side of God and to have the help of various lightning-hurling saints, particularly Santa Juanita de la Cruz, Santa Barbarita Centella, Santa Barbarita Doncella, and Santa Teresita de Jesús. In addition, the ranks of the good weather spirits include many *ahuaque*, or rain spirits, beings also known as *espíritus* or *aires del tiempo* (weather spirits).

The rain spirits are organized into local militarylike groups that correspond to local shrines on mountainsides, often at the mouths of caves. They fight with lightning that they make with slings and cartridges of gunpowder. Similarly, villagers use exploding rockets to fend off hail storms.[6] Although the rain spirits are generally thought to be good spirits, their lightning bolts can leave illness-causing *aires* in the ground.

People who are struck by lightning and survive the ordeal are understood to have an obligation to serve the weather spirits. Being struck by lightning is thought to give one a gift for controlling bad weather and curing *aire* illness and other afflictions. Those who agree to serve in this fashion are called *sirvientes* (servants), *graniceros*, or *trabajadores temporales* (weather workers).

Graniceros believe that they can revive persons who have been struck by lightning. Using a red *jícara* filled with water and geranium petals, they perform a ceremony similar to the one for curing *susto* described earlier.

Those who survive a lightning strike without such treatment may suffer for months or even years from insomnia, loss of appetite, and disquieting encounters with spirits. In this event, relief is likely to come only when the victim has been treated by a *granicero* and agrees to serve the weather spirits. After making a commitment, the person is inducted into the local group of *graniceros* in a ceremony called a "coronation," which *graniceros* from the surrounding region attend. The rain spirits are summoned with rockets and offerings of white flowers, chicken *mole*, fruit, bread, tobacco, alcohol, candles, and incense.

The principal servant, called the *mayor*, keeps two *jícaras* as "signatures" to represent the obligation of each servant and his or her spouse. The unity of the *mayor*, the servants, and the local rain spirits is symbolized by three pairs of small polychrome angels that represent the servant and spouse; two other pairs are placed at the shrine in the countryside, two are kept by the *mayor*, and two by his servant. Each servant also "plants" a cross on a table in his home.

Don Lucio's table is oriented on an east-west axis. In the middle is a small, wooden image of a house or church, topped with a cross and framed by small crosses at each side. Images of the Virgen de Guadalupe and small clay images of angels are stationed in the house and near its entrance. To the right, the east end of the table, is a large jug of water that he calls *agua blanca* (white water) or *agua de ceniza* (water with ashes), which contains good spirits. Immediately to the left of the house is a second large jug of water containing the spirits of lightning; its water is described as clear or "green." A third jug at the west end of the table is said to contain spirits of "bad waters," "tempests," the Water Snake, and lightning. Don Lucio uses it to combat evil: "Con el malo, lo malo se controla" (Evil is controlled with evil). The *jícaras*, which are said to represent the earth (as well as signatures of his servants), are kept under the table, along with a set of the black and red dolls used in curing *aire* illness (see chapter 9).

The most important *granicero* shrine in central Mexico is Alcaleca (house of rain), a cave on the side of the volcano Popocatépetl. *Graniceros* near Tlayacapan have their own local shrine, an altar in the crux of a forked tree in a clearing on a nearby mountainside, a spot where two *graniceros* in the local group were struck by lightning. The altar holds two crosses. On the trail leading to the clearing, there is a small tree with a cross that serves as a door to the clearing.

In early May and again in early November, at the beginning and end of the rainy season, roughly, each group of *graniceros* makes a journey to its shrine or to Alcaleca. The ceremony in May falls on the second, the eve of the day of the Santa Cruz; in November it is on the fifth, the church's day for honoring the relics of saints and a date that closely follows All Saints' and All Souls' Days. At the beginning of the rainy season the *graniceros* ask for good rains; at the end, they give thanks to the spirits for all they have done for the campesinos.

The November that I participated in the ceremony, we approached the clearing on foot and horseback, stopping at the cross marking the doorway to the clearing. We built a fire to produce coals for the censers and attached marigolds to the cross. Holding his censer and facing the cross, Don Lucio greeted the spirits:

> Ave María Purísima, Ave María Santísima.
> In the name of the Holy Trinity,

> God the Father, God the Son, and God the Holy Spirit. . . .
> Weather-working angels,
> local groups from the districts and those of the governing place,
> from all the surrounding countryside who pass on this day,
>   to receive these garden flowers,
> Santa Juanita de la Cruz, madre de Jesús Cristo.
> Señor San Miguel Arcángel, you will be our guide and
>   our protector on this day. . . .

The other participants joined in praises and prayer, and then Don Lucio continued:

> Ave María Purísima, Ave María Santísima,
> Mother Cross serene, now lightning struck.
> Here where you are struck, this little tree,
> in this field of God,
> arms open, awaiting good weather and bad,
> tempests, hail showers, and storms,
> you are the one who suffers for us,
> and for our fields and our crops,
> beloved mother, receive this comfort and happiness from heaven,
> that we have come to glorify you on this day,
> on this very day.

The group then moved forward and entered the clearing, where it sang praises to the Señor de Chalma and the Santa Cruz. At the shrine, Don Lucio stood on a stump facing Popocatépetl, singing and inviting the spirits to attend and partake of the aroma of incense. Each servant then faced the crosses at the altar one at a time, making the sign of the cross with a censer and thanking the weather spirits personally. The altar was cleared of dirt and old flowers and decorated with fresh marigolds. At the foot of the tree candles were lit and an offering was made of chicken *mole*, bread, fruit, alcohol, and tobacco. After the spirits were served, members of the group shared the meal.

The ceremony in May is similar except that palm fans, brooms, and *jícaras* also are offered to the spirits and small polychrome angels are placed on the altar. The figures, painted pink, red, white, and light blue, represent the rain spirits or soldiers who struggle with the bad weather spirits. The following November they will be found tarnished and broken, casualties of the rainy season. In May the flowers included in the offering are predominantly white, such as gladiolus and baby's breath.

The sinister weather spirits include the Culebra de Agua, the Torito, evil winds, the spirits of hail, the rainbow, and some of the rain spirits. Generally, Don Lucio spoke of the rain spirits as though they were good, but he implied that their clouds could be turned to evil purposes by the bad spirits, and on occasion he seemed to say even some of the rain spirits are bad.

Similarly, some *graniceros* are known to use their gifts for evil. Don Lucio described how a weather worker in another community sent a large black cloud toward Lucio's hamlet. As the threatening cloud hovered above and lightning crashed all about him, Don Lucio used his palm fan and broom to send the cloud back to where it came from. He said that a *granicero* must know how to speak to the spirits "in anger." Even well-intentioned *graniceros* must know how to propitiate and control evil weather spirits.

Besides housing various crosses and being a shrine for the worship of San Miguel Arcángel, lightning saints, and the rain spirits, Alcaleca is associated with the Culebra de Agua, the Torito, and the spirits of hail. This same dualism is seen in Don Lucio's household shrine: the clay angels are placed on top of the table, but underneath are small clay images of a horseman, coyote, little bull, snake, and other creepers and crawlers.

9. Los Aires

In earlier chapters we considered images of the woman but only touched on the subjective experience of women. In this chapter I shall say more about female experience through the description and analysis of demonic affliction. An examination of the symbolism of symptoms and curing procedures will indicate something of the emotional stress and deprivation that go with the woman's role and will at the same time round out my demonstration of the systematic character of traditional culture.

The emotional experience of women in Tlayacapan must be understood in the context of patriarchal values and sexual mores in general and women's relationships with husbands and fathers in particular. Both men and women suppress their sexuality within the marital relationship, but women do so under the rule of male authority. And since it is a matter of cultural values that women should be more spiritual and less "natural" than men, they are denied the opportunities men have for the expression of their needs and emotions outside the home. I suggest in this chapter that womens' denial of nature leads to its conversion into physical ailments that, say the villagers, are caused by *los aires*. I argue that *aire* affliction is a symbolic transformation of natural and spiritual reproduction and so, for women, a variation on the biblical theme that a woman's fate is one of conception, pain, and conflict with the serpent. Given that *los aires* pose a special menace to children, beliefs about them cohere also with the apocalyptic vision of Satan as the persecutor of the Child as well as the Woman.

Los Aires

One informant said that *los aires* are dark-skinned beings who prefer to attack people with light skins. Male *aires* tend to pester women, whereas female *aires* harry men. *Aires* may attack any part of the body, although not infrequently they are attracted to the genitalia. They molest fetuses and cause miscarriages and deformities; and on at least one occasion, an *aire* is said to have impregnated a woman with six piglets. They have been known to

make a man's testicles swell to "the size of soccer balls." *Aires* also cause
nightmares about being eaten by ants or being chased by snakes, bulls, or
black men (an *aire* came to one woman in her dreams as a black man who
tried to lie on top of her). Not all dreams about *aires* are unpleasant,
however. The night after her husband took some of the fertile tailings from
an anthill to spread on his field, Lucia danced with little male *aires* around
the anthill in her dream.

People are more vulnerable to the *aires* at certain times and under certain
conditions, for example, when they are overheated or have just finished a
meal. Whenever one is warm, say, on getting out of bed, one must be careful
not to go directly outside.

In addition to the harm they can do to fetuses and genitalia, *aires* cause
earaches, headaches, rashes, pimples, cold sores, blisters, warts, eye sores,
tics, twitches, inexplicable pains, anesthesia, paralysis, and palsy, especially
of the facial muscles. An *aire* made one woman walleyed as she was
crossing a bridge.

When the *aires* are not molesting villagers, they seem to spend much of
their time eating. Once, returning from the fields with Don Lucio and
Lucina, his daughter-in-law, I was asked, as we crossed over a barranca on a
small bridge, whether I smelled anything peculiar. Could I not smell the
garlic? The *aires*, they said, were having lunch. It seems that people often
are attacked because they bother *aires* as they are eating.

Foods, medicinal herbs, and illnesses in Tlayacapan are said to be either
"hot" or "cold." These qualities, which are metaphysical more than
physical, do not necessarily describe temperature in the ordinary sense. As a
rule, illness results from the excess of one or the other of the two qualities
and is treated with herbs of the opposite quality (Ingham 1970a). Because
aires are cold, they are treated with hot herbs. The usual home remedy
involves "cleaning" (that is, stroking) a patient's body with such warming
herbs as sweet basil, rue, Santa María, *zopilote*, *estafiate*, myrtle,
peppermint, *salverial*, *cordoncillo*, or *pirú*. If this treatment fails to bring
relief, the patient may seek the help of a curer, who may be a shaman who
specializes in curing illnesses caused by weather spirits. Since *aires* have
volition, a mere application of herbs is not always efficacious. They must be
appeased. The curer communicates with them in dreams or visions to learn
how they were offended (for example, the patient stepped on their food) and
to determine what might mollify them (for example, an offering of food).

The curer "cleans" the patient twice daily with *aire* herbs for three days;
on the fourth day, a single, more elaborate rite is performed. During this
seventh and final treatment the curer cleans the patient with the herbs and
then with a variety of other objects, among them a set of fourteen small clay
figurines that are manufactured in the barrio of Santa Ana by the same
families that make clay figurines for All Saints' and All Souls' Days. Unlike

these other dolls, however, the *aire* dolls are painted black with red stripes. The set makes up a centerpiece depicting the patient, curer, and patient's spouse, two men on horseback, two women holding chickens, two bulls, a coyote with a chicken in its mouth, a snake, a lizard, a scorpion, a centipede, a toad, and a bird called a *huilota*, with attached whistle. The number of dolls is fixed by custom, but their form is somewhat variable; one doll maker, for example, includes a tarantula when asked to make a set. Other objects employed in the rite include twenty-four cigarettes, a bottle of rum, a black chicken, unsalted tamales, unsalted green or red *mole*, bread, chocolate, bananas, lemons, red tulips, an egg, *chile pasilla*, and a homemade broom. Pairs of cigarettes are tied with red yarn to all the dolls except for the centerpiece and bird.

Before beginning to clean the patient, the curer arranges the ritual items on a table covered with red paper. When all are in place, he sprinkles them with rum and begins to clean the patient, passing each object (herbs, food, figurines, and black chicken) over the patient's entire body one at a time in a series of gentle stroking motions, starting at the head and working down to the feet. People say that the black chicken may die or go blind from the badness it absorbs. When the curer is finished, he places the ritual objects in a basket and shares some rum with the patient and attending family. Last, the curer takes the basket to the anthill, blowing the whistle along the way to attract the *aires*, and offering rum to passersby for their protection. He continues to blow the whistle until he reaches the anthill. There he greets the *aires* respectfully, announcing that he has brought them a meal. He lays out the red paper, sprinkles rum over it, spreads out the entire offering, including the now-dead chicken and other items of food, and sprinkles more rum. Again he speaks to the *aires*, telling them that they have been served and given their due and now they must leave the patient in peace.

Illness produced by *los aires* is less serious than the condition known as *mal aire*. The latter is caused by more sinister *aires* or *espíritus malos* (evil spirits), often the spirits of murder victims. Witches can intentionally direct evil air at a victim using a technique known as *aire echado* (thrown air). A mixture of salt, cooking oil, egg, and bones and earth from the grave of a murder victim is formed into a ball and thrown against the victim's house. The mixture may cause illness to the householders or bring about their economic ruin. Salt used in witchcraft is said to make money slip through one's fingers like sand. Salt alone can achieve this effect if it is placed on a five-centavo coin and thrown on a rooftop. The salt must be borrowed from seven married couples.

Don Lucio treats the illness by first making the sign of the cross before the patient and praying. Then he asks the patient to stand next to a brazier for a treatment "with fire." The smoke from one or more "hot" herbs combines with that of burning incense to rid the patient of the bad spirit. Don Lucio facilitates the process by holding his blessed palm (that is, woven strips from a frond blessed on Palm Sunday) in the rising smoke and then stroking the patient with it.

The curing of *aire* illness can have erotic connotations. One day when Doña Petra complained about a rash on her leg that she thought had been caused by *aires*, María teased her, saying that Don Otilio might be willing to "clean" her with his underwear. Don Otilio, jumping at the chance to rib Doña Petra a little, admitted that he would be delighted to oblige. He said he would even clean her leg "right up to the top!" Not surprisingly, men are often suspicious of the relationships between their wives and male curers. One husband was seized with jealousy when he came home and found his wife seated on the bed being cleaned by a strange man; she, however, continues to insist, "He never touched me!"

Los Aires, the Evil Eye, and Children

The *aires* of the ground are prone to attack fetuses and newborns. They are but one of several types of miasmata that menace children. Babies and youngsters are also subject to *mal de ojo* (evil eye) or *daño* (harm), an affliction attributed to persons who have "strong vision." When such a person admires a child and experiences envy—a hot emotion—looking at the child will cause it harm. Children are more vulnerable to the evil eye than adults because their blood is "weak," "sweet," or "cool." The physically attractive child is especially apt to attract the glance of a covetous adult and so is more likely to suffer the sickness. By contrast, ill-tempered children, whose blood is more like that of adults, and unattractive children are less affected.

The standard diagnostic and curing procedure is first to rub the afflicted child with an unbroken chicken egg. The curer then taps the egg in the sign of the cross on the edge of a glass of water, cracks the shell, and drops its contents into the water. If bubbles arise from the yolk, if an eye or whirlwind forms in the albumen, or if part of it turns white (as if cooked by the hot vision), then the child is thought to have the sickness. If the yolk also rolls over in the glass, then the child's ailment is indeed grave. The symptoms of *daño* include hot hands, feet, and head, a cold trunk, and diarrhea and vomiting. Often, people say, the left eye fills with pus and closes. When a child dies of the sickness, the eye may even come out of its socket. The child with evil eye sickness is said to smell like a rotten egg. The forehead may have a salty taste, and the curer, having licked it, may feel like throwing up the next day.

In addition, the young victim is rubbed or cleaned with *chile pasilla* (hot), alum (hot), and *jarilla* (cool). The egg, which is said to be cool, apparently collects most of the badness. The alum and *chile pasilla* may be burned in the hearth. A male or female image of the culprit appears in the burned alum. If the child truly has the evil eye sickness, the smoke from the *chile pasilla* will not irritate the eyes of the people who are present at the curing ritual, yet the perpetrator will have bloodshot eyes the next day. Any herbs that may remain after the treatment are thrown into the street. Following the cleaning with the egg and herbs, the child also may be rubbed with the inside of a woman's skirt or slip, the ends of a woman's hair, or a man's underwear (one curer told me that she was losing her hair from having cured so much evil eye sickness). If after three treatments the patient does not improve, he or she may be held in the smoke from the burning *chile pasilla*, alum, and three pieces of garbage gathered from each of the four corners of the village plaza. Although the practice is unusual, one woman, heeding the advice of a compadre, sought relief from evil eye sickness for her child by asking the priest for *evangelios*. Following the same logic applied in the treatment of *susto* described earlier, she selected several godfathers and godmothers: the former were drunkards and the latter, prostitutes.

Certain amulets offer protection: a seed called *ojo de venado* (deer's eye) or a little sachet of garlic, clove, or cumin. The child may be dosed with a spoonful of cooking oil in which a scorpion has been boiled, or the child's forehead may be crossed with cooking oil. Rings, earrings, and bracelets of gold or sea coral also are effective preventives because they absorb the harm. Although most persons who have strong vision are unaware of the danger they pose, those who do know that they possess the evil eye can take certain precautions to protect children. They may try to avoid susceptible children altogether, of course, but, failing this, they may give them perfunctory spankings, as if to say they do not find the children so attractive, or, paradoxically, they may kiss them, as if to show they intend no harm.

People also speak of *aire de basura* (garbage air). It may be given off by men or women who have had sexual relations recently, but it is emitted especially by prostitutes or loose women. *Aire de basura* is hot and similar to the offending agent in evil eye sickness. It is said that some years ago a loose woman visited a friend, the mother of a young child, just after having had sexual relations in the barranca. Shortly after the visit the child's left eye began to run and eventually the iris and pupil turned entirely white.

People need not engage in illicit sex to be carriers of garbage air; the *aires*, wafting into the streets, can contaminate innocent people who then pass the evil on to children. One sometimes sees men passing time on their doorsteps before entering their houses. They are delaying entrance because they do not want to convey an *aire* to an infant indoors. By resting for a few moments, they cool down, which motivates any *aire* to leave. People who are hot with anger also can cause *daño de muina* (harm from anger), a sickness similar to evil eye sickness.

Garbage air sickness is treated by some people in the same manner as evil eye sickness. More often, the eye is washed with an infusion prepared by boiling the umbilical cord of the first-born son. (The dried cord is kept in a piece of cloth and used a little at a time.) One woman reported treating garbage air successfully by cleaning the child with a black chicken.

Belief in evil eye sickness may be part of the constellation of beliefs about *aires*.[1] *Aire* illness, evil eye sickness, garbage air illness, and harm from anger are all similar. Presumably, in evil eye sickness the adult's eye made hot by the passion of sex or envy expels an *aire* or, alternatively, attracts an *aire* and then becomes a vehicle for transmitting it to a child. This hypothesis explains the similarities among the diagnoses and treatments for the several conditions.

Eggs are used to diagnose and cure evil eye sickness and the various *aire* ailments. The presence of both evil eye sickness and *aire* sickness is indicated by small "whirlwinds" in the albumen. Black chickens, routinely called in to cure afflictions caused by the *aires* of the anthill, may also be used to treat garbage air sickness. Because *aires* like to eat garlic, garlic is an amulet against the evil eye; like gold or sea coral, it draws the *aire* away from the wearer's person and into the amulet itself. Moreover, both evil eye sickness and *aires* affect the victim's eye—usually the left—and indeed have a special attraction to eyes, which no doubt accounts for the popularity of the deer's eye as a charm against the evil eye. In support of this interpretation, it may be noted that in medieval Europe evil spirits were thought to enter and leave the body through the eye. Salves to protect eyes from evil spirits were made with garlic and other worts, salt, butter, and sheep's grease (Moss and Cappannari 1976:3).

Aire and the Soul

In Tlayacapan and in nearby communities villagers recognize three types of soul. The *espíritu* comes from God and infuses a person with the "breath of life." It rests at the back of the head at the top of the spinal column but also courses through the bloodstream. The *alma* (soul) or *ánima* is sometimes called the container of the spirit, although the notions soul and spirit often seem to be used interchangeably. When usage is more precise, the understanding may be that the soul is closer to the body than the spirit; it is also known as *la sombra*, a part of the soul mentioned earlier (see chapter 4). One part of the *sombra* may be in the heart, although most of its components, palpable in twelve pulses, are distributed among the major joints of the body. The remarks of some informants imply that these components fall asleep or retreat toward the heart when a person is frightened. Others say that the shadow-soul leaves the body. Because the shadow-soul is in the bloodstream, it shares the quality of a person's blood.

People who have "weak" or "cool" or "sweet" blood are apt to have noble or delicate characters, whereas those with "strong," "hot," or "bitter" blood are more inclined to have "strong" characters: they may be given to more vice and sin but are less likely to suffer *sustos*. The greater instance of *sustos* among children than adults is explained in folk terms by the belief that children tend to have weak blood.

Evil spirits are said to derive from persons who had strong spirits in life. The visible manifestation of a ghost, usually seen as an amorphous white shroud, is said to be the person's shadow-soul. In Tecospa people distinguish the *espíritu*, the *sombra*, and the *aire de noche* (night-air soul). The last has a malevolent quality; clothed in the *sombra*, it appears after death as a ghost (Madsen 1960:167, 187). In Tepoztlán the *espíritu* is a guardian angel that looks after the soul, which, in contrast to the *espíritu*, is closer to the body and suffers for its sins after death; the "soul," presumably the *sombra*, is said to be a white, foamlike presence that can become a ghost after death (Lewis 1951:278, 415).

Funerary ritual in Tlayacapan demonstrates the connection between *aire* and the soul. The ritual focuses on appeasing the soul of the deceased, removing all residue of the dead person from the house, and making sure that the body and shadow-soul are properly buried in the cemetery.

After death the body of the deceased is dressed in new clothes and socks. If the person died in bed, the bed is removed and a cross of sand and lime is figured on the floor. The corpse is then laid on the cross in sign of penance; a child's body is not placed on the floor but on a table, because children are considered innocent. When a coffin has been obtained from a local carpenter or mortuary shop (in Cuautla or Yautepec), it is placed on a stand above the cross. A wake lasts throughout the night following the death, and the funeral and burial usually are held the next day. In the funeral procession, the women wear dark *rebozos* and walk single file in two lines in front of the casket. The women carry candles and green lemons on sticks; the lemons are stuck with a pine twig on top and a piece of clove in the middle. The casket is carried by relatives of the deceased and is followed by the band and men, who respectfully carry their hats in their hands. The procession moves to the church, where a mass is held. At its conclusion, passing bells signal that the procession is about to continue to the cemetery. After the burial the compadre *de la cruz* covers the lime cross in the home with flowers. Men drink *toros* (rum and Coke) and everyone is served coffee, sweet rolls, and soup.

For each of seven nights after the funeral, rosaries and prayers are said in the house of the dead person, and participating friends and compadres bring candles and flowers. On the eighth day, or a week later, a rosary is held at the hour of death. In preparation, a mat is laid over the cross and the deceased is figured with clothing on the mat. To the left side of the clothes are placed a glass of water, fruit, votive candles, cigarettes, *mole*, and chocolate. On the right side are a whole chicken, more fruit, and tamales. The prayer specialist directs the placement of all the objects. Mats for the mourners are placed on the opposite side of the room. Incense is lit and the prayer specialist recites from an old prayer book for about an hour, occasionally instructing the godmother of the cross to sprinkle the mat with holy water. *Mole* is then served. The godfather of the cross makes sure that everyone is well supplied with cigarettes. The offering to the deceased is removed and replaced with a wooden cross. Some guests leave, but others stay in an all-night vigil; children who remain play special funeral games. The wooden cross is supplied by the compadres *de la cruz*, who have taken it along with a bouquet of gladiolus and baby's breath to the priest for his blessing.

The next day the wooden cross is raised and the flowers, cross of sand and lime, and wax droppings from the many candles are ceremoniously swept up by the godparents with a new broom. The rite is called "raising the *sombra*." The sweepings are placed in a small box or two and, along with the cross, are taken to the church and then to the cemetery. The boxes and broom are buried at the grave site and the cross is placed over the grave.

Significantly, the homemade broom used to "raise" the *sombra* is of the same type used by *graniceros* to manipulate the weather and to clean homes of evil spirits. These ritual brooms and the placement of *sombra* in the cemetery imply that the bonemeal and grave dirt in *aire echado* contain *sombra*. Given that the bones and dirt are taken from the grave of a murder victim, this inference is also supported by statements that the offending spirit in *mal aire*—an illness caused by an evil spirit undirected by a witch—is usually that of a murder victim. The bonemeal and grave dirt in *aire echado*, in other words, contain the *sombra* and *aire de noche* of the buried man and therefore convey his malevolence and desire for vengeance. *Aire echado*, then, is related to *mal aire* and what in Tecospa is called night-air sickness. According to Madsen (1960:187),

Ghosts send an evil-air called "aire de noche" (night air) or "espanto" (fright). When a man dies by violence his spirit soul goes to hell while his night-air soul, contained in his shadow-soul, roams the earth frightening the living.

Night-air sickness in Tecospa is treated with the smoke of a brazier, much as Don Lucio treats *mal aire* near Tlayacapan. Interestingly, in Tecospa they also treat night-air sickness by cleaning the patient with a black chicken, part of the treatment for afflictions caused by *aires* of the anthill in Tlayacapan.

Concepts of the soul and their relation to *aire* illness appear to be rooted in pre-Hispanic belief. According to López Austin (1980:197-262), the ancient Nahuas recognized three vital centers or forces in the body. One was the *teyolia*, which was in the heart in life and became a bird after death. Following the Spanish Conquest, the concept of the *teyolia* evidently merged with the Catholic concept of the spirit. In Tlayacapan people liken the spirit of a dead person to a white dove, pigeon, or butterfly (see Lewis 1951:278).

The Nahuas also believed that each person had a *tonalli*, a type of soul that constituted a person's vital warmth. The word *tonalli* derives from *tona* (to make heat). Tonatiuh, the name of the sun, contains the same root. The *tonalli* was thought to give a person strength, vigor, and warmth and was closely associated with the *tléyotl* (from *tletl*: fire), a person's reputation. Tonatiuh was the principal source of heat or vitality. Like the *sombra*, the *tonalli* was divided into various parts.

The *ihíyotl*, the third vital force in the Nahuatl conception of the person, was located in the liver and gave off harmful emanations. Belief in the *ihíyotl* apparently persists in what the people of Tecospa call the night-air soul and in the belief, found in Tlayacapan and elsewhere, that anger, which causes an overflow of bile in the liver, is a source of harmful *aire*.

Vetancurt observed that smoke was used to remove *aires* that caused madness, and Sahagún's informants mentioned a smoke termed *ehecapatli* (medicine for *aires*), which was used with children who suffered from an *aire* or the effects of a thunderbolt. Ponce wrote, "They also attribute sicknesses of children to winds and clouds, and say *cualani in eecame, cualani in ahuaque* [the winds are annoyed, the owners of the rain are annoyed], and they blow the winds making their incantations to them" (López Austin 1972:403). The *tlaloque*, or rain gods, were held to be responsible for gout in hands and feet, contractions, paralysis, and stiff necks. To remedy these ailments, offerings were made to the god of wind, the goddess of water, or the god of rain. Xipe Totec was thought to cause pustules and eye sickness (Sahagún 1956:1:65, 72). Quetzalcoatl, the god of wind, was said to be the advocate of tumors, eye diseases, catarrh, and coughing (Durán 1967:1:66). The *cihuapipiltin*, the spirits of women who died in childbirth, caused paralysis and palsy. Traveling together in the air, they appeared whenever they sought human spirits. Often the spirits they took were those of children. The *cihuapipiltin* were appeased with offerings of small figures of butterflies and lightning made from bread. Tezcatlipoca was known, among other things, as the Night Wind, and presumably took the form of a wind, but he could also appear as a "shadow." He caused leprosy, boils, gout, itch, and dropsy in those who failed to do proper penitence (Sahagún 1956:1:49-50, 277).

The evidence for European influence, however, is equally strong. A priest in Tlayacapan explained to me that there were two traditions about the soul in the church. In the Thomistic-Aristotelian view, the soul and spirit were inseparable; in the Augustinian-Platonic view, the soul was the life force, whereas the spirit represented the highest portion of a person's being. This latter view may have been the more common among the laity of Europe from medieval times through the sixteenth century, and obviously it is the view that better corresponds to current beliefs in northern Morelos. In Europe it was thought that there were three types of spirit, each associated with a special organ: the natural spirit, or highest part of the soul, was in the head; the vital spirit was in the heart; and the animal spirit was in the liver. Some authorities added a generative spirit and placed it in the sex organs. In any case, the several spirits traveled about the body in the blood (Cruttwell 1951).

The Bible associates the soul with breath and wind. The Holy Ghost itself is a breath or wind (2 Thes 2:8; Jn 3:8). Moreover, the conventional rendering of the Holy Ghost as a dove demonstrates that the identification of spirits with birds in northern Morelos may be European as well as pre-Hispanic. In the Middle Ages, gold and silver doves were hung near baptismal fonts to represent the Holy Ghost. Evil spirits are also windlike in traditional Christian imagery. The Devil is "the prince of the power of the air" (Eph 2:2). Origen, a Father of the church, mentions the idea that demons are fine and thin, "as if formed by air," and adds that because of their grossness they haunt the denser parts of bodies and frequent unclean places (Origen 1869:1:6; 1872:2:259).

The coldness of *los aires* and their libidinal qualities may have both pre-Hispanic and European origins. Many of the illness-causing gods in the pre-Hispanic pantheon were associated with water and fertility. In European folklore, the Devil is said to assume the form of "a cold, north wind," and accounts of his sexual relations with women mention the icy coldness of his penis (Williams 1941:162). Indeed, the Devil is said to lack seed. To reproduce, he and other demons took the form of succubi to have intercourse with men, thereby stealing their semen, and then, as incubi, impregnated women with the pilfered semen (Institoris 1970:21-29). In Spain incubi and succubi are known as *duendes* and, similarly, *duendes* in Tlayacapan are sexually precocious. In the Nahuatl community of Atla, Puebla, villagers refer to *los aires* as *wendes*, an obvious corruption of *duendes* (Montoya Briones 1964:159). This usage is not found in Tlayacapan, but resemblances are present between the two. There are indications that *los aires*, like goblins, tend to be the spirits of children. It is mostly fetuses and children who are killed by *los aires*, and offerings made to them as part of the treatment of the illnesses they cause are notably similar to the offerings that are made to the spirits of dead children during All Saints' celebrations. Both goblins and *los aires* are dwarfish and libidinous creatures who have associations with the Devil. Whether they are separate but similar figures, as in Tlayacapan, or one and the same, as in other Nahuatl communities, clearly they are comparable to devils and demons in European folk belief: they are erotic but cold; if they are not sterile, their generative powers are perverted and malignant.

Spirit, Aire, and Reproduction

The *aires* of the ground and evil spirits, then, represent components of the soul that are closest to a person's natural being, namely the shadow-soul in the blood and the night-air soul in the liver. In traditional Nahuatl culture of northern Morelos, the *yeyecame*, or *aires*, of the ground, contrast with the *ahuaque*, or rain spirits. The latter are called *aires del tiempo* (airs of the weather) or *espíritus*, suggesting their connection with the higher part of the soul. They may inhabit the ground, but they also move above it, just as evil spirits may surface on earth but reside in Hell. The good rain spirits at least are seen as angels and are under the command of San Miguel Arcángel. In short, they belong to the company of saints and to the domain of the Holy Spirit.

Demonic and holy spirits of all kinds have generative properties. I have already noted the role of the Holy Spirit in human procreation and baptism, and the beneficial influence of the saints and rain spirits on the fertility of animals and crops. In this chapter we have seen that the *aires* of the ground have libidinal qualities; indeed, one might even say they are seminal: as a ghost, the *sombra* appears as an amorphous, white presence. Let us consider the roles of different types of spirit in generation in more detail.

1. In baptism, a combination of water, special ingredients, and Holy Spirit produces spiritual regeneration and rebirth and remission of sins. Baptism cleanses the person of Original and actual sin. Parallels with natural procreation are several. The preparation of the baptismal font and the rite of baptism are replete with explicit and implicit allusions to sexual coitus and natural birth. The baptismal font is like a womb. The candle represents God, the Father. Instead of natural parents, there are spiritual parents. The water is made fertile with oil. The salt placed in the initiate's mouth and the oil used to make the cross on the forehead are said to have the power to exorcise sin.

In the chapter on ritual kinship, I noted the similarity between baptism and the blessing of seeds, animals, and instruments of production with holy water. They are part of a complex in which persons and things are rendered fertile and incorporated into the church through a symbolic rite of procreation.

2. Jesus was conceived in Mary by the Holy Spirit (Mt 1:8). Unlike Eve and other women before her, Mary conceived without succumbing to the temptation of the flesh; the Annunciation was a triumph over the serpent. Various Fathers of the Church and at least one pope held that the fertilizing Holy Ghost came to Mary as a dove that breathed into her ear.[2]

3. Villagers mention three ingredients when talking about natural procreation: the menstrual blood in the woman's womb, the man's *naturaleza* or semen, and the "breath of life" or spirit, which comes from God. The first two are essential but not sufficient conditions for life, which cannot occur without God's intervention. Natural conception, then, is a moral complexity. On the one hand, it is a natural process and so is heir to the curse of Eve. As village beliefs about scorpions imply, the woman in submitting to sexual intercourse succumbs, like Eve, to the serpent. Pregnancy is therefore a

matter of shame and is said to be a "sickness." In this regard, village attitudes follow those of early Church Fathers. Augustine thought that sexual intercourse between husband and wife was a venial sin and, as noted earlier, that it was instrumental in the transmission of Original Sin from one generation to the next. Clement of Alexandria even believed that the Holy Spirit vacates the soul during orgasm (Murphy and Erhart 1975:7-8). Yet conception occurs with the direct participation of the Holy Spirit. God decides whether conception is to occur and supplies the breath of life.

4. *Aire* illness is a demonic mimesis of spiritual generation and regeneration. *Aires* are more preternatural than spiritual and they engender monstrous births or affliction. They live in anthills, the soil of which is prized for its fertility. They are especially attracted to sex organs. Male *aires* are drawn to women and lie on them as they sleep. *Aires* are said to have impregnated one woman with piglets. Whereas in natural coitus men engender a "sickness" that issues in a child, *aires* produce only a barren sickness.

Both evil eye sickness and *aire* illness are treated by rubbing the patient with an egg, which of course is an ovum enclosed in a nutritive fluid and a hard shell. The egg has explicit sexual connotations in other domains of village life: "egg" is slang for the male testicle. In the context of curing, however, its connotations are more bisexual and, perhaps, primarily feminine. Albumen has a semenlike appearance, especially when soft boiled. In diagnosis, any *aires* that have affected the patient become visible in the egg white, whereas the yolk is said to represent the patient. Since the patient is usually female, we may surmise that the egg's ability to attract and absorb *aires* is a representation of the sexual relation between male and female.

I have noted that a child may be cleansed of evil eye sickness with street garbage, hair, and underwear. The use of these articles is understandable, given the libidinal character of *aires* and the assumption, considered earlier, that the evil eye is a medium for their transmission. Underwear, of course, covers the sexual parts and absorbs their scent and, presumably, their force. Underwear, like eggs, has a special attraction for *aires* and, apparently, an ability to overpower them.[3] Similarly, hair is highly charged with *naturaleza*, the vital energy present in semen. Villagers say that women with long hair tend to be skinny, implying that hair drains the body of its force. Long, loose hair—as in the figure of the Llorona—has sexual connotations. Ordinarily, women are careful to comb and braid their hair before appearing in public. Not to do so would be to seem wanton. The street—and the garbage found in it—is associated with illicit sexuality and vice in general. We may surmise, then, that the objects used in cleansing patients of *aire* are efficacious because they are charged with libidinal energy.

In Tepoztlán salt and yarrow leaves are used to clean a patient with *aire* illness (Lewis 1951:280). In Tlayacapan there is evidence pointing to a hidden significance in salt and, in particular, an affinity between salt and spirits, both bad and good: when a nursing woman becomes pregnant, her milk is said to turn salty; salt is an ingredient in *aire echado*, along with egg and oil; a bewitched house or field is said to be "salted"; salt is taken after a meal for protection against *aires*; the food offered to *aires* is cooked without salt; the forehead of a child afflicted with evil eye sickness may taste salty; spilling salt portends bad luck; and salt is used in the blessing of holy water.

Tepoztecans may use salt in curing *aires* because it, too, has a sexual quality and hence the power to absorb the offending spirits. In a comparative study of superstitions about salt, Jones (1964:22-109) concluded that salt symbolizes body fluids, especially semen. Salt, he observed, is notable for its durability and permanence as well as its power to preserve organic matter. In various cultures it is associated with the essence of life, and it may be used to promote fecundity and prevent barrenness and impotence. Regarding central Mexico, however, it may be more apt to say that salt represents not so much semen as an essence of several analogous procreative substances (that is, semen, Holy Spirit, and demonic spirit). Admittedly, it may seem contradictory to take salt for protection against *aires* or to clean a patient with foods lacking salt, on the one hand, and to use salt and yarrow leaves to cure people, on the other. The contradiction may be more apparent than real, though. Salt may attract *aires* because it has the power to bind procreative substance, yet it may also repel them by strengthening the potential victim's natural aspect. One folk curer explained that the *aires* do not bother him because he has "strong, bitter blood," whereas those with sweet blood are more vulnerable. By this reasoning, offering *aires* saltless food may be a way of reducing their potency.

In any event, it should now be clear why *aire echado* is compounded of egg, salt, oil, and bones and earth from a grave. The egg, salt, and oil have the power to bind the *sombra* and *aire de noche* contained in the bones and cemetery dirt. The mixture, we may infer, is modeled after baptismal water and holy water. The first contains holy oil and the second is blessed with salt, and both are suffused with the Holy Spirit. Similarly, *aire echado* contains oil, salt, egg, and a sinister spirit. It is, in effect, a black version of the baptism-blessing complex. It uses the same or similar elements but produces illness or death, the antithesis of spiritual rebirth. It may also induce economic misfortune, an effect that can be caused by the evil use of salt alone. Salt, we may assume, absorbs the fertility in fields and money, rendering them sterile, yet salt is also present in holy water, which is beneficial. Apparently, salt has the power to exorcise *and* bind spiritual substance.

The small clay figurines used to cure *aire* illness are among the most intriguing elements in the curing paraphernalia, and are reminiscent of supernatural beings described elsewhere in this book: the men on horseback suggest *pingos*, or devils; the coyote represents the Devil's dog; and the images of bulls may correspond to the Little Bull, the malevolent weather spirit. The dolls suggest that the *aires* are somehow affiliated with the Devil. Indeed, the Devil assumes the form of a whirlwind, the most dangerous of *aires*, and he is present as well in ghosts, rainbow air, and *mal aire*, or what in Tecospa is called "night air."

Earlier I noted that the European Devil assimilated some of the characteristics of the pre-Hispanic Tezcatlipoca. The latter was known, among other things, as Yoalli-Ehecatl (Night Wind) and he dominated Quetzalcoatl, the god of wind (also known as Night Wind; Garibay 1965:23), and other deities associated with wind, rain, and fertility. Offerings to the *aires* may derive from pre-Hispanic offerings to such deities, but they may derive as well from the cult of Tezcatlipoca. The priests connected with his cult covered themselves from head to foot with a black soot made from the pitch of the torch pine, except when they needed more power and courage, at which times they covered their bodies with a special ointment made by mixing tobacco, morning glory seeds, soot, and the ground-up remains of burned spiders, scorpions, centipedes, lizards, snakes, and hairy black worms. This concoction, which was called "food for the gods" and "divine medicine," was applied to sick children and adults (Durán 1967:1:51-53). Actual creepers and crawlers are not ground up with tobacco for the *aires* offering today, but cigarettes are attached to their images.

The various forms of generation compose a structure consisting of the spiritual, natural, and the demonic. Spiritual or supernatural generation is one extreme. In virgin birth and baptism the masculine generative agent is the Holy Spirit, and the male's *naturaleza* is absent. The other extreme is demonic affliction and demonic impregnation, again without the intervention of masculine *naturaleza*. As in spiritual generation, the male element is windlike, but demonic and unnatural. Natural reproduction, meanwhile, is morally ambiguous; since it perpetuates Original Sin but requires God's influence, we might say it is the middle or mediating element.

Demonic Generation	*Natural Generation*	*Supernatural Generation*
aire illness	sexual reproduction	baptism
		virgin birth

Los Aires and Women

Aire illness affects women more than men. Men occasionally attribute a fever blister or rash to *los aires*, but women seek treatment for the condition more often than men and present more worrisome symptoms.

These trends are not peculiar to Tlayacapan. Women suffer from spirit possession and spirit intrusion more often than men do in many traditional agrarian societies. I. M. Lewis (1971) hypothesizes that spirit possession is an oblique expression of women's resentment of male dominance and prerogatives. He notes that an ailing woman may legitimately shirk domestic duties, however much discomfort and inconvenience it may cause her husband. Furthermore, during treatment, she may escape from the home, receive compassionate care from a charismatic curer, and socialize with other women in like circumstances. Lewis observes that women who are being treated for demonic affliction often join a cult group that forms around the shaman or curer. He calls these groups "peripheral" cults because they focus on alien and minor deities, ghosts, and weather spirits rather than on the high gods of received religion. In such cults trance and other altered states of consciousness have the subjective meaning of placing the devotee in a more desirable relation with the spirit world. As evil spirits are exorcised and spiritual blessings are received, affliction gives way to positive spiritual experiences and even ecstasy.

Lewis draws mostly on African materials, but his description of peripheral cults works well for central Mexico also. Groups of *graniceros* involve women in ritual activities, and women, more often than men, consult the *graniceros* for treatment. Euphoric experiences are encouraged in various ways. *Graniceros* go into trances and seek visions, traditionally with the aid of morning-glory seeds. During the curing of *aire* illness patients are lulled into relaxation while being stroked and censed with aromatic herbs. As part of her treatment, a woman may take a sweat bath with her curer; both undress for the occasion, and the heat is apt to leave them both feeling pleasantly exhausted. Pilgrimages to the shrines of the rain spirits in May and November encourage feelings of camaraderie with other devotees and communion with the spirit world.

Lewis's description of peripheral religion also fits spiritualism and spiritism, the cults that are replacing the *granicero* complex in the treatment of *aire* illness. It is difficult to say how many women in Tlayacapan participate in these more modern cults, since a certain amount of secrecy surrounds them. One spiritist practitioner ventured that many village women are involved, and for what it is worth, most of my female informants visit centers of one cult or the other. It is apparent, too, that the cults appeal primarily to women (see Finkler 1980). In 1966 there was a group of about ten mostly female spiritualists in Tlayacapan led by a medium from another village. Other women frequented spiritualism or spiritism centers in Oaxtepec, Cuautla, and Mexico City.

Spiritualism was founded in the nineteenth century by a priest named Roque Rojas, who went into trance and later took the name of Father Elias.

Eventually, he was identified with the prophet Elijah and the Holy Spirit. In spiritualism, mediums known as *peristales* or *sacerdotisas* establish communication with the Holy Spirit, Father Elijah, and dead beings. The medium enters into "ecstasy," a condition that one informant likened to being dead. Treatment methods might include herbal potions and cleansings, communication with the spirit, and *pases magnéticos*, a process of communicating "electricity" to the patient. The mediums are usually female, but the spirits who are thought to really effect the cure are often male.

Spiritism is a rival sect, founded by the Frenchman Allen Kardec in the mid-nineteenth century. Kardec taught that spirits of the dead, both good and evil, were in regular communication with the spirits of the living. In spiritism centers, mediums are also used to put patients in contact with powerful curers. Often they are hypermasculine figures like Pancho Villa and Cuauhtemoc, the last ruler of the Aztecs. Spiritist curers also cure by cleaning. Along with the familiar herbs and eggs, they like to use a cheap perfume called Siete Machos, "Seven He-Men" (see Madsen and Madsen 1969:64-75). One woman, whose mother is an avid spiritist, keeps a bottle of the perfume around the house and applies it whenever she is not feeling well or before she leaves the house.

Lewis's review of the literature shows that sexual themes—veiled and explicit—are pervasive in the beliefs and customs of peripheral cults. Spirits tend to have erotic attributes, and trance states may mimic sexual pleasure and climax. Lewis suggests that this sexual imagery may reflect anxiety about fertility. He notes that the ancient Greeks interpreted hysteria—a condition that corresponds to spirit intrusion elsewhere—as a consequence of delayed motherhood. According to Plato, the "womb is an animal which longs to generate children." When it remains barren, it becomes distressed and moves about the body, cutting off respiration and causing disease (see Veith 1965:7-8).

We can surmise that anxieties about fulfilling reproductive expectations may play a part in the *aire* complex in Tlayacapan also. *Aires*, we have seen, are thought to attack fetuses and they can interfere with normal reproduction in still other ways. There is, moreover, an understanding that women should marry and have children, and they are expected to take good care of those children. Since women are far more involved in child care than are men, they are the ones who are blamed when children become sick and die. The fact that *aires* also attack infants and children, then, may express the stresses women experience in trying to fulfill the maternal role.

It is unclear, however, whether this line of thought accounts for the intimation of sexual gratification in *aire* affliction or the even more apparent mimicry of sexual relationship in the treatment of affliction. In reality, women's feelings and wishes may be more complex than Lewis implies. Anger about men's prerogatives and anxieties related to the performance of mothering may be part of the picture, but there is reason to suppose that women are also ambivalent about motherhood and frustrated in their sexuality. They are rewarded for motherhood and certainly find satisfaction in the care of children, especially in holding and nursing infants, but far more than men they bear the pain and frustration of the traditional system of reproduction. They endure the discomfort of pregnancy, the pain of childbirth, and the labor of child care, as well as the guilt associated with illness and death in the family. At the same time, they are less likely to experience sexual pleasure in reproduction. They are not expected to enjoy marital sex, and the way it occurs in some cases virtually ensures that they will not enjoy it. Moreover, the deprivations of postpartum sexual abstinence fall mainly on women, since, unlike men, they are not free to seek extramarital sexual and pseudosexual gratification.

Symbolically, *aire* affliction exaggerates these aspects of the woman's condition; it represents the negative side of sexuality and substitutes illness for pregnancy and the birth of real children. At the same time, however, it provides women with a facsimile of the immoral gratification that men enjoy, that is, forbidden pleasure without the burdens of child care. It allows for women's needs for affectionate and pleasurable interaction with men, and in the relationship with the curer or spirit person, replaces an asexual or unpleasurable relationship with a positive relationship with erotic overtones. In the traditional *granicero* cult, the curer, a charming, sympathetic male shaman, sensually strokes the patient's body with objects, many of which are unambiguously masculine and phallic. In more modern cults, a medium may place the patient in communication with powerful, primordial males or even the Holy Spirit itself. The womb, in other words, longs not merely to generate children; it longs for the natural pleasure afforded by the act of reproduction.

Further support for this emendation of Lewis's argument can be found in the pre-Hispanic symbolism in the *aire* complex and in what modern Western medicine has learned about *aire*-like afflictions. Recalling that the dolls used in the treatment of *aire* affliction probably derive from the cult of Tezcatlipoca, consider the ribald tale about how Tezcatlipoca managed to become the son-in-law of Huemac, the ruler of Tula. Huemac, the story goes, had a beautiful daughter whom all the young noblemen of Tula coveted. Then one day Tezcatlipoca appeared in the marketplace in the guise of a stranger, a seller of chiles ("chile" was probably a metaphor for penis, as it is today), and without a stitch of clothes. The princess happened by and saw his outsized sexual organ. Returning to the palace, she kept thinking about what she had seen and was overcome with passion. Indeed, her desire made her sick, and her entire body swelled up. When Huemac learned of her plight, he ordered the stranger's arrest. Huemac's agents searched the countryside, only to find him where he first appeared, in the marketplace vending his green chiles. They took him to the palace, where he was questioned and told that he would have to cure the princess. Although he feigned protest, claiming that he was but a mere seller of chiles, he was washed, barbered, clothed, and sent into the princess's bedroom. Thereupon he joined her in bed and made her well (Sahagún 1956:1:281-282).

The tendency for women to suffer *aire* illness more often and more seriously than men, and the symptoms of the condition (for example, neuralgias, anesthesia, tics and twitches, paralysis, and temporary loss of sight and hearing) strongly suggest that it is a folk category for conversion hysteria,[4] the same ailment that Plato attributed to movements of the womb. The modern understanding of hysteria owes a great deal to the pioneering investigations of Breuer and Freud (1955; see also Freud 1953). They demonstrated that the physical symptoms of hysteria can be traced to hidden thoughts and feelings, themselves the products of real or imagined sexual trauma in childhood and patriarchal and prudish family values and relationships. Among the forbidden thoughts and feelings were wishes for sexual pleasure and pregnancy, often in incestuous and adulterous relationships, and anger and resentment about male privilege and hypocrisy.

Freud's insights represent a major step forward in the understanding of hysteria and still have anthropological implications, but it is interesting to note that they were not entirely original. They can be traced to Plato, of course, but they also had more immediate precursors in nineteenth-century medical observation and speculation. In 1853, well before the publication of the work of Breuer and Freud, Robert Carter wrote:

It is reasonable to expect that an emotion, which is strongly felt by great numbers of people, but whose natural manifestations are constantly repressed in compliance with the usages of society, will be the one whose morbid effects are most frequently witnessed. This anticipation is abundantly borne out by the facts; the sexual passion in women being that which most accurately fulfills the prescribed conditions, and whose injurious influence upon the organism is most common and familiar. Next after it in power, may be placed those emotions of a permanent character, which are usually concealed, because disgraceful or unamiable, as hatred or envy; . . . (quoted in Veith 1965:201)

Susto

Encounters with *mal aires* can provoke a *susto*, or fright illness, a condition that may render the victim more vulnerable to the harmful effects of the evil spirit. Once the person's *sombra* has been frightened or lost, he or she feels a bone-chilling sensation of coldness.

O'Nell and Selby (1968) observe that *susto* is more common among women than men in two Oaxacan communities and explain the sex difference by noting the more stressful nature of the female role, citing some of the same factors that I mention in my interpretation of the etiology of *aire* illness. My information on *susto* in Tlayacapan, which is based mostly on the reports of priests and folk curers, indicates that the incidence of the illness is roughly the same for men and women, but I suspect that it is really more common among women, since they are more apt than men to treat themselves and so less likely to consult a specialist. In any event, *susto* in women may be an emotional reaction to their predicament, as O'Nell and Selby propose, although I would add that, in contrast to *aire* illness, it tends to be a depressive or anxiety-type reaction, often to loss or separation.

The differing dispositions of the libido in *aire* illness and *susto* are consistent with this view. In *aire* illness, the libido is suppressed but active; it simply seeks indirect expression in physical symptoms and imaginary encounters with demonic spirits. In *susto* there is a more radical loss of libido; the treatment with *evangelios*, which is the favored form of treatment for adults, clearly has the purpose of restoring natural or sexual vitality (the godparents, recall, are either youths or persons of unsavory character). The use of the color red in the giving of a scapular and the *sombra* ritual further suggest that treatment aims at strengthening the libidinal content of the blood and *sombra*.

Both *aire* illness and *susto* may be related to economic anxieties. In *aire echado*, the spiritual and physical harm done to the victim may be compounded by economic misfortune. *Susto* also is linked to misfortune. One woman suffered a severe *susto* that lasted for several months when her purse, which contained several hundred pesos, was snatched from her when she was shopping in the marketplace in Cuautla. Stories are told about men who have suffered *sustos* while hunting for buried treasure or attempting to strike bargains with the Devil. It is understood that rich villagers have long had the habit of burying money in their homes and that the evil spirits of the rich remain on earth after death to guard their money. So, when someone moves into the house of a former wealthy owner and digs up the floor in an effort to find buried treasure, he may meet a ghost and suffer a *susto* in the process. He may also encounter the Devil. The latter regards anything of the earth as his; he may move buried treasure to prevent its discovery or appear with the aim of trading the treasure for the seeker's soul.[5]

In short, several outcomes are possible: one may appropriate tainted wealth or fail to appropriate it; and in the process one may lose or bargain away one's soul. The moral is now familiar: successful commerce in a fallen world requires a strong spirit and strong blood. Those who are too noble in spirit and too weak in blood are most apt to suffer victimization.

10. Syncretism and Social Meanings: An Overview

In this study of Tlayacapan I have shown that traditional culture is a meaningful and coherent whole, a consistent system of Catholic themes and images. I have also tried to elucidate the social and psychological implications of this Catholicity. Folk religion, I have emphasized, is not an institution but rather a way of life. And in making these arguments about the encompassing and informing rationality of folk Catholicism, I have contended that indigenous customs are more consistent than inconsistent with orthodox precepts and sensibilities.

In this chapter I summarize and elaborate this interpretation of syncretism. Drawing on ethnohistorical arguments in previous chapters, I show that significant elements of the deep structure of the pre-Hispanic world view persist in present-day beliefs and practices, but I also show that they are embedded in, and subordinated to, Catholic beliefs and symbols. I then review my arguments about the experiential implications of this religious syncretism and conclude with observations on culture change.

Syncretism

By most accounts, the missionary friars of the sixteenth century found a receptive audience in the Mexican Indians. The natives converted in multitudes and dedicated themselves with enthusiasm to the construction of religious buildings. Within a generation of such promising beginnings, however, friars were increasingly skeptical about the completeness of the conversion. Growing familiarity with pre-Hispanic religion suggested that the acceptance of Christian beliefs and practices was superficial: saints were being treated like anthropomorphic deities and old gods were still being propitiated at mountainside caves; and at their fiestas, the Indians were given to drunkenness and other vices.

Mexican Catholicism continues to impress observers, clerical and anthropological, as a heterodox mixture of indigenous and ecclesiastical elements. William Madsen (1967), a perceptive student of syncretism in the central highlands, describes the folk religion of the region as "Christo-paganism." He notes that some saints and conceptions of the soul and hereafter have strong indigenous components. At the same time, he observes the predominance of Catholic forms and suggests that the conversion to Catholicism either eliminated or altered major features of the pre-Hispanic pantheon. The militaristic gods Tezcatlipoca and Huitzilopochtli, he writes, were discredited by the Conquest and so played no part in the ensuing folk religion. Their place was taken by the Marian figure of Guadalupe, whose phenomenal popularity following her appearance on the Hill of Tepeyac ensured the nominal success of Catholicism but also gave it a peculiar character. The Virgen de Guadalupe appears to be a fusion of the pre-Hispanic goddess Tonantzin and a Spanish Guadalupe but, as Madsen notes, she preserves few if any of Tonantzin's distinguishing characteristics.

My analysis of syncretism in Tlayacapan suggests a slightly different interpretation. The store of Christian customs that was transmitted to Mexico in the sixteenth century was already a blend of orthodox and pre-Christian culture. Syncretism in Mexico did not so much dilute Catholicism as enrich a tradition that was already heterodox by virtue of its historical mission and its own theological dialectics. As it accommodated itself to diverse pagan traditions, Catholicism elaborated an extensive pantheon of saints and demons, and by postulating the importance of virtue and spirit, it asserted the reality of evil and nature. So by the time of the Conquest of Mexico, Catholicism was predisposed to assimilate pagan religions. In Mexico the parallels with pre-Hispanic religion were substantial, and the result of conversion was a folk Catholicism that was at once more Catholic and more pagan than the lay religion found elsewhere in Catholic countrysides.

Tezcatlipoca and Huitzilopochtli, patrons of elite power and imperial domination in Aztec society, may have been discredited by the Conquest but they did not disappear; instead, they merged with the Devil and his agents. Before the Conquest, Huitzilopochtli and Tezcatlipoca were strongly associated with war and fire, symbols of domination and appropriation. In conformity with these attributes, they were patrons of the nobles or professional warriors. Xipe Totec, Quetzalcoatl, and many of the other gods associated with water and fertility, by contrast, were advocates of agriculture and craft production and therefore enjoyed more popularity among the commoners, who were farmers and artisans. The fertility gods were the objects of domination and appropriation by the militaristic gods. Throughout Middle America, the arrival of Cortés and the conquistadors was perceived as the expected return of Quetzalcoatl and was the occasion for revolt against the reigning militaristic deities and their earthly representatives (see Bricker 1981). In time, of course, the image of the Spaniards diversified. Some became respected members of local communities but, generally speaking, they assumed the same dominant position once occupied by pre-Hispanic elites. Predictably, these Spaniards were associated with the Devil and his agents, who had taken the place of Tezcatlipoca and Huitzilopochtli.

Tonantzin and various other fertility gods, popular among the commoners in pre-Hispanic society, were overlaid by Adam and Eve, the Holy Family, and various saints, figures that symbolized the preoccupations of common peasants with fertility and kinship. The introduction of lay Catholicism and the resulting syncretism, in other words, allowed a reinterpretation of the meanings of pre-Hispanic deities that was more in keeping with the class interests of the commoners. It appealed to the same millenary hopes that were expressed in the expectation that Quetzalcoatl would return.

The evidence for Tezcatlipoca's fusion with the European Devil is substantial. The Devil in Tlayacapan today, like the pre-Conquest Tezcatlipoca, is associated with the color black, death, wealth, the coyote, whirlwinds, phallic sexuality, and vice and sin. Mixcoatl, a god who in some contexts at least appears to have been closely related to Tezcatlipoca, was replaced by Harlequin and the bullfighter, ritual figures with demonic qualities.

The god Huitzilopochtli, another symbol of elite power and Aztec domination, was probably replaced by the morally tainted figure of the Chinelo. The latter likely derives from the European commedia dell' arte, and yet the physical resemblance between it and Huitzilopochtli is striking; moreover, there are many allusions in Carnival to the pre-Hispanic Aztecs. Huitzilopochtli and the warriors of the sun, then, were assimilated into or replaced by the agents of the Devil, among them Judas, the Pharisees, and other characters in the Harlequinade, especially Pantalone and Pulcinella.

The Virgen de Guadalupe's appearances before the humble Indian Juan Diego are supposed to have occurred near a shrine to Tonantzin, and some images of the Virgin Mary in central Mexico are called "Tonantzin." Yet, Tonantzin-Cihuacoatl resembled Eve more than the Virgin Mary. At the same time, there was a stronger basis for identifying Mary with Chalchiuhtlicue, the female counterpart of Tlaloc. Chalchiuhtlicue, like the Virgen de Guadalupe, wore a blue dress (Durán 1967:1:266) and, in other guises, was known as Chicomecoatl and Xilonen, both of whom were virgins. As a goddess of tender maize, Xilonen was a symbol for fertility and rejuvenation, similar in this regard to Xipe Totec. Among present-day weather workers, crosses represent the Virgin, presumably because a cross held the dying Christ just as the Virgin held Christ as a baby. In any case, the crosses are "planted" and are closely associated with maize. (This association between the cross, the Virgin, and maize in the uplands of Morelos, incidentally, is not peculiar. Olivera [1979] has described the resemblance between the cult of the crosses today and the pre-Hispanic celebrations for Chicomecoatl in a Nahuatl community in Guerrero.)

Nonetheless, a fusion of the Virgin and Tonantzin makes a measure of symbolic sense. Tonantzin was an Eve-like goddess and Mary is understood to be the Second Eve. Eve was innocent and, therefore, much in the mold of Mary until she was tempted by the serpent. Mary, the Second Eve, triumphed over the serpent and invoked Eve's pre-fall innocence; she complements the Eve of the Fall. The appearance of the Virgin on Tepeyac, then, was an apposite symbol for the spiritual conquest of pagan Mexico; it implied continuity but also transformation.

The Virgen de Guadalupe stands on a crescent moon. This moon, we can surmise, has pagan and possibly natural connotations. In Tlayacapan crescent moons are worn by the Moors in the Dance of the Santiagueros. In European religious paintings, the Virgin of the Immaculate Conception stands on a huge serpent or both a serpent and a crescent moon, imagery that endures in Tlayacapan and elsewhere in central Mexico. In Tlayacapan the Virgen de la Concepción stands on a serpent, the Virgen de la Apocalipsis in the chapel of Altica surmounts a globe and a seven-headed serpent, and the Virgen de Guadalupe of course stands on a crescent moon. The moon, it may be noted, was worshiped in various pagan religions in the Old World; the Roman Diana, the goddess of the moon and hunting, for example, sometimes wore a crescent moon around her neck. The figure of Mary may stand on the moon as well as on the serpent because she has transcended the cycle of natural reproduction and the temptations of the flesh associated with Eve and other pagan female figures.

There are, then, two Eves: the innocent Eve and the Eve of the Fall, although both are one. These considerations may explain why young girls dress as Malinches for the fiesta of the Virgen de Guadalupe. La Malinche evokes the negative side of Eve inasmuch as she is associated with the Llorona, but she is also connected, through her association with Eve, to Mary. The practice implies that Malinche is identified with the Virgin, and indeed "Malinche" is a diminutive form of "Mary." Young girls are asexual, like Eve before the Fall. Interestingly, even the Llorona wears a wedding dress, a symbol of virginal purity.

Other correlations between pre-Hispanic deities and saints are suggested by the ethnographic material. Tlaloc was apparently replaced by Saint John the Baptist, the patron saint of Tlayacapan. Facets of Quetzalcoatl may endure in various forms. Recall that he was an ambiguous, tricksterlike figure who was associated with wind and rain. Together with Cihuacoatl, he was linked with the deer, and thus could represent the victim of the hunt as well as the hunter. As god of the West he played a part in the procreation of the human race. He was also associated with drunkenness and the gods of maguey beer. Following his death he became Tlahuizcalpantecuhtli, god of the morning star. Thus remnants of Quetzalcoatl in the West may be present in the Hunters, ritual bulls and the supernatural Little Bull and Water Snake, Adam, and the old men who dance with the Tenanches. Tlahuizcalpantecuhtli, Quetzalcoatl in the East, has been replaced by San Miguel Arcángel, the morning star and leader of the good weather spirits.[1]

The *nagual* may be another in the series of figures that preserves characteristics of Quetzalcoatl. The latter, along with Cihuacoatl and the Cihuapipiltin, was a patron of the thief-witch before the Conquest. The contemporary thief-*nagual* not only preserves the characteristics of the Aztec thief-witch but also has conspicuous similarities with Quetzalcoatl himself. Like Quetzalcoatl, he transforms himself into an animal and is closely associated with alcoholic intoxication.

Table 9 summarizes how the principal gods of the four quarters in the pre-Hispanic cosmos were replaced by and assimilated into Christian figures. The Devil, the Hunter, and Death replaced the indigenous gods of the North, whereas the Devil's agents absorbed the figure of Huitzilopochtli, a god who in the period of conversion must have epitomized pagan idolatry. Quetzalcoatl, Cihuacoatl, and other gods of the West were redefined as Adamic figures, whereas Xipe Totec, Tlahuizcalpantecuhtli, Chalchiuhtlicue, and Tlaloc were replaced, respectively, by Christ or the Christ Child, Saint Michael, Mary, and John the Baptist.

Table 9
Syncretism in Tlayacapan

Pre-Hispanic	Post-Hispanic
North	**Devils and Demons**
Tezcatlipoca	Devil
Mixcoatl	Hunter
Mictlantecuhtli	Death
West	**Adamic Figures**
Quetzalcoatl	Adam, Cortés, *Nagual*
Cihuacoatl	The Weeper, La Malinche
Deer	Bull
South	**Agents of the Devil**
Huitzilopochtli	Chinelo
Warriors of the Sun	Moors, Pharisees, Judas
East	**Holy Figures**
Xipe Totec	Christ Child, Shepherds
Chalchiuhtlicue	The Virgin
Tlahuizcalpantecuhtli	Saint Michael the Archangel
Tlaloc	Saint John the Baptist

This syncretism effected a melding of structure as well as symbolic content. The pre-Hispanic relationship between the hunter and the deer and the similar one between Tezcatlipoca and Quetzalcoatl merged with the relationship between the Devil and Adam and Eve, represented in part by the theme of the primordial hunt in which the Devil is the hunter and the deer, bear, or bull is an Adamic creature.

Similarly, the relationship between Xipe Totec and Huitzilopochtli was replaced after the Conquest by dramatizations of the persecution of Christ by the Devil's agents. In Tlayacapan both the Christ of the Crucifixion and the Niño Dios have Xipe-like attributes. Maize seeds are blessed on Holy Saturday, recalling Xipe's association with maize. And just as the skins of Xipe impersonators were saved, the clothes worn by the Niño Dios in previous years are treasured in a large box. Xipe and Christ were alike in being personifications of victimization in their respective religions, but there was another conspicuous parallel calling for the assimilation of the one to the other. Like the various *calpulli* gods were identified with Xipe in the festival of Tlacaxipehualiztli, the images of the saints that replaced the *calpulli* gods were understood to represent persons who had modeled their lives after Christ's example. Moreover, in the festival of Tlacaxipehualiztli, the Xipe warriors were subordinated to Huitzilopochtli-Tonatiuh and the warriors of the sun, just as the Chinelos are said to be the enemies of the Christ Child. Another vestige of the sacrificial combat between the Xipe warriors and those of Huitzilopochtli-Tonatiuh may be found in the dance of the Santiagueros, and yet another may be present in the juxtaposition of the Aztec dancers and the Pastoras.

Reproduction: The Root Metaphor

In both pre-Hispanic religion and sixteenth-century Hispanic Catholicism, reproduction was what the philosopher Stephen Pepper (1942) has called a "root metaphor," a concept so basic and prolific that it informed an entire world view.

The slaying of the deer in ancient Mexico was a metaphor for sexual intercourse. Similarly, the killing of a bull or mock cow in Hispanic culture had Adamic connotations; it represented the temptation of Adam and Eve by the Devil and the beginnings of death and natural procreation.

The sacrifice of Xipe warriors in pre-Hispanic ritual was associated with agricultural fertility and renewal. Dramatizations of the passion and resurrection, the Hispanic counterparts of this ritual, also alluded to regeneration. The death of Christ on the cross at the hands of agents of the Devil conveyed the possibility of spiritual regeneration and everlasting spiritual life: baptism, the rite of spiritual regeneration, is a representation of the Passion and resurrection.

In ancient Mexico ancestors of clans and tribes were thought to have lived in caves; the Aztecs, for example, traced their beginnings to Chicomoztoc, the Seven Caves or Seven Barrancas. Caves were vaginalike passageways to the womb of the world. Indeed, the codices represent mystic impregnation with an arrow or a calendrical sign for motion penetrating a hill (Elzey 1976). According to the *Anales de Cuauhtitlan*, sexual dualism was the essence of the supreme mystery of divinity: the lord of the flesh appeared in red and covered the earth with cotton; the lady of the flesh appeared in black and endowed the earth with solidity (Codex Chimalpopoca 1945:8). An allusion to this sexual union of the upper and nether worlds also occurs in the Codex Borgianus (see fig. 10). Quetzalcoatl and Tlaloc are seen in the West and East, respectively. Tlazolteotl is in the North. Her head is covered with cotton, a symbol for both rain and semen, and the sign for death protudes from her vulva and that for wind, from her anus. Meanwhile, a lizard extends from the genitals of the male god in the South.

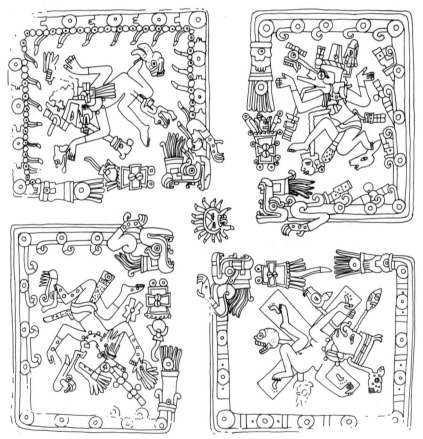

Fig. 10. Cosmic Procreation (after Codex Borgianus, Seller 1963:plate 72)

The four regions of the Mexican cosmos symbolized different phases of the life cycle. West or Tamoanchan was where intercourse took place. North, the interior of the earth, was presumably the locus of gestation. East was associated with rebirth and renewal. South was identified with the youthful virility of Huitzilopochtli, the hummingbird. West was also the place of dying, whereas the underworld was the resting place for the dead. Sexual intercourse was analogous to death.

The four regions, conceptualized as points on an axis mundi, were reducible to three because East and West composed the midpoint on the axis. Above was the realm of the sun, a region known as Omeyocan (Two Place); below was Mictlan (Land of the Dead); and on the surface of the earth were Tamoanchan and Tlalocan, fertile regions associated with moisture and caves (see Elzey 1976; fig. 11).

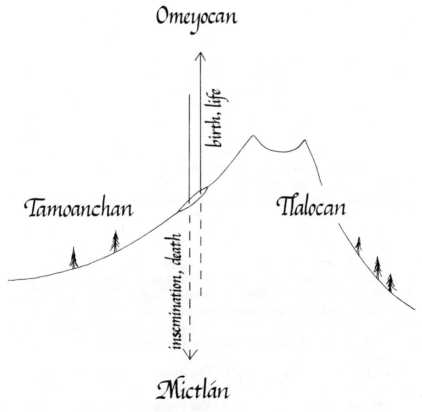

Fig. 11. The Axis Mundi

The axis mundi or vertical organization of space apparently merged with Christian notions of heaven, earth, and Hell and the corresponding categories of spirit, nature, and the demonic. Omeyocan became Heaven and Mictlan became Hell. Caves and mountainside altars resemble Tlalocan inasmuch as they are associated with Mary, saints, and benevolent rain spirits. Miraculous springs and the barrancas, conceived as invocations of the River Jordan, also recall Tlalocan; the water of Chalchiuhtlicue, the goddess of Tlalocan, was used to cleanse the newborn child in a rite reminiscent of baptism. Ordinarily, however, barrancas are associated with *naguales* and the Llorona, as well as *los aires* and goblins; caves are dwelling places for the Devil and evil weather spirits; and sinkholes are associated with rainbows. Openings in the earth's surface, then, also recall the Edenlike Tamoanchan, the region of rain and procreation in the West (fig. 11).

Homes, streets, and fields occupy points on a continuum between these two poles. The house, as we have seen, has strong associations with nature. The area at the rear of the house is an invocation of Eden or primordial, pristine nature. This nature, however, is subject to both negative and positive supernatural influence. By fomenting sexual lust, the Devil affects the natural bond between husband and wife; indeed, custom implies that Original Sin is transmitted through marital sexuality. What is more, agents of the Devil may cause a house to become "salted" and infested with evil spirits. By the same token, God, through the instruments of blessings and the sacraments, has a spiritualizing influence on house and marriage. Once sanctified, the house even takes on attributes of a chapel or church. The moral connotations of the street and field also vary, depending on the activities of evil beings and rites of sanctification.

All the symbolic categories of space just mentioned are inflected with the notion of reproduction: the home is the locus of biological and social reproduction; the street is characterized by illicit reproduction and aggressiveness phrased in sexual terms; and even agricultural production in the fields is commonly expressed in reproductive idiom. Seeds are planted in the ground; plants are "born" when they break through the ground; they are cared for and fed with fertilizer; they become sick with diseases; and they "mature" and die. Reproduction is sometimes phrased in agricultural terms, as when a woman complained that her husband "only plants children," but this inversion of the usual construction merely confirms the similarity between the two activities.

The Devil's cave, the barrancas, and anthills have strong sexual and Adamic connotations. Meanwhile, sacred places are associated with spiritual reproduction. Supernatural influence on reproduction and production is itself couched in reproductive metaphor. Human beings are "regenerated" through baptism and seeds, plants, animals, and other forces of production are made fertile through benedictions and blessings. The Holy Spirit also enters into the conception of new human offspring. Demonic forces, by contrast, may have an adverse effect on reproduction, infants, and young children. Demonic affliction can be understood as a parody or inversion of blessings and baptism.

The concept of the soul offers another illustration of reproductive metaphor. As we have seen, the soul is closely linked with natural force in the blood and has a conspicuous similarity to semen. The soul, then, resembles labor power and biological generativity, the two potentialities that are essential to the production and defense of material wealth as well as the creation of a family. In congruence with these metaphorical implications, the Devil seeks to divest a person of the soul, just as sinister others pose a threat to one's material possessions and sexual prerogatives or seek to abuse the self sexually or in other ways.

Along with informing conceptions of space and the activities that occur within them, the theme of reproduction runs through the folk festivals and ritual like a leitmotif. The dancing of the Tenanches, Carnival, mock bull and deer slaying, and bull riding all evoke primordial, pre-Christian animality. Christmas celebrates Christ's virgin birth and prefigures the coming reign of spiritual relations. Fiestas for the saints are analogous to saint's day celebrations for individuals and Christmas. Just as there are nine nights of posadas before Christmas to symbolize Mary's pregnancy, the fiestas for the saints and crosses are preceded by nine days of rosaries. Easter recapitulates Christ's death, entombment in a cavelike sepulchre, and rebirth. Christ lives, dies, returns to the womb of the earth, and then is born again. As in ancient Mexico, death is a return to the place of origins, parturition in reverse. Funerary ritual endures for nine days, whereupon the shadow-soul is ceremonially raised from the floor and taken to the cemetery to be buried.

Social Implications

The social characteristics of the pre-Hispanic gods and the manner in which they were assimilated into Christian figures strongly suggest that the process of syncretism was not merely intellectual. As rational as it may have been, it took account of real conditions. It gave structure and meaning to social stratification, barrio organization, communal tenure, and the organization of production and reproduction.

The social organization and communal land tenure of the barrio during the colonial period remained much as they were before the Conquest. Barrio members continued to enjoy the use of barrio communal land in exchange for support of the group's religious festivities, which were organized by its highest-ranking members. The kinship ideology of the *calpulli*, itself largely fictitious, gave way to a conception of solidarity based on spiritual kinship. Meanwhile, the European image of the Devil came to personify the enemies of the Indian community. Spaniards replaced Indian nobles as the ruling class, and just as Tezcatlipoca had been linked with the pre-Hispanic nobles, the Indians pictured the Devil as an hacendado or Spanish gentleman and suspected actual Spaniards of having exchanged their souls for the Devil's money.

The locus of evil and the boundary between the forces of good and evil, however, fluctuated as a matter of perspective. For their part, the Spaniards viewed themselves as Christians and Indians as heathens in need of more religious instruction. Meanwhile, attributions of evil in either direction were curtailed when persons were drawn, either through compadrazgo or mutual participation in fiestas, into a common circle of spiritual kinship. The opposition between nature and spirit and especially the ambiguity in nature—the fact that it subsumes the Devil's agents as well as ordinary children and pagan peoples not yet incorporated into the spiritual family— were germane to these processes of manipulating and moderating the conflict between good and evil. The notion that nature can be incorporated into the spiritual family through baptism and benedictions allowed the legitimation of both wealth and the instruments of production.

These ambiguities in the opposition between good and evil were further compounded by the value of natural strength and even a measure of evil in the struggle with evil, a phenomenon we have examined in detail. As we have seen, men identify with fighting saints, for example, during the festivals of Santiago and the Señor de la Exaltación, but they also appropriate the power of the primordial animal and even play the role of the Devil himself at times. In Carnival men of the barrios, the descendants of Indians, dress as Chinelos or pagan warriors (that is, in the guise of Huitzilopochtli), in opposition to the wealthy villagers or Spaniards who live on or near the plaza. Thus attired, they make a mockery of the Spaniard's stereotype of the Indian and reaffirm the value and necessity of their own indigenous, natural origins, although not without a hint of ironic sarcasm: the Chinelo sports green eyes and a heavy, phallic beard, as if to say that it is really the Spaniard who is the pagan warrior and enemy of Christ. The rivalry between the dance groups or barrios in Carnival is no less evident, however, and reflects the importance of social solidarity in defending the communal lands and political interests of the barrios.

Besides examining the importance of the categories of nature and spirit for the phrasing of relations between self and others, I have noted their relevance to familial roles, particularly as they bear on reproduction. The cycle of reproduction has two phases: sex and nursing. Attitudes toward reproduction are fraught with ambivalence because there are hardships and pleasures, disadvantages and advantages to having children. Taking such considerations into account, parents in every society arrive at a characteristic rate of reproduction. In rural Mexico, the rate has been a mean of slightly more than six children born live to each couple by completion of the fertile years, a statistic that represents a considerable curbing of biological fecundity. The curbing has been achieved in large part through prolonging the asexual or nursing phase of reproduction. Reproduction and restraint are reflected in two sets of supernatural figures: Adam and Eve, who represent carnal relations; and Joseph and Mary, who, in contrast, are images of asexual, self-sacrificing parents.

The complementarity of the two sets of images is not always harmonious. Women often accuse men of terminating the period of postpartum abstinence too soon; men may insist on having sexual relations either to beget more offspring or simply to satisfy their sexual needs. In either event, a man ignores his wife's identification with the Virgin. Moreover, men often feel more amorous when they have been drinking, and this proclivity reinforces the association between men and animality, vice, and sex in the minds of women. For them, the drunken husband is more like the serpent than Adam. Male drunkenness does not necessarily have this effect, however. Often it is a concomitant of sexual and pseudosexual behavior outside the home that, by displacing sexuality away from the wife, supports her virginal qualities.

The analysis of *aire* affliction and women's own statements indicate their ambivalence toward sex and their resentment of male dominance and male behavior in the street. Women are naturally inclined to enjoy sex but the marital arrangement and the regulation of reproduction impose special hardships on them; hence, they are likely to lead to sexual frustration as well as anger about male dominance and prerogatives. Cultural restrictions on men's behavior are less severe. When men are in the street, cultural norms permit them to give either direct or symbolic expression to their sexual needs. The mores grant women less latitude. In this context, *aire* illness provides women with a comparable symbolic outlet for their suppressed needs and feelings.

Change

During the 1970s traditional marital relations and sexual mores began to change. Fewer couples were observing a long period of postpartum sexual abstinence, and the desire was increasing among both men and women for smaller families and there was a corresponding acceptance of modern birth control. Young women, at least, were becoming more vocal about their disapproval of the traditional double standard for male and female sexuality. Television in particular was exposing villagers to modern notions of symmetrical marriage relations and women's rights. It seems likely that these trends will affect the traditional association between sexuality and demonic images.

The figure of the Devil is losing its earlier importance. In the traditional imagery, the Devil was a Spanish gentleman or horseman. The passing of the colonial order has rendered this image obsolete. The Revolution of 1910 lessened the power of the Spanish elite in the village, and in the *tierra caliente* it reduced the number and influence of the sugarcane refineries. No longer barons of rural estates who sometimes appear on horseback, the modern owners and administrators of the refineries are bureaucrats undistinguished by feudal pretensions.

There is still evil in the world, as any villager will testify, but it is somehow less amenable to personification. Noting that the Devil hardly appears any more, one informant said, "The only devils nowadays are our children." Education, television, and travel are making the villagers more skeptical. The existence of spooks and demons has become less credible, and the entertainment they once provided has been replaced by television soap operas and knowledge of the outside world. The night, when illuminated by electric street lights, is not nearly as eerie as it once was.

The disintegration of the barrio communal land system has tended to undermine barrio solidarity and, hence, support for barrio fiestas. A gradual trend toward the secularization of barrio landholdings may have been under way soon after Mexico's independence from Spain, but it became the general condition on the eve of the Revolution of 1910, when the so-called Reform Laws were put into full effect. The recent campaign of the clergy against the *mayordomías* has also taken its toll. Increasing participation in the market economy, with its attendant consumerism, may further discourage ritual expenditures.

As we have seen, modern conditions can reinforce traditional expressions of spiritual kinship. Cash cropping and wage labor have underscored the importance of interfamily alliances. The labor needs and equipment expenses associated with tomato planting in particular have encouraged cooperative ventures and efforts to remain on good terms with day laborers, perhaps explaining why mayordomos are often tomato planters. Villagers, it was also noted, use compadrazgo relations to find employment for their children.

Nonetheless, if what is happening in other parts of Middle America is any indication, we can expect continuing participation in the market eventually to erode enthusiasm for the saints, thereby completing the work begun by liberal politicians in the nineteenth century and progressive clergy in the twentieth century. The forces of change are widespread in Middle America. In many communities they have created a receptive environment for Protestant missionaries. Protestants do not hold fiestas to venerate the saints nor do they sponsor sacraments by serving as godparents. Having deemphasized the idiom of ritual kinship and the importance of Mary, Protestants have little motivation to appropriate the power of primordial nature or to struggle like fighting saints with the forces of evil. Unencumbered by the obligations of ritual kinship and the expenses of drinking and playing the roles of pagan warrior or fighting saint, they are free to focus on capital formation, the activity that once marked a person as the Devil's pawn. The church, not unaware of the repercussions of economic change for the faith, has sought to respond to them. In Tlayacapan, as elsewhere in the region, it has experimented with downplaying the saints, perhaps with the aim of preempting the economic advantages of converting to Protestantism—but not without reinforcing anticlericalism and forsaking its own historical commitment to communality.

Notes

Chapter 2: Setting, People, and Village

1. See Romanucci-Ross (1973) for an account of violence and factionalism in a *tierra caliente* community.

2. Ibid.:157. The mean percentage of church marriages in the *tierra templada-fría* is 72 compared with 55 in the *tierra caliente* (see Estados Unidos Mexicanos [1963, 1971]).

3. For a discussion of the relation between ethnicity and communal land in Morelos, see Lomnitz-Adler (1979). For a detailed study of ethnicity in relation to land tenure in the highland Maya area of southern Mexico, see Collier (1975).

4. The figure for private land is based on my 1966 house-to-house census. The figure for ejidos is based on my census and a Departamento Agrario census that was conducted in 1966. The figure for communal land derives from my census and data given by de la Peña (1980). The figures are no doubt approximations; I suspect they err on the low side by 10 to 15 percent. For additional information on land tenure in Tlayacapan and nearby communities, see de la Peña (1980) and Varela (1984a).

5. For a detailed discussion of political organization and activity in Tlayacapan, see Varela (1984a).

Chapter 3: History

1. See Barlow (1963). Following personal communication from Alfredo López Austin, I have made several changes in Barlow's suggested translation. See also Garibay K. (1958:173-185).

2. Unpublished document cited by Warman (1970).

3. Horacio Crespo, personal communication.

4. *El Globo y Estandarte Mejicano*, 18 May 1849, p. 4.

5. Archivo de la Reforma Agraria (ARA), Morelos, Expediente 5/108.

6. Estados Unidos Mexicanos (1902).

7. Horacio Crespo, personal communication.

8. Loose letters in Archivo Municipal, Tlayacapan.

9. ARA, Morelos, Expediente 5/108.

10. Ibid.

11. These statistics are based on information found in Civil Registers and Estados Unidos Mexicanos (1963, 1971, 1983). Birth rates from 1940 to 1964 are based on

registered births. The 1980 birth rate is an estimate based on the 1980 census.

Chapter 4: The Family

1. For psychologically oriented interpretations of the male role in other Latin Catholic societies, see Brandes (1980), Dundes and Falassi (1975), and A. Parsons (1964).

2. According to Don Lucio, *pericón* is very "hot" and disturbs the mind when taken internally. It is sometimes applied externally for medicinal purposes. For a discussion of its use in Tepoztlán, see Bock (1980).

3. Other ethnographers have commented on the significance of the distinction between house and street in Latin culture, for example, Gudeman (1976b), O'Nell and Selby (1968), A. Parsons (1964).

4. Once I saw a man grab another's penis and hold it for a minute or so while his victim did his best to act as though nothing were happening.

5. Oscar Lewis (1951:362) found this same custom in Tepoztlán.

6. In one such joke, Burro loses his penis and Monkey finds it and takes it home with him. At the next town meeting, Burro asks if by chance anyone has found his missing member. Monkey starts to raise his hand but Mrs. Monkey grabs it and tells him to keep quiet.

7. See McClain (1975:40) for a description of similar beliefs in Jalisco.

8. In an important study of fertility regulation in a Mexican community, Shedlin and Hollerbach (1978) described the use of herbal abortifacients and noted the presence of conceptual ambiguity about the state of early pregnancy. Moreover, they found the same ambivalence about reproduction that I have found in Tlayacapan.

9. For more discussion of this point, see Bongaarts (1975). The birth positions of dead children were not always properly recorded in the interviews with the 140 women. Table 4, therefore, only includes women who reported no infant or child deaths.

10. See Bushnell (1958:263).

Chapter 5: Ritual Kinship

1. I am indebted to Stephen Gudeman for this insight (personal communication, and Gudeman [1976a]).

2. Foster (1979:159-160) suggests that the godfather minimizes envy by dispensing coins to others who have not shared directly in the good fortune of the infant's birth.

3. The characteristics of barrio-chapel systems in Middle America have been examined in detail by Thomas (1979). His survey has delineated eight traits in such systems: (1) tutelary saint, (2) annnual fiesta, (3) *mayordomia* circulated within the barrio, (4) saint's lands, (5) chapel, (6) communal labor service, (7) civil lands, and (8) *principales*, or respected elders or former mayordomos. Colonial Tlayacapan apparently had all of these characteristics, but Thomas knows of no contemporary community that has them all. He suspects that the institution of saint's lands has European antecedents but it also has indigenous origins (personal communication).

Chapter 6: The Faces of Evil

1. Taussig (1977) has discussed beliefs about the sterility of the Devil's money in Colombia.

2. Brandes (1981b) has examined the association between the woman and the Devil in Spain.

3. For an insightful discussion of social marginality and witchcraft attributions in a Mexican community, see Selby (1974).

Chapter 8: The Struggle with Evil

1. This expression is similar to one recorded by Pitt-Rivers (1961:89) in Spain: "El hombre como el oso, mientras más feo más hermoso" (The man is like the bear, the uglier the prettier).

2. Untitled document dated 11 April 1765, Documentos del Archivo Municipal, Tlayacapan, Morelos.

Comparative data from other parts of Middle America also show the association of the bull with both the Spaniard and the Devil (Ichon 1973:440; Moore 1979). Laughlin (1976:41), for example, recorded the dream of a Zinacanteco informant in which a Ladino appeared mounted on a bull and challenged the Indian dreamer to fight the bull. The Indian grabbed the bull by the horns, but one broke off; he then grabbed the bull by the remaining horn and the legs and succeeded in throwing it to the ground. With the help of others he killed it. When the dreamer awoke and told the dream to his wife, she said, "A devil is tormenting you." The dream did not make the man sick, he said, because he managed to kill the bull in his sleep.

3. For a suggested etymology of *cuete*, see Guerrero Guerrero (1980:24).

4. The names given to cantinas tend to support my view that drinking is a struggle with primordial nature and the forces of evil. Among the various names of drinking establishments collected by Guerrero Guerrero (1980) in Hidalgo are the following: El Campeonato, La Gran Victoria, El Triunfo del 3 de Mayo, El Gran Combate, Waterloo, El Gran Infierno, El Invencible, El Gran Susto, El Triunfo de la Onda Fría, and El Harem.

5. These observations on the political implications of the large barrios and dance groups in Tlayacapan have been stimulated by Claudio Lomnitz-Adler's (1982:230-291) very interesting discussion of the situation in neighboring Tepoztlán.

6. In San Andrés, Tepoztlán, offerings of gunpowder and pulque are made in certain caves when rain is needed (personal communication, Diane Ryesky).

Chapter 9: *Los Aires*

1. Michael Kearney (1972:54; 1976) has insightfully observed the essential similarity between evil eye and *aire* in Ixtepeji, Oaxaca. My interpretation builds on this insight by specifying the mechanism underlying the similarity.

2. Jones (1964:266-373). In Jones's view, the dove and breath of God are symbolic equivalents of penis and semen in natural procreation. His interpretation, although similar to mine, is too reductionistic in that it ignores the manifest meaning of the Annunciation and its place within a whole structure of diverse forms of reproduction. Spirit is similar in function to semen but opposes it, like spirit versus nature.

3. This ability of underwear to absorb *aire* informs a witchcraft technique in Tlayacapan. According to one curer, a witch may make a doll from the dirty underwear of the intended victim. After the doll has been placed in a corner of the witch's house with some cemetery dirt and prayed over for nine nights, as in a funeral,

it is taken to the cemetery and buried with a picture of the victim. Presumably, the image absorbs a *sombra* from the dirt.

4. Finkler (1980) also suspects that *aire* illness may be a folk category for conversion hysteria and related conditions.

5. For another view of treasure tales in Mexican peasant society, see Foster (1964).

Chapter 10: Syncretism and Social Meanings: An Overview

1. Among the Cora, Elder Brother (also known as Deer Person among the Huichol) is identified with the morning star and San Miguel Arcángel (Grimes and Hinton 1972:92).

Bibliography

Alarcón, Hernando Ruiz de
1953   *Tratado de las supersticiones y costumbres gentílicas que oy viuen entre los indios naturales de esta Nueva España, escrito en México, año de 1629.* In *Tratado de las idolatrías, supersticiones, dioses, ritos, hechiceras y otras costumbres gentílicas de las razas aborígenes de México.* Vol. 2. Edited by Francisco del Paso y Troncoso, pp. 17-180. Mexico City: Ediciones Fuente Cultural.

Aramoni, Aniceto
1965   *Psicoanálisis de la dinámica de un pueblo (México, tierra de hombres).* Mexico City: B. Costa-Amic.

Asad, Talal
1983   "Anthropological Conceptions of Religion: Reflections on Geertz." *Man* 18:237-259.

Barlow, R. H.
1963   "Remarks on a Nahuatl Hymn." *Tlalocan* 4:185-192.

Barrett, Ward
1970   *The Sugar Hacienda of the Marqueses del Valle.* Minneapolis: University of Minnesota Press.

Benítez, Fernando
1980   *Los indios de México.* Vol. 5. Mexico City: Ediciones Era.

Bermúdez, Maria Elvira
1955   *La vida familiar del mexicano.* Mexico City: Antigua Librería Robredo.

Bivar, A. D. H.
1975   "Mithra and Mesopotamia." In *Mithraic Studies: Proceedings of the First International Congress of Mithraic Studies.* Vol. 2. Edited by John R. Hinnells, pp. 275-289. Manchester: Manchester University Press.

Blaffer, Sarah C.
1972   *The Black-man of Zinacantan: A Central American Legend.* Austin: University of Texas Press.

Bock, Philip K.
1980   "Tepoztlán Reconsidered." *Journal of Latin American Lore* 6:129-150.

Bonfil Batalla, Guillermo
1968 "Los que trabajan con el tiempo: notas etnográficas sobre los graniceros de la Sierra Nevada, México." *Anales de Antropología* 5:99-128.
1971 "Introducción al ciclo de ferias de cuaresma en la región de Cuautla, Morelos, México." *Anales de Antropología* 8:167-202.
Bongaarts, John
1975 "Why High Birth Rates Are So Low." *Population and Development Review* 1:289-296.
Bowlby, John
1980 *Attachment and Loss.* Vol. 3. *Loss: Sadness and Depression.* New York: Basic Books.
Bragaglia, Anton Giulio
1953 *Pulcinella.* Rome: Gherardo Casini Editore.
Brandes, Stanley H.
1979 "Dance as Metaphor: A Case from Tzintzuntzan, Mexico." *Journal of Latin American Lore* 5:25-43.
1980 *Metaphors of Masculinity: Sex and Status in Andalusian Folklore.* Philadelphia: University of Pennsylvania Press.
1981a "Cargo versus Cost Sharing in Mesoamerican Fiestas, with Special Reference to Tzintzuntzan." *Journal of Anthropological Research* 37:209-225.
1981b "Like Wounded Stags: Male Sexual Ideology in an Andalusian Town." In *Sexual Meanings: The Cultural Construction of Gender and Sexuality.* Edited by Sherry B. Ortner and Harriet Whitehead, pp. 216-239. Cambridge: At the University Press.
Breuer, Josef, and Sigmund Freud
1955 *Studies on Hysteria. The Standard Edition of the Complete Psychological Works of Sigmund Freud.* Vol. 2. Edited and translated by James Strachey. London: Hogarth Press.
Bricker, Victoria Reifler
1973 *Ritual Humor in Highland Chiapas.* Austin: University of Texas Press.
1981 *The Indian Christ, the Indian King: The Historical Substrate of Maya Myth and Ritual.* Austin: University of Texas Press.
Bushnell, John
1958 "La Virgen de Guadalupe as Surrogate Mother in San Juan Atzingo." *American Anthropologist* 60:261-265.
Caro Baroja, Julio
1965 *El Carnaval (análisis histórico-cultural).* Madrid: Taurus Ediciones.
Carrasco, Pedro
1976a "Los linajes nobles del México antiguo." In *Estratificación social en la Mesoamérica prehispánica,* by Pedro Carrasco et al., pp. 19-36. Mexico City: Centro de Investigaciones Superiores and Instituto Nacional de Antropología e Historia.
1976b "Estratificación social indígena en Morelos durante el siglo XVI." In *Estratificación social en la Mesoamérica prehispánica,* by Pedro

Carrasco et al., pp. 102-117. Mexico City: Centro de Investigaciones Superiores and Instituto Nacional de Antropología e Historia.

Chevalier, François
1963   *Land and Society in Colonial Mexico: The Great Hacienda.* Edited and foreword by Lesley Byrd Simpson. Translated by Alvin Eustis. Berkeley & Los Angeles: University of California Press.

Christian, William A., Jr.
1981   *Local Religion in Sixteenth-Century Spain.* Princeton: Princeton University Press.

Codex Chimalpopoca
1945   *Códice Chimalpopoca. Anales de Cuauhtitlan y leyenda de los soles.* Translated by Primo Feliciano Velázquez. Mexico City: Imprenta Universitaria.

Codex Magliabechiano
1970   *Codex Magliabechiano.* Edited by Ferdinand Anders. Graz, Austria: Akademishche Druck-u. Verlagsanstalt.

Collier, George A.
1975   *Fields of the Tzotzil: The Ecological Bases of Tradition in Highland Chiapas.* Austin: University of Texas Press.

Conrad, Jack Randolph
1957   *The Horn and the Sword: The History of the Bull as Symbol of Power and Fertility.* New York: E. P. Dutton.

Cook de Leonard, Carmen
1966   "Robert Weitlaner y los graniceros." In *Summa anthropológica: en homenaje a Roberto J. Weitlaner,* pp. 291-298. Mexico City: Instituto Nacional de Antropología e Historia, Secretaría de Educación Pública.

Cordry, Donald
1980   *Mexican Masks.* Austin: University of Texas Press.

Correa, Gustavo
1960   "El espíritu del mal en Guatemala: ensayo de semántica cultural." In *Nativism and Syncretism,* by Munro S. Edmonson et al., pp. 37-103. Middle American Research Institute, 19. New Orleans: Tulane University.

Corwin, Arthur F.
1963   *Contemporary Mexican Attitudes toward Population, Poverty, and Public Opinion.* Latin American Monographs, 25. Gainesville: University of Florida Press.

Crespo, Horacio, and Herbert Frey
1982   "La diferenciación social del campesinado como problema de la teoría y de la historia, hipótesis generales para el caso de Morelos, México." *Revista Mexicana de Sociología* 44:285-313.

Crumrine, N. Ross
1983   "Symbolic Structure and Ritual Symbolism in Northwest and West Mexico." In *Heritage of Conquest: Thirty Years Later.* Edited by Carl Kendall et al., pp. 247-266. Albuquerque: University of New Mexico Press.

Cruttwell, Patrick
1951   "Physiology and Psychology in Shakespeare's Age." *Journal of the History of Ideas* 12:75-89.
De Curiel, Andrés
1905   "La relación de Totolapa y su partido." *Papeles de Nueva España.* Vol. 6. Edited by Francisco del Paso y Troncoso, pp. 6-11. Madrid.
Deiss, Lucien
1976   *It's the Lord's Supper: The Eucharist of Christians.* Translated by Edmond Bonin. New York: Paulist Press.
De la Peña, Guillermo
1980   *Herederos de promesas: agricultura, política y ritual en los altos de Morelos.* Mexico City: Centro de Investigaciones Superiores del Instituto Nacional de Antropología e Historia.
Díaz del Castillo, Bernal
1956   *The Discovery and Conquest of Mexico:1517-1521.* Edited by Genaro García. Translated by A. P. Maudslay. New York: Farrar, Strauss, & Cudahy.
Díaz-Guerrero, Rogelio
1961   *Estudios de psicología del Mexicano.* Mexico City: Antigua Librería Robredo.
Douglass, Carrie B.
1984   "*Toro muerto, vaca es*: An Interpretation of the Spanish Bullfight." *American Ethnologist* 11:242-258.
Driesen, Otto
1904   *Der Ursprung des Harlekin. Ein Kulturgeschichtliches Problem.* Berlin: Alexander Duncker.
Dundes, Alan, and Alessandro Falassi
1975   *La Terra in Piazza: An Interpretation of the Palio of Siena.* Berkeley & Los Angeles: University of California Press.
Durán, Fray Diego
1967   *Historia de las indias de Nueva España e Islas de la Tierra Firme.* 2 vols. Edited by Angel Ma. Garibay K. Mexico City: Editorial Porrúa.
El Guindi, Fadwa, and Henry A. Selby
1976   "Dialectics in Zapotec Thinking." In *Meaning in Anthropology.* Edited by Keith H. Basso and Henry A. Selby, pp. 181-196. Albuquerque: School of American Research-University of New Mexico Press.
Elu de Leñero, María del Carmen
1969   *¿Hacia dónde va la mujer mexicana?* Mexico City: Instituto Mexicano de Estudios Sociales.
Elzey, Wayne
1976   "Some Remarks on the Space and Time of the 'Center' in Aztec Religion." *Estudios de Cultura Nahuatl* 12:315-334.
Estados Unidos Mexicanos
1902   *Censo y división territorial del Estado de Morelos. 1900.* Mexico City: Oficina Tip. de la Secretaría de Fomento.
1963   *VIII censo general de población. 1960. Estado de Morelos.* Mexico

City: Secretaría de Industria y Comercio, Dirección General de Estadística.
1971   *IX censo general de población. 1970. Estado de Morelos.* Mexico City: Secretaría de Industria y Comercio, Dirección General de Estadística.
1983   *X censo general de población y vivienda. 1980. Estado de Morelos.* Vol. 1., tomo 17. Mexico City: Secretaría de Programación y Presupuesto, Instituto Nacional de Estadística, Geografía e Información.

Finkler, Kaja
1980   "Non-Medical Treatments and their Outcomes." *Culture, Medicine and Psychiatry* 4:271-310.

Foster, George M.
1953   "Cofradia and Compadrazgo in Spain and Spanish America." *Southwestern Journal of Anthropology* 9:1-28.
1960   *Culture and Conquest: America's Spanish Heritage.* New York: Wenner-Gren Foundation for Anthropological Research.
1963   "The Dyadic Contract in Tzintzuntzan, II: Patron-Client Relationship." *American Anthropologist* 65:1280-1294.
1964   "Treasure Tales, and the Image of the Static Economy in a Mexican Peasant Community." *Journal of American Folklore* 77:39-44.
1979   *Tzintzuntzan: Mexican Peasants in a Changing World.* Rev. ed. New York: Elsevier North Holland.

Freud, Sigmund
1953   *Fragment of an Analysis of a Case of Hysteria. The Standard Edition of the Complete Psychological Works of Sigmund Freud.* Vol. 7. Edited and translated by James Strachey. London: Hogarth Press.

Fromm, Erich, and Michael Maccoby
1970   *Social Character in a Mexican Village: A Sociopsychoanalytic Study.* New Jersey: Prentice-Hall.

García Pimentel, Luis
1904   *Relación de los obispados de Tlaxcala, Michoacán, Oaxaca y otros lugares en el siglo XVI. Manuscrito de la colección del Señor Don Joaquín García Icazbalceta.* Mexico City: Casa de García Pimentel.

Garibay K., Angel Ma.
1958   *Veinte himnos sacros de los Nahuas.* Mexico City: Universidad Nacional Autónoma de México.
1965   *Teogonía e historia de los mexicanos: tres opúsculos del siglo XVI.* Mexico City: Editorial Porrúa.

Greenberg, James B.
1981   *Santiago's Sword: Chatino Peasant Religion and Economics.* Berkeley & Los Angeles: University of California Press.

Grijalva, Juan de
1624   *Crónica de la orden de N. P. S. Augustín en las prouincias de nueva españa, en quatro edades desde el año de .1533 hasta el de .1592.* Mexico City: En el religiosíssimo conuento de S. Augustín, y imprenta de Ioan Ruyz.

Grimes, Joseph E., and Thomas B. Hinton
1972   "Huicholes y coras." In *Coras, huicholes y tepehuanes.* Edited by

Thomas B. Hinton, pp. 73-97. Mexico City: Secretaría de Educación Pública and Instituto Nacional Indigenista.

Gudeman, Stephen
1972   "The *Compadrazgo* as a Reflection of the Natural and Spiritual Person." *Proceedings of the Royal Anthropological Institute of Great Britain and Ireland for 1971*, pp. 45-71.
1975   "Spiritual Relationships and Selecting a Godparent." *Man* 10: 221-237.
1976a   *Relationships, Residence and the Individual: A Rural Panamanian Community.* London: Routledge & Kegan Paul.
1976b   "Saints, Symbols, and Ceremonies." *American Ethnologist* 3:709-729.

Guerrero Guerrero, Raúl
1980   *El pulque: religión, cultura, folklore.* Mexico City: Secretaría de Educación Pública-Instituto Nacional de Antropología e Historia.

Hicks, W. Whitney
1974   "Economic Development and Fertility Change in Mexico, 1950-1970." *Demography* 11:407-421.

Hilgers, Joseph
1911   "Novena." *The Catholic Encyclopedia.* Vol. 11. Edited by Charles G. Herbermann et al., pp. 141-144. New York: Robert Appleton Company.

Horcasitas, Fernando, and Douglas Butterworth
1963   "La Llorona." *Tlalocan* 4:204-224.

Hunt, Eva
1977   *The Transformation of the Hummingbird: Cultural Roots of a Zinacantecan Mythical Poem.* Ithaca: Cornell University Press.

Ichon, Alain
1973   *La religión de los totonacas de la sierra.* Translated by José Arenas. Mexico City: Instituto Nacional Indigenista.

Ingham, John M.
1964   "The Bullfighter: A Study in Sexual Dialectic." *American Imago* 21:95-102.
1969   *Culture and Personality in a Mexican Village.* Ph. D. dissertation, University of California, Berkeley. Ann Arbor: University Microfilms.
1970a   "On Mexican Folk Medicine." *American Anthropologist* 72:76-87.
1970b   "The Asymmetrical Implications of Godparenthood in Tlayacapan, Morelos." *Man* 5:281-289.
1971   "Time and Space in Ancient Mexico: The Symbolic Dimensions of Clanship." *Man* 6:615-629.
1984   "Human Sacrifice at Tenochtitlan." *Comparative Studies in Society and History* 26:379-400.

Institoris, Henricus
1970   *Malleus Maleficarum.* Edited and translated by the Rev. Montagu Summers. New York: Benjamin Blom.

Jones, Ernest
1964   *Essays in Applied Psycho-Analysis.* Vol. 2. New York: International

Universities Press.

Kahl, Joseph A.
1967   "Modern Values and Fertility Ideals in Brazil and Mexico." *The Journal of Social Issues* 23 (4):99-114.

Kearney, Michael
1972   *The Winds of Ixtepeji: World View and Society in a Zapotec Town.* New York: Holt, Rinehart, & Winston.
1976   "A World-View Explanation of the Evil Eye." In *The Evil Eye.* Edited by Clarence Maloney, pp. 175-192. New York: Columbia University Press.

Kelly, Phyllis B.
1979   "A Model of Population Increase in the Mazahua Region, Mexico." *América Indígena* 39:371-380.

Kurath, Gertrude Prokosch
1949   "Mexican Moriscas: A Problem in Dance Acculturation." *Journal of American Folklore* 62:87-106.

Lafaye, Jacques
1976   *Quetzalcoatl and Guadalupe: The Formation of Mexican National Consciousness, 1531-1813.* Foreword by Octavio Paz. Translated by Benjamin Keen. Chicago: University of Chicago Press.

Laughlin, Robert M.
1976   *Of Wonders Wild and New: Dreams from Zinacantan.* Smithsonian Contributions to Anthropology, 22. Washington, D. C.: Smithsonian Institution Press.

Leñero Otero, Luis
1968   *Investigación de la familia en México: presentación y avance de resultados de un encuesta nacional.* Mexico City: Instituto Mexicano de Estudios Sociales.

Lewis, I. M.
1971   *Ecstatic Religion: An Anthropological Study of Spirit Possession and Shamanism.* Harmondsworth, England: Penguin Books.

Lewis, Oscar
1951   *Life in a Mexican Village: Tepoztlán Restudied.* Urbana: University of Illinois Press.

Lomnitz-Adler, Claudio
1979   "Clase y etnicidad en Morelos: una nueva interpretación." *América Indígena* 39:439-475.
1982   *Evolución de una sociedad rural.* Mexico City: Fondo de Cultura Económica.

López Austin, Alfredo
1972   "El mal aire en el México prehispánico." In *Religión en Mesoamérica. XII Mesa Redonda.* Edited by Jaime Litvak King and Noemi Castillo Tejero, pp. 399-408. Mexico City: Sociedad Mexicana de Antropología.
1980   *Cuerpo humano e ideología: las concepciones de los antiguos Nahuas.* Vol. 1. Mexico City: Universidad Nacional Autónoma de México.

Loucky, James
1979   "Production and the Patterning of Social Relations and Values in Two Guatemalan Villages." *American Ethnologist* 6:702-722.
Madden, David
1975   *Harlequin's Stick, Charlie's Cane: A Comparative Study of Commedia dell' arte and Silent Slapstick Comedy.* Bowling Green, Ky.: Bowling Green University Popular Press.
Madsen, William
1960   *The Virgin's Children: Life in an Aztec Village Today.* Austin: University of Texas Press.
1967   "Religious Syncretism." In *Handbook of Middle American Indians.* Vol. 6. Edited by Robert Wauchope, pp. 369-391. Austin: University of Texas Press.
Madsen, William, and Claudia Madsen
1969   *A Guide to Mexican Witchcraft.* Mexico City: Minutia Mexicana.
Martin, Cheryl English
1982   "Haciendas and Villages in Late Colonial Morelos." *Hispanic American Historical Review* 62:407-427.
McAndrew, John
1965   *The Open-Air Churches of Sixteenth-Century Mexico: Atrios, Posas, Open Chapels, and Other Studies.* Cambridge, Mass.: Harvard University Press.
McClain, Carol
1975   "Ethno-Obstetrics in Ajijic." *Anthropological Quarterly* 48:38-56.
McClelland, David C.
1964   *The Roots of Consciousness.* Princeton, N.J.: D. Van Nostrand Company.
McGinn, Noel F.
1966   "Marriage and Family in Middle-Class Mexico." *Journal of Marriage and the Family* 28:305-313.
Montoya Briones, José de Jesús
1964   *Atla: etnografía de un pueblo nahuatl.* Mexico City: Instituto Nacional de Antropología e Historia.
Moore, Alexander
1979   "Initiation Rites in a Mesoamerican Cargo System: Men and Boys, Judas and the Bull." *Journal of Latin American Lore* 5:55-81.
Morrisroe, Patrick
1907   "Blessing." *The Catholic Encyclopedia.* Vol. 2. Edited by Charles G. Herbermann et al., pp. 599-602. New York: Robert Appleton Company.
Moss, Leonard W., and Stephen C. Cappannari
1976   *"Mal' occhio, Ayin ha ra, Oculus fascinus, Judenblick:* The Evil Eye Hovers Above." In *The Evil Eye.* Edited by Clarence Maloney, pp. 1-15. New York: Columbia University Press.
Murphy, Francis X., and Joseph F. Erhart
1975   "Catholic Perspectives on Population Issues." *Population Bulletin* 30 (6). Washington, D.C.: Population Reference Bureau.

Nelson, Cynthia
1971   *The Waiting Village: Social Change in Rural Mexico.* Boston: Little, Brown & Company.

Niklaus, Thelma
1956   *Harlequin Phoenix; or the Rise and Fall of a Bergamask Rogue.* London: The Bodley Head.

Olivera, Mercedes
1979   "Huemitl de Mayo en Citlala: ¿ofrenda para Chicomecoatl o para la Santa Cruz?" In *Mesoamerica: homenaje al doctor Kirchoff.* Edited by Barbro Dahlgren, pp. 143-158. Mexico City: Instituto Nacional de Antropologia e Historia.

O'Nell, Carl W., and Henry A. Selby
1968   "Sex Differences in the Incidence of Susto in Two Zapotec Pueblos: An Analysis of the Relationships between Sex Role Expectations and a Folk Illness." *Ethnology* 7:95-105.

Origen
1869-72   *The Writings of Origen.* 2 vols. Edited by the Rev. F. Crombie. In *Ante-Nicene Christian Library.* Vols. 10, 23. Edited by the Rev. A. Roberts and J. Donaldson. Edinburgh: T. and T. Clark.

Parsons, Anne
1964   "Is the Oedipus Complex Universal? The Jones-Malinowski Debate Revisited in a South Italian 'Nuclear Complex.' " In *The Psychoanalytic Study of Society.* Vol. 3. Edited by Warner Muensterberger and Sidney Axelrad, pp. 278-301, 310-326. New York: International Universities Press.

Parsons, Elsie Clews
1936   *Mitla: Town of Souls; and other Zapotec-speaking Pueblos of Oaxaca, Mexico.* Chicago: University of Chicago Press.

Parsons, Elsie Clews, and Ralph L. Beals
1934   "The Sacred Clowns of the Pueblo and Mayo-Yaqui Indians." *American Anthropologist* 36:491-514.

Paz, Octavio
1961   *The Labyrinth of Solitude: Life and Thought in Mexico.* Translated by Lysander Kemp. New York: Grove Press.

Peñalosa, Fernando
1968   "Mexican Family Roles." *Journal of Marriage and the Family* 30:680-689.

Pepper, Stephen Coburn
1942   *World Hypotheses: A Study in Evidence.* Berkeley & Los Angeles: University of California Press.

Pitt-Rivers, J. A.
1961   *The People of the Sierra.* Chicago: University of Chicago Press.

Pohl, Mary
1981   "Ritual Continuity and Transformation in Mesoamerica: Reconstructing the Ancient Maya *Cuch* Ritual." *American Antiquity* 46:513-529.

Ramírez, Santiago
1961   *El mexicano: la psicología de sus motivaciones.* 3d ed. Mexico

City: Editorial Pax-México.

Ramírez, Santiago, and Ramón Parres
1957   "Some Dynamic Patterns in the Organization of the Mexican Family."
International Journal of Social Psychiatry 3:18-21.

Redfield, Robert
1930   *Tepoztlán, a Mexican Village: A Study of Folk Life.* Chicago: University of Chicago Press.
1941   *The Folk Culture of Yucatan.* Chicago: University of Chicago Press.
1953   *The Primitive World and its Transformations.* Ithaca: Cornell University Press.
1955   *The Little Community: Viewpoints for the Study of a Human Whole.* Chicago: University of Chicago Press.

Ricard, Robert
1966   *The Spiritual Conquest of Mexico: An Essay on the Apostolate and the Evangelizing Methods of the Mendicant Orders in New Spain: 1523-1572.* Berkeley & Los Angeles: University of California Press.

Robelo, Cecilio A.
1885   *Revistas descriptivas del Estado de Morelos.* Cuernavaca: Imprenta del Gobierno de Morelos.

Rojas Rabiela, Teresa
1973   "La cerámica contemporánea de Tlayacapan, Morelos, Mexico." *Anales de Antropología* 10:241-264.
1980   "Una relación inédita de Tlayacapan, Morelos en el siglo XVIII (1743)." *Cuicuilco* 1:59-62.

Roman Missal
1951   *The Roman Missal.* Introduction by Adrian Fortescue. New York: Macmillan.

Romanucci-Ross, Lola
1973   *Conflict, Violence, and Morality in a Mexican Village.* Palo Alto, Cal.: National Press Books.

Sahagún, Fray Bernardino de
1950-69 *Florentine Codex: General History of the Things of New Spain*, Bk. 1. Translated by Charles E. Dibble and Arthur J. O. Anderson. Salt Lake City: University of Utah, and Sante Fe: School of American Research.
1956   *Historia general de las cosas de Nueva España.* 4 vols. Edited by Angel María Garibay K. Mexico City: Editorial Porrúa.

Selby, Henry A.
1974   *Zapotec Deviance: The Convergence of Folk and Modern Sociology.* Austin: University of Texas Press.

Seler, Eduard
1963   *Códice Borgia.* 3 vols. Translated by Mariana Frenk. Mexico City: Fondo de Cultura Económica.

Serna, Jacinto de la
1953   *Manual de ministros indios.* In *Tratado de las idolatrías, supersticiones, dioses, ritos, hechicerías y otras costumbres gentílicas de las razas aborígenes de México.* Vol. 1. Edited by Francisco del Paso y

Troncoso, pp. 40-368. Mexico City: Ediciones Fuente Cultural.

Shedlin, Michele Goldzieher, and Paula E. Hollerbach
1978   "Modern and Traditional Fertility Regulation in a Mexican Com-
        munity: Factors in the Process of Decision Making." Working Papers.
        New York: Center for Policy Studies, The Population Council.

Smith, W. Robertson
1889   *Lectures on the Religion of the Semites.* New York: D. Appleton.

Smith, Waldemar R.
1977   *The Fiesta System and Economic Change.* New York: Columbia
        University Press.

Stycos, J. Mayone
1955   *Family and Fertility in Puerto Rico: A Study of the Lower Income
        Group.* New York: Columbia University Press.

Taussig, Michael
1977   "The Genesis of Capitalism amongst a South American Peasantry:
        Devil's Labor and the Baptism of Money." *Comparative Studies in
        Society and History* 19:130-155.

Thomas, Norman D.
1979   "The Mesoamerican Barrio: A Reciprocity Model for Community
        Organization." In *From Tzintzuntzan to the "Image of Limited Good."*
        Edited by Margaret Clark, Robert V. Kemper, and Cynthia Nelson, pp.
        45-58. Berkeley: Kroeber Anthropological Society Papers 55-56.

Varela, Roberto
1984a   *Procesos políticos en Tlayacapan, Morelos.* Cuadernos Universitarios,
        11. Mexico City: Universidad Autónoma Metropolitana.

1984b   *Expansión de sistemas y relaciones de poder.* Mexico City: Universi-
        dad Autónoma Metropolitana.

Veith, Ilza
1965   *Hysteria: The History of a Disease.* Chicago: University of Chicago
        Press.

Warman, Arturo
1970   "La banda de Tlayacapan." Preface to the record, *La Banda de
        Tlayacapan.* MNA-08. Mexico City: Secretaría de Educación Pública.

1976   *... Y venimos a contradecir: los campesinos de Morelos y el estado
        nacional.* Mexico City: Centro de Investigaciones Superiores de
        Instituto Nacional de Antropología e Historia.

Warren, Kay B.
1978   *The Symbolism of Subordination: Indian Identity in a Guatemalan
        Town.* Austin: University of Texas Press.

Williams, Charles
1941   *Witchcraft.* London: Faber & Faber.

Williams, Raymond
1981   *Culture.* Glasgow: Fontana.

Wolf, Eric R.
1957   "Closed Corporate Peasant Communities in Mesoamerica and Central
        Java." *Southwestern Journal of Anthropology* 13:1-18.

1959   *Sons of the Shaking Earth.* Chicago: University of Chicago Press.

Womack, John, Jr.
  1969   *Zapata and the Mexican Revolution.* New York: Alfred A. Knopf.
Woods, Barbara Allen
  1959   *The Devil in Dog Form: A Partial Type-Index of Devil Legends.* Folklore Studies, 11. Berkeley & Los Angeles: University of California Press.
Zorita, Alonso de
  1963   *Life and Labor in Ancient Mexico: The Brief and Summary Relation of the Lords of New Spain.* Translated, with introduction by Benjamin Keen. New Brunswick: Rutgers University Press.

Index

Abortion, 68, 69. *See also* Birth; Conception, theory of; Midwives; Reproduction
Acahual, padrinos de, 76. *See also* Godparenthood
Advent, 122
Agape, 91
Agriculture: kitchen garden, 58; peanut, 45; rice, 45; sugarcane, 46; tomato, 45, 46, 47. *See also* Communal land; Land tenure
Ahuaque (rain spirits), 157-160
Aire echado, 163, 168; symbolism of, 173
Aire illness, 191; and conversion hysteria, 178; erotic connotations of curing of, 164; symbolism of, 177; symptoms of, 162; treatment of, 162-164
Aires, 116, 143, 161-179; attracted to genitalia, 161; behavior of, 162; and birth of piglets, 161; and bulls, 147; as cause of miscarriages, 161; and newborns, 67; and reproduction, 170-174; and the soul, 166-170; and women, 174-178
Albures (verbal barbs), 144-145
Alcaleca, 105
All Saints' and All Souls' Days, 137-138
Alma. See Soul
Altica, barrio of, and la Virgen del Apocalipsis, 122
Alum, 164. *See Also Aires; Aire* illness;

Eggs
Anima. See Soul
Ash Wednesday, 127
Atchalán, 154
Atlatlahuacan, 10
Augustinians, 33-34
Axis mundi, pre-Hispanic, 188

Baptism, 79, 82; symbolism of, 80, 171; theological rationale for, 78-79
Barrancas, 103-105
Barrio-chapel complex, 15-18; in colonial period, 36-38; construction of chapels in, 33; crosses, 18; economic basis of, 4; in Independence period, 39; interbarrio rivalry, 18; and marriage, 18-19
Birth: delivery, 67; intervals, 69-70; post- care, 67; rates, 45. *See also* Abortion; Conception, theory of; Midwives; Reproduction
Bivar, A. D. H., 149-150
Blessings, 83. *See also* Godparenthood
Blood, 164, 179. *See also Aires; Aire* illness
Bock, Philip K.: on barrios, 4; on Chinelos, 128
Bonfil Batalla, Guillermo, 134
Braceros, 45. *See also* Agriculture
Breuer, J., and S. Freud, 178. *See also Aires; Aire* illness
Bullfighter, as Harlequin, 148, 149
Bullfight, symbolism of, 148
Bulls, 146-151; and *aires*, 147; blood